Point Taken

A Brief Thematic Reader

Elizabeth Penfield

University of New Orleans

PEARSON

Longman

New York   Boston   San Francisco
London   Toronto   Sydney   Tokyo   Singapore   Madrid
Mexico City   Munich   Paris   Cape Town   Hong Kong   Montreal

Senior Vice President and Publisher: Joseph Opiela
Senior Acquisitions Editor: Lynn M. Huddon
Marketing Manager: Deborah Murphy
Senior Supplements Editor: Donna Campion
Production Manager: Ellen MacElree
Project Coordination, Text Design, and Electronic Page Makeup: Nesbitt Graphics, Inc.
Cover Designer/Manager: Nancy Danahy
Cover Image: Copyright © Getty Images, Inc.
Manufacturing Buyer: Roy Pickering
Printer and Binder: R. R. Donnelley & Sons Company
Cover Printer: Coral Graphic Services

For permission to use copyrighted material, grateful acknowledgment is made to the copyright holders on pp. 289–292, which are hereby made part of this copyright page.

Library of Congress Cataloging-in-Publication Data

Point taken : a brief thematic reader / [compiled by] Elizabeth Penfield.
    p. cm.
ISBN 0-321-11740-9
    1. College readers. 2. English language—Rhetoric—Problems,
exercises, etc. 3. Report writing—Problems, exercises, etc.
I.Penfield, Elizabeth, 1939-
PE1417.P575 2003
808'.0427—dc22

                                                    2003017141

Copyright © 2004 by Pearson Education, Inc.

Please visit our website at http://www.ablongman.com

ISBN 0-321-11740-9

3 4 5 6 7 8 9 10—DOH—06 05 04

CONTENTS

1 Identity   7

2   Relationships   39

6　The Media　　　　　　　　149

7 Education   176

"[T]he entitlement benefits all Californians by encouraging the best students to stay in the state for college." Fletcher

"Abigail Thernstrom's argument against California's expansion of scholarships for needy students who perform well in high school . . . demonstrates elitism and defeatism." Mockler

"Though Harvard's deluge of A's and honors may be an extreme case, experts say grade inflation in higher education is a nationwide problem that started in the permissive 1960s and '70s and grew with ensuing decades."

"Some time ago, I received a call from a colleague who asked if I would be the referee on the grading of an examination question. He was about to give a student a zero for his answer to a physics question, while the student claimed he should receive a perfect score and would if the system were not set up against the student."

"In the new lingua franca of higher education, students are 'consumers of our product' in one conversation or presentation and 'inputs'—a part of what we sell—in the next."

"Named 'the world's premier application essay editing service' by the New York Times Learning Network and 'one of the best essay services on the Internet' by the Washington Post, Essay Edge has helped more applicants write successful personal statements than any other company in the world."

8 Language

"Being a woman is hard work. Not without joy and even ecstasy, but still relentless, unending work."

9 Ecology   **228**

10 The Internet and Technology   260

Rhetorical Guide

Modes of Discourse

Description

Narration

Process

Example

Definition

Comparison

Causal Analysis

AIMS OF DISCOURSE

Self-Expression

Exposition

Argument

PREFACE

The term *point taken* is rooted in understanding and reason. Think of an argument during which you make a particularly good case for your position. The response may be "Point taken," recognition that your opponent understands your position and has been persuaded to accept it. So too this book includes selections that explain and argue so that students may do the same, reaching an understanding of the texts and evaluating the reasoning behind them. That's another way of saying that *Point Taken* emphasizes analytical reading and writing.

You'll find that emphasis in the 60 short selections and 3 letters to the editor that come from a variety of contemporary sources on a variety of topics. The 10 topics are contemporary as well: Identity, Relationships, Scenes and Places, Work, Popular Culture, The Media, Education, Language, Ecology, and the Internet and Technology. No matter what the topic, however, the selections are short, well written, and engaging. They lend themselves to being read critically and to analytical discussions and writing assignments.

In *Point Taken* you will find:

* An overview of analytical reading
* Chapter introductions that connect the topics to the lives of the students
* Information about each author and the selection's context
* Questions or short assignments to prepare the student for the selection
* Suggestions for analyzing and discussing the texts
* Suggestions for brief as well as extended writing responses
* Suggestions for papers that compare selections
* Diversity of authors, styles, subject matter, genres, and sources
* Complete selections, not excerpts

I welcome comments and suggestions, although a book this size is limited in the number of topics and selections that can be included. You can write to me in care of Longman's English Editor, 1185 Sixth Avenue, New York, NY 10036 or send an email to <epenfiel@uno.edu>.

The Topics

The theme of each chapter lends itself to analysis, both oral and written. Starting with topics closer to personal experiences—Identity, Relationships, and Scenes and Places—students are asked to step back from the subject and view it critically. From there, the topics broaden to categories still familiar but less personal: Work, Popular Culture, The Media, and Education. The last three—Language, Ecology, and the Internet and Technology—deal with subjects perhaps more removed but nevertheless accessible.

The Selections

Each of the 10 topics is illustrated by six selections. Though the topics vary, every selection is organized around a thesis, sometimes implied rather than stated but always there. Because most of the pieces are short, fewer than 1,000 words, readers can identify how the thesis is supported and can critically examine the evidence on which it rests, testing its validity.

Looking at the table of contents, you will find many familiar names—Margaret Atwood, Willie Morris, Amy Tan, John McPhee, Maya Angelou, Peter Mathiessen—but you'll also see some that are not so familiar even though they may have won awards for journalism or science writing. Well known or not so well known, the authors included in this book provide a variety of perspectives, representing different interests, occupations, genders, cultures, and ages.

As you would expect, most of the selections are essays, some fitting the familiar category of the personal essay in the classic style of Bacon and Lamb—analytical meditations on subjects such as family relationships, citizenship, or learning a new language. Others are expository pieces that explain the essence of a place, for instance, or redefine the work ethic, or speculate about what technology may offer in the future. And, of course, you'll also find selections that argue—television news emphasizes too much violence or has crossed the line from news to entertainment, for example, or that the business model of management should not apply to universities.

Each chapter also contains a "non-essay," an example of a specialized subgenre such as travel writing, letters to the editor, dictionary entries, or an interview, Web page, advice column, obituary, or book review. In some cases, the source is outside of the print mainstream of nonfiction and journalism, drawn instead from the electronic media or college newspaper or from a specialized journal or alumni magazine. As a result, students learn how writing is shaped for different audiences and media.

The Rhetorical Modes and Aims

Although the book is best described as a thematic reader, anyone who emphasizes the various modes of organization will also find a rhetorical guide to both modes and aims. Under "Modes of Discourse" you will find the selections sorted according to their primary means of organization: description, narration, process, example, definition, comparison, and causal analysis. Because the book emphasizes analytical reading and writing, you'll find more selections fitting causal analysis and definition than description and narration. You'll also discover that the selections listed under process are not the simple how-to variety but the more sophisticated descriptive or historical type.

As for the aims of discourse, self-expression, exposition, and argument are all represented. The selections listed under self-expression are more the classic meditative sort, not the touchy-feely or egocentric kind. Exposition includes selections that explain or explore their subjects, and those exemplifying argument state a debatable thesis supported by evidence.

The Apparatus for Reading and Writing

The book begins with a short expository essay on analytical reading, not because students don't know how to read but because, often, they don't read critically enough. The essay identifies the main problems students have when reading about an unfamiliar topic or confronted with a complex issue and suggests ways to address those problems. Although the emphasis, as you might expect, is on reading as an active intellectual activity, this introductory essay is intended as a base line so that teachers can then develop the ideas as they like, applying their own advice and, perhaps, examples of annotated reading.

Each selection is introduced by a brief biography of the writer and information about the place of publication so that the reader is aware of the overall context for the piece. "Before You Read" then provides a lead-in to the selection, perhaps raising a question that ties the student's experience to the subject or emphasizing a key term. You'll find that these prompts may be used for an initial discussion or a short writing assignment.

Suggestions for reading and writing follow each selection. "Reading: Responding to the Text" includes four questions that ask students to take a close and critical look at the text, analyzing its organization, assessing its effectiveness, testing assertions, and the like. Two sets of suggestions for writing then follow: "Writing: Brief Response" and "Writing: Extended Response." The two brief assignments can be used as notebook or journal entries or to start off classroom discussion. They are directly related to what the students read, asking, for example, about the appropriateness of a title or the validity of a particular assertion. The longer two assignments at times call for textual analysis and at times for research. Most of them can be completed within a week, though some can be easily adapted to longer research papers, done individually or as group projects. Each chapter ends with "Comparing the Selections," four writing assignments that focus on two or more selections and require close analytical rereading. Some focus, for instance, on the ideas the texts have in common, asking the students to make a case for the more effective presentation; others may emphasize the texts' contrasting styles or ask students to test differing assertions against their own experience, using examples from the texts. Again, the emphasis is on critical reading and analytical writing.

The Instructor's Manual

The Instructor's Manual to accompany *Point Taken* does the obvious—augment the text—but does so in a slightly different way. Instead of answering the questions, it discusses the questions as a whole, sometimes suggesting another approach to the text, sometimes pointing out a possible pitfall, sometimes proposing an easier path into discussion. And as for the writing assignments, each one is augmented by advice on how to implement it, suggestions on how to adapt the assignment for group work, and how to go about gathering information, taking notes, revising, and the like.

Acknowledgments

Point Taken would never have existed without the ideas, advice, and support of Lynn Huddon, to whom I owe many thanks. I am also grateful to many others for their help in bringing this book to publication: Theodora Hill for her good taste and good judgment and her help with the more onerous tasks involved in preparing a manuscript; Louis Bruno for his careful copyediting (though we disagree about the placement of prepositions); Janet Nuciforo for her patience and skill in seeing the manuscript through the various stages of production; and Cynthia Taylor for her advice and help with the instructor's Manual. The following reviewers all provided comments and guidance that improved the manuscript in various stages: Rachel Bell, Skyline College; Angelika Carroll, Albuquerque Technical Vocational Institute; Linda Clegg, Cerritos College; Linda Conway, Howard College; Tracy D. Duckart, Humboldt State University; Cheryl Elsmore, California State University–Santa Barbara; Jeff Glauner; Park University; Steven Luebke, University of Wisconsin–River Falls; Lyle W. Morgan, Pittsburgh State University; and Pauline Woodward, Endicott College. And, of course, I thank my students, for they have taught me a great deal over the years.

ELIZABETH PENFIELD

Reading
Analytically
Identifying with the Text

1   The process of writing is active, but once a writer is finished with the text, it's dead until a reader brings it back to life. Sure, if what you're reading is straightforward, such as a set of directions, you can passively absorb information in rote fashion—first do this, then do that, and so on. But anyone who has tried to put together a barbeque grill or hook up home theater components or read a computer manual knows that even seemingly simple directions often take some interpretation. Few texts are readerproof.

2   Move from simple directions to complex ideas, and reading becomes more complex. Think, for example, of some of the textbooks you might have in chemistry or economics or the more elusive works of James Joyce or William Faulkner. All of a sudden, the prose becomes dense, meaning obscure, reading far more time-consuming, perhaps a chore. Somewhere between the two extremes of directions and complexity, however, lie the selections you'll be reading here.

3   You'll be reading these selections critically, and critical reading cannot be separated from critical thinking. The ability to think abstractly, weigh opinions, sort through facts—everything involved in the ability to reason—distinguishes human beings from most other life forms. And as a thinking human being, you bring to what you read all of your experiences, ideas, values, and knowledge. Thinking and reading critically enables you to deal with words that you don't know, experiences that are quite unlike your own, values you disagree with, ideas that you hadn't thought of before. Reading becomes a way of learning, a way of increasing your vocabulary, broadening your experience, testing your values, coming up with new ideas.

1

4   Even though you've been reading one way or another all the years you've been in school, some advice may be helpful. For a start, forget the idea of a book being something sacred, something that can't be marked up, written in, even thrown across the room. Choose a weapon—pencil, pen, highlighter—and use it to underline and make notes in the margins. If you can't bring yourself to do that, then use a reader's notebook, a place to write down your responses to what you're reading—ideas you question, words you need to look up, and the like.

5   Skip the title of a selection? Don't. Writers often spend a lot of time working on their titles, titles that tip you off not only to the subject but also sometimes to the authors' attitudes toward those subjects. "A Black Fan of Country Music Tells All," the title of Lena Williams' essay, tells you its author is black and likes country music, but the "Tells All" taps into the idea of confession, a notion that makes sense given the stereotypical musical tastes some associate with African-Americans—jazz, rap, blues, Motown, and the like. So, begin your reading by thinking about a selection's title and then move on. After you've finished the piece, go back and think about its connections to its title.

6   Hit a word or name you don't know? Mark it. Don't just skip over the word, see if the sentence helps explain its meaning (it probably does). If it doesn't, you'll need to look up the word in a dictionary, but not right away. It's easy to get so lost searching through the dictionary that you lose sight of what you're reading, and you don't want to have the words get in the way of your overall comprehension. You can always write down any word you don't know, look it up later, then come back to the original sentence and review it within the larger context of the whole piece.

7   Struck by an idea that you disagree with? Write "Bull!" or some such in the margin, or copy it over in your notebook with a question mark beside it. After you've finished reading, reconsider the idea. In the meantime, try to keep an open mind, puzzling out how the idea relates to others and checking to see what evidence the writer supplies to support it. Try to understand the writer's line of reasoning by putting yourself in the person's place and accepting the major premise. If, for instance, the first paragraph can be summed up by "All Ds and Fs should be abolished," grant the writer that idea, jot down "Sez who?" or some such, and keep track of the supporting evidence. By the end of the selection, you'll be

able to rethink your first responses and discover if they still make sense.

8   Confused by what may be the main point? Look for the controlling thesis, the central assertion. Think of an assertion as a claim that has an arguable point, a value judgment as opposed to a fact: "Raises should be based on merit not seniority" states an assertion; "Raises are often based on seniority" states a fact. Consider the difference between "College football provides a training ground for professional players" and "College football produces professional players at the expense of academic programs." One is fact, the other opinion. Often, you can use the idea of information to test out the difference. Facts contain known or easily verifiable information; anyone who follows professional football knows that most played college ball. The idea that college football may take away from academic programs, however, may be a new idea—an assertion that needs to be backed up by evidence to be credible.

9   Note each assertion or claim and the supporting facts as you read along by putting a check in the margin or summing it up in your notebook. Then, when you've finished reading, ask yourself what the piece is about, its subject. Write it down. If you were reading a piece titled "The Hidden Costs of Education," for instance, you might first note that the writer has narrowed the subject of the title to students who don't live on campus. Then, perhaps, as you read you marked a number of statements that were backed up by examples: "A car and even public transportation can eat up your dollars"; "The price of text books keeps rising"; "You can be pressured into a 'life style' of expensive clothes and dates"; "Tuition may not include lab fees, student activity charges, and the like." Summarize those ideas in one sentence and you can identify the writer's major point in a simple statement—"A college education often costs non-resident students far more than they expect"—or a more elaborate version, "The unanticipated costs of transportation, textbooks, a new way of life, and unexpected fees can bankrupt the non-resident student." Either way, you've identified the thesis, the writer's major assertion about the subject.

10   Puzzled by how you're supposed to respond? Consider the possibilities. Perhaps the writer is simply trying to explain, explore, or report on a problem, process, or scene. As the reader, your only job is to understand it. On the other hand, maybe the writer wants you to accept a particular idea or position. In that case, you need to

identify just what that idea is and what sort of response the writer wants you to have—to rethink your position, adopt the opinion, take a particular action. But keep in mind that not all writing is serious; don't forget the kind that only asks for a laugh.

11   Can't figure out how the selection is organized? Reread it, exploring various possible patterns. Try general to specific. A piece on the cost of a college education, for instance, might move from the general idea that it's too high to the specifics of why it is so. Or perhaps the selection works from the specific to the general, beginning with the cost of tuition and then exploring why it is so high. Or perhaps the writer chooses to organize the piece using problem and solution, stating the problem—high cost—and then proposing ways that it can be reduced.

12   Consider, too, how the train of thought is linked together. If you were reading about the West Nile virus disease, the writer would probably define the disease so you know just what it is, show how it differs from other viral diseases by using comparison and example, explain how it is caused and its effects, discuss its stages, and dramatize how you feel if you contract it. To make the piece more interesting, the writer might begin it with a story about someone who died of the disease. Definition, comparison, example, analysis, description, and narrative all can provide building blocks that shape how a text is organized.

13   Find a fact that seems dubious or a source that seems suspicious? Mark it. Come back to it later, after you've finished the piece and have had some time to think about it. Theodore Roosevelt came up with the expression "weasel words" for vague terms that should set off alarms, words such as *arguably, significantly, substantially, somewhat, virtually,* and so on. Spot an assertion that uses one of them and you should respond with "Who says?" Assuming the "fact" is tied to a source, you can judge its reliability. A person who is quoted may be reporting a personal experience, but personal experience may only provide anecdotal evidence, for what's true for one person may not be true for another. Even eyewitness accounts are often suspect, as any trial attorney can tell you. Watch out, too, for unnamed sources. News stories that cite sources such as a "member of the administration" or a "high-level official" may be quoting someone whose views are reliable or someone who has something to gain. Without a name, you don't know.

14   If you see a name, check it out to discover if the person is really an "expert" or "authority." Look up the source on the Internet or in the library and examine the person's credentials. Mick Jagger knows music, but think twice if he's quoted on family values. And if a reporter or text is cited, make sure that source can be believed; the *New York Times* or *Wall Street Journal* is apt to be more reliable on national issues than the *Tin City Express*. As for numbers and statistics, examine the larger context. If 8 out of 10 doctors support the idea of euthanasia, make sure that they aren't members of the Hemlock Society. With so much information available electronically, it's all the more important to evaluate sources. Anyone can put up a Web site, and absolute truth is elusive.

15   Confused, bothered, overwhelmed by the writer's style? Bear with it, but after a few minutes, put down the selection and go do something else. Then go back and start again, from the beginning. Try to hear the words, not just see them. Don't worry about starting, stopping, backtracking—it's what all good readers do. It might help to circle similar ideas and link them with lines; the result may reveal the pattern of thought that perplexed you.

16   If you added up all these suggestions and reached the conclusion that reading is a vigorous and dynamic act, you're right. What's described here is critical reading—not critical in the sense of judging harshly, but critical in the sense of questioning, weighing evidence, evaluating, comparing your world to the one the writer has created on the page, and reaching a reasoned conclusion. This kind of analytical reading is what education is all about, and it doesn't stop when the bell rings or the degree is awarded. Think of it as an internal and intellectual Energizer Bunny.

Identity

Introduction

We live in a world where identity can be reduced to a photo on a driver's license, a passport, or a badge that permits access to a particular building or area. More sophisticated methods involve fingerprints, voice recognition, or the pattern of a retina—anything that makes a person unique. But uniqueness goes much deeper than that. It is the sum of all that you are.

If you were to take a moment to jot down a list of all the ways you can be identified, the length might surprise you. Gender, age, marital status, occupation, income, ethnicity, nationality would probably head the list, but other bits of information help turn such basic facts into a picture: color of eyes and hair, height, weight, skin tone, a scar or tattoo, body type. The items on such a list are concrete, easy to measure, yet the description falls far short of the person. Much more difficult to define are the traits that make up personality—kinds of intelligence, range of emotions, and the like. More difficult still are those categories related to memories, past experiences, beliefs, ethics, ideals, ideas, and attitudes. To say a person is a Democrat or a Republican, for instance, merely puts a label on a complex network of beliefs, glossing over finer distinctions, for instance that someone can be a Republican on economic policies and a Democrat on social issues.

Even obvious categories can be slippery. Our culture draws a line between child and adult, but the line varies. The armed forces put it at 18, but the legal age for alcohol is 21, while the one for a driving license varies from state to state. And surely everyone knows an adult still stuck in childhood and a child more mature than many an adult.

Differences and similarities help define a person. If you were to analyze your identity, you would probably find yourself drawing upon comparison, contrast, and description to define yourself. Or you might consider why you are the person you are, examining causes and effects. And if a particular place or event epitomizes your identity, that might be a good place to start your essay.

As you read the selections that follow, read each first for its basic meaning.

What group or groups does the author identify with and why?

If you had to use one word to summarize the writer's identity, what would it be?

What is that identity in conflict with and why?

How, if at all, is that conflict resolved?

How would you characterize the writer's attitude toward identity: Is it proud? Puzzled? Amused? Apologetic? Angry? What?

What have you learned from the essay?

Then when you reread each selection, be aware of how the writer defines that identity.

What comparisons does the writer use?

What examples?

Assuming the subject's identity is different from your own, how does the writer make it real to you?

To what extent can you identify with the subject?

How is that identification brought about?

While it's obvious that a sense of identity is important to all of us, it's particularly important to anyone who is a member of a minority, for that person's sense of self is defined in noticeable ways by what he or she is and is not. Keep those distinctions in mind as you read the selections by Henry Han Xi Lau, Brent Staples, and Bharati Mukherjee, all of whom write about the ways in which their identities are challenged. Three other selections, those by Leo Reisberg, Naomi Wolf, and Edward L. Hudgins, examine different ways of belonging, forming identities by campus groups, gender and profession, and nationality. Some of the selections deal with individual identity, some with cultural identity, but each focuses on "Who am I?" and "How do others see me?"

Myths and Misconceptions
Interview with Naomi Wolf

Andy Steiner

Naomi Wolf was working on her PhD at Princeton University when she adapted her dissertation into The Beauty Myth: How Images of Beauty Are Used Against Women, *a best-seller published in 1991. As the title of the book implies, Wolf is concerned with issues that affect women, an interest that runs through all of her work as she tries to re-define and revive feminism. She has explored the relationship between women and politics in* Fire with Fire: The New Female Power *(1993), girls, women, and sexuality in* Promiscuities: The Secret Struggle for Womanhood *(1997), and women, childbirth, and the medical industry in* Misconceptions: Truth, Lies and the Unexpected on the Journey to Motherhood *(2001). Her essays have been published in print media as diverse as* Ms., Glamour, *the* Wall Street Journal, *and the* New Republic. *The interview that follows appeared not long after the events of September 11, 2001, in the* Utne Reader, *a journal founded in 1983 by Eric Utne that reprints articles from what it terms "alternative media sources." Andy Steiner, the interviewer, is a Senior Editor at* Utne. *He begins his interview by first summarizing some information about Naomi Wolf and then goes on to ask her about her roles as woman, feminist, mother, and author.*

Before You Read   Based on the brief biographical information above, what questions would you ask Naomi Wolf?

1   The chronic chronicler of a generation, feminist author Naomi Wolf writes books that get people talking. Her first, the international best-seller *The Beauty Myth,* launched a debate about female body image that continues to rage today. She followed that stunning debut with *Fire with Fire,* which focuses on women and power, and *Promiscuities,* a book about young women's emerging sexuality. Over the past decade, Wolf's way with words and telegenic personality have earned her the title "the Gloria Steinem of the '90s." The former Rhodes scholar gained notoriety when she

was tapped as a high-paid "image consultant" for Al Gore's 2000 presidential campaign.

2   While Wolf's books are always thoroughly researched works, they usually weave in some measure of personal experience, an element that has helped assure her a loyal fan base. When word got out that Wolf was pregnant with her first child, readers knew it was only a matter of time before she published something about it. Sure enough, seven years and two children later, Wolf is out with *Misconceptions* (Doubleday, 2001), her critique of pregnancy and birth in America.

3   Though many say they saw it coming, Wolf insists that she didn't set out to write about motherhood. "It wasn't my goal," she says. "But as I lived the experience of becoming a mother, the words just started flowing out of me." Wolf and her husband, David Shipley, have two children, Rosa, 6, and Joey, 1. She spoke with senior editor Andy Steiner from her home in New York City.

4   *You recently moved from the suburbs to an apartment in New York City. How do you like raising children in a bustling urban area?*

5   Large cities can be really wonderful and community-based places to raise children, partly because you are away from the tyranny of automobiles. I love that in this city kids can run in and out of stores where they know the storekeepers, and they see a wide variety of people on the street. For me, living in the suburbs contributed to the postpartum depression that I wrote about in *Misconceptions*. Our culture makes the experience of new motherhood a particularly isolating one, and I found that the suburban environment is especially isolating for women and the children they care for. Every day, our suburb became this ghost town of white women and their babies. Sure, you could go to the playground and be with the other moms, but you got the feeling that you were still living at the margins of American life, away from the rest of the world.

6   *What sorts of books are you reading to your children?*

7   We're really interested in books about girls being smart and tough and strong. One of our favorites is a version of *Cinderella* called *Cindy Ellen*. She is a cowgirl who wins the prince by being the most daring rider at the rodeo. Rosa also loves the *Magic Tree House* books, which are full of girls and boys having daring adven-

tures. I've realized lately how subversive some of the old children's favorites are, like *Mary Poppins*. She's quite a role model. She has magical powers and can turn everything upside down. I also loved Laura Ingalls Wilder's *Little House* books when I was growing up. I'm hoping to lure Rosa into that world, because the idea of being a little girl facing a big adventure is exciting and timeless.

8 *What magazines do you read?*

9 These days I find myself turning to the newsmagazines, unfortunately. Also *The New Yorker,* and other local publications like *New York* and *The New York Observer* and the *New York Post.* I've been moved to see this city and the people who live here reel and recover and adapt to life under siege. For a truly global city, New York seems very local, almost like a small town these days. I wouldn't have talked like this before 9/11, but there is a new sense of this being a hometown as well as an international city.

10 *It sounds like you've developed pretty serious reading tastes. Do you read anything for fun?*

11 Some people may find this surprising for a feminist, but I love *Better Homes and Gardens*. Decorating and housekeeping magazines have been a guilty pleasure of mine for years. It's almost like my fascination with reading about how to make a pillow intensifies the more I come face to face with my lack of skills in that department. I'm not interested in the high-end, classy stuff of this genre like *Martha Stewart Living.* What I'm really interested in is mainstream mass market magazines with recipes for Halloween cookies.

12 *A lot of young feminists seem to have rediscovered the domestic arts. What's that all about?*

13 Well, home has become more and more important to us as a nation, and young feminists aren't immune to that. I also think the second wave of feminists, the women who came just before this, felt they had to turn their backs on a lot of things that traditionally provided pleasure for women, like home life, domesticity, being maternal, sexuality. Now younger women are embracing those things again, but with more attitude. For instance, knitting in public has become one of the ultimate in-your-face things a feminist can do. If you don't want to be politically correct at work, you can always pull out your knitting at a meeting.

14 *In the Fall 2001 issue of* Brill's Content, *author Katie Roiphe wrote a scathing review of* Misconceptions. *How do you respond to your critics?*

15 Constructive criticism is always helpful, and since I know my books are controversial and I take strong positions, it only seems fair that people should be able to write what they want in response. Still, I am often surprised that the tone of some reviews can be so vehement. I often wish that all criticisms were of my *ideas* and not of me personally. But generally I feel so well supported by my readers and I receive so much critical support that I am happy that someone is engaging in the debate.

16 While I often hate Roiphe's conclusions, I respect her take-no-prisoners style. I'm happy as a feminist that there's a new generation of young women who feel comfortable holding strong, independent opinions.

17 *In the past, you've written about your interest in spirituality. Are there any contemporary religious teachers that you find enlightening?*

18 There are so many inspirational voices out there right now, people who are making spirituality available and accessible to everyone. I've been interested in learning about the historical Jesus, especially in the teachings of Reverend John Shelby Spong and the Jesus Seminar people. I'm also a big fan of Buddhist teacher Sharon Salzberg, a friend and mentor of mine and the author of *A Heart as Wide as the World*. I also have great respect for Thich Nhat Hanh.

19 *What kind of music do you listen to?*

20 I listen to a lot of Irish and Scottish folk music. I lived in that part of the world for a few years, and I continue to be inspired by how those musicians are reclaiming an old tradition and making it relevant for today. My kids enjoy a great CD called *Reggae for Kids*.

21 *What television shows do you watch?*

22 Now, unfortunately, we've been watching a lot of CNN. And then there are the children's shows *Arthur* and *Dragon Tales,* which I don't find as repulsive as some of the children's programming that's out there. I've paid my *Barney* dues.

23 *With two young children at home, do you and your husband ever make it to the movies?*

24   We do see more on video than we used to, but I still see more than a lot of mothers do. I loved *Bridget Jones's Diary*. I liked that it was literate, and that an average-sized girl got the guy. I also really liked *High Fidelity*. I'm 38, so I don't identify as a boomer, but I'm not a Gen X'er, either. There aren't that many cultural artifacts that appeal to people my age. *High Fidelity* was completely it. And I loved *Crouching Tiger Hidden Dragon*. I should also say I absolutely loved *Charlie's Angels*. This new wave of strong, crazy heroines in film is salutary. In the same vein, I liked Angelina Jolie's character in *Lara Croft: Tomb Raider*. I think it's cool that we have villains and commandos who are women. Another aspect of the female psyche is being acted out.

25   ***Are you seeing any media trends that disturb you?***
26   Dissent has become unpopular overnight in this country. I don't think patriotism has to mean consensus or the quashing of the principled interrogation of our leaders. Suddenly it feels like we're living in 1958. I'm afraid in this atmosphere of fear there will be dark repercussions for us over the long term. It's important to remember that we can wage a war without giving up the things like dissent that truly make America great.

Reading: Discussing the Text

1. Steiner's summary that precedes the interview is intended to provide background about Wolf and at the same time engage the reader to read on. To what extent does it succeed?
2. Consider the image of Wolf that Steiner creates in his summary. How well does it fit the Naomi Wolf of the interview?
3. Wolf's academic credentials are impressive—Yale undergraduate, Rhodes scholar, Princeton graduate school. What does that information contribute to your understanding of Naomi Wolf?
4. How would you characterize Wolf's identity? What evidence can you find for what you infer are her priorities?

Writing: Brief Response

1. Would you like to meet Naomi Wolf? Using evidence from the essay, explain why or why not.
2. Spend five minutes or so writing down your associations with the word *feminist*. What one-sentence generalization can you infer from your list?

Writing: Extended Response

1. While there's only so much that an interview can cover, it should do justice to its subject. Use your library or the Web to get a fuller sense of Wolf. Given what your research reveals, evaluate Steiner's interview. For instance, you can examine the interviewer's questions: Are they the right ones? Do they probe deeply enough? Is there more that you want to know?

2. Use the selection as a rough guide for how to conduct an interview that brings out the most important aspects of a person's life—in Wolf's case those are her career, family, opinions, and interests. Select a person from your own family to interview and draw up a list of questions to consider. Then, when you interview the person, use the list as a guide and record your questions and the responses. You can then edit the interview into written form, eliminating the *hems* and *haws* but remaining true to what was said. The result may well be a valuable addition to your family's history.

I Was a Member of the Kung Fu Crew

Henry Han Xi Lau

New York City is still in many ways a city of neighborhoods, many of which are ethnic ones. The Chinatown that Henry Han Xi Lau writes about is one of the oldest, and it's where you can still walk down the street and not hear a word of English. To Lau, it's also home, even though he and his family have moved to Brooklyn, which like Manhattan, is one of the city's five boroughs or districts. A sophomore at Yale University at the time he wrote this essay, Lau describes the people and places of Chinatown, defining it as "ghetto." The piece was published in the New York Times Magazine *on October 19, 1997. After the essay came out, Lau objected to the way it had been edited, calling it a "warped presentation" in a later piece he wrote for* Discourses, *an undergraduate journal at Yale (you can find his critique reprinted in* Microcosm, *a Web journal published by Rice University). What's missing, according to Lau, is the "resourcefulness and hard-working side of ghettoness." See what you think.*

Before You Read   Look up *ghetto* in an unabridged dictionary so that you can discover its origin as well as have a clear understanding of the word's denotative meaning. How have you heard or read it used?

1   Chinatown is ghetto, my friends are ghetto, I am ghetto. I went away to college last year, but I still have a long strand of hair that reaches past my chin. I need it when I go back home to hang with the K.F.C.—for Kung Fu Crew, not Kentucky Fried Chicken. We all met in a Northern Shaolin kung fu class years ago. Our *si-fu* was Rocky. He told us: "In the early 1900's in China, your grand master was walking in the streets when a foreigner riding on a horse disrespected him. So then he felt the belly of the horse with his palms and left. Shortly thereafter, the horse buckled and died because our grand master had used *qi-gong* to mess up the horse's internal organs." Everyone said, "Cool, I would like to do that." Rocky emphasized, "You've got to practice really hard for a long time to reach that level."

2   By the time my friends and I were in the eighth grade, we were able to do 20-plus pushups on our knuckles and fingers. When we practiced our crescent, roundhouse and tornado kicks, we had 10-pound weights strapped to our legs. Someone once remarked, "Goddamn—that's a freaking mountain!" when he saw my thigh muscles in gym class.

3   Most Chinatown kids fall into a few general categories. There are pale-faced nerds who study all the time to get into the Ivies. There are the recent immigrants with uncombed hair and crooked teeth who sing karaoke in bars. There are the punks with highlighted hair who cut school, and the gangsters, whom everyone else avoids.

4   Then there is the K.F.C. We work hard like the nerds, but we identify with the punks. Now we are reunited, and just as in the old days we amble onto Canal Street, where we stick out above the older folks, elderly women bearing leaden bags of bok choy and oranges. As an opposing crew nears us, I assess them to determine whether to grill them or not. Grilling is the fine art of staring others down and trying to emerge victorious.

5   How the hair is worn is important in determining one's order on the streets. In the 80's, the dominant style was the mushroom cut, combed neatly or left wild in the front so that a person can appear menacing as he peers through his bangs. To gain an edge in grilling

now, some kids have asymmetrical cuts, with long random strands sprouting in the front, sides or back. Some dye their hair blue or green, while blood red is usually reserved for gang members.

6   Only a few years ago, examination of the hair was sufficient. But now there is a second step: assessing pants. A couple of years ago, wide legs first appeared in New York City, and my friends and I switched from baggy pants. In the good old days, Merry-Go-Round in the Village sold wide legs for only $15 a pair. When Merry-Go-Round went bankrupt, Chinatown kids despaired. Wide-leg prices at other stores increased drastically as they became more popular. There are different ways of wearing wide legs. Some fold their pant legs inward and staple them at the hem. Some clip the back ends of their pants to their shoes with safety pins. Others simply cut the bottoms so that fuzzy strings hang out.

7   We grill the opposing punks. I untuck my long strand of hair so that it swings in front of my face. Nel used to have a strand, but he chewed it off one day in class by accident. Chu and Tom cut their strands off because it scared people at college. Jack has a patch of blond hair, while Tone's head is a ball of orange flame. Chi has gelled short hair, while Ken's head is a black mop. As a group, we have better hair than our rivals. But they beat us with their wide legs. In our year away at college, wide legs have gone beyond our 24-inch leg openings. Twenty-six- to 30-inch jeans are becoming the norm. If wide legs get any bigger, they will start flying up like a skirt in an updraft.

8   We have better accessories, though. Chi sports a red North Face that gives him a rugged mountain-climber look because of the jungle of straps sprouting in the back. Someone once asked Chi, "Why is the school bag so important to one's cool?" He responded, "Cuz it's the last thing others see when you walk away from them or when they turn back to look at you after you walk past them." But the other crew has female members, which augments their points. The encounter between us ends in a stalemate. But at least the K.F.C. members are in college and are not true punks.

9   In the afternoon, we decide to eat at the Chinatown McDonald's for a change instead of the Chinese bakery Maria's, our dear old hangout spot. "Mickey D's is good sit," Nel says. I answer: "But the Whopper gots more fat and meat. It's even got more bun." Nel agrees. "True that," he says. I want the Big Mac, but I buy the two-cheeseburger meal because it has the same amount of meat but costs less.

10   We sit and talk about ghettoness again. We can never exactly articulate what being ghetto entails, but we know the spirit of it. In Chinatown toilet facilities we sometimes find footprints on the seats because F.O.B.'s (fresh off the boats) squat on them as they do over the holes in China. We see alternative brand names in stores like Dolo instead of Polo, and Mike instead of Nike.

11   We live by ghettoness. My friends and I walk from 80-something Street in Manhattan to the tip of the island to save a token. We gorge ourselves at Gray's Papaya because the hot dogs are 50 cents each. But one cannot be stingy all the time. We leave good tips at Chinese restaurants because our parents are waiters and waitresses, too.

12   We sit for a long time in McDonald's, making sure that there is at least a half-inch of soda in our cups so that when the staff wants to kick us out, we can claim that we are not finished yet. Jack positions a mouse bite of cheeseburger in the center of a wrapper to support our claim.

13   After a few hours, the K.F.C. prepares to disband. I get in one of the no-license commuter vans on Canal Street that will take me to Sunset Park in Brooklyn, where my family lives now. All of my friends will leave Chinatown, for the Upper East Side and the Lower East Side, Forest Hills in Queens and Bensonhurst in Brooklyn. We live far apart, but we always come back together in Chinatown. For most of us, our homes used to be here and our world was here.

Reading: Discussing the Text

1. In his later essay, Lau points out that the profile that ran in a Chinese newspaper, the *World Journal,* emphasized Yale, but the *Times* played up "punk imagery" and put Yale "all the way at the bottom of the page, printed in small letters." To what extent does the *Times* minimize Lau's education?

2. What reasons can you think of for the title of Lau's group? Consider its initials and the standard association with them. What is the effect of the contrast?

3. Lau may have moved away from Chinatown, but he is still very much a part of its community. How would you characterize that community and its values?

4. Assuming you are unfamiliar with Chinatown, what examples does Lau use to describe it? To what extent does he make it come alive?

Writing: Brief Response

1. Think about the kinds of clothes you wear and write a brief description of them. Then take a hard look at your list and write a notebook entry about how they might identify you.
2. At some point, you and your friends probably constituted a group or crew. Write an entry in which you explain what brought you together and your shared values.

Writing: Extended Response

1. Each generation usually ends up with at least one label or tag—the Baby Boomers, the Yuppies, or some such. What label works for your generation? Write an essay that explains your choice, providing examples to prove your point.
2. A sense of community can arise from friendships, neighborhoods, religious affiliation, workplace, school, and the like. Think about the community that holds particular meaning for you and write an essay that analyzes that meaning. Make sure that all the points you make in your essay add up to one main assertion.

Proliferation of Campus Clubs
Too Much of a Good Thing

Leo Reisberg

If you have ever done any research on education, then you probably already know the Chronicle of Higher Education. *A weekly that is also available on line and possibly as an electronic resource through your campus library, the* Chronicle *is an excellent source of information on anything to do with colleges and universities, both here and abroad. In addition to all sorts of statistical data—enrollments, faculty salaries, and the like—it also covers any topic that affects higher education, whether it be testing, law suits, grant opportunities, meetings, Internet resources, information technology, or campus crime. The range of issues is as large as the world we live in. Leo Reisberg is a reporter for the* Chronicle, *writing stories as varied in subjects as ACT and SAT math scores and witches on campus. No matter what the subject, you'll find that articles in the* Chronicle *are built around the kind of paragraphing you find in journalistic writing—short paragraphs that break down information to fit the physical space of a news column. Reisberg's article on campus clubs appeared in the September 29, 2000, issue.*

Before You Read   Use an unabridged dictionary to look up *balkanization*. What examples can you think of where the word would be appropriate?

1   Just days after arriving at the University of Virginia for orientation, the new batch of freshmen ambled through a crowded outdoor field, where they faced one of their first tests in college decision-making: the student-activities fair.

2   A woman twirling a Hula-Hoop announced a 44-hour dance marathon. A student wearing an *X-Files* T-shirt hawked the Psi Phi Club, a group of science-fiction buffs that he aptly dubbed "the unfraternity." And in the middle of one row of tables, wedged between the University Christian Fellowship and the University Democrats, sat the founders and only two members of the University Crohn's and Colitis Association.

3   One unwitting freshman wandered to that table, signed the group's mailing list, and only then asked, "What's it about?"

4   Greg Guignard (who has Crohn's disease) and Emmett Lynskey (who has ulcerative colitis) explained that the club, which started last spring, is a campus offshoot of a national organization for people with gastrointestinal disorders. One of their goals, Mr. Guignard told him, is to form a support group for other students with the disease.

5   The freshman responded by nodding his head blankly. "Oh, um, OK," he said, his eyes darting around toward other booths. Then he walked away, in search of groups that might better fit his interests.

6   With more than 250 groups recruiting at the activities fair, there was something for just about everyone: hip-hop fans, origami enthusiasts, stand-up comics, Christians who are athletes, Christians who are nurses, and international students from Hong Kong.

7   Student organizations are mushrooming at campuses across the country. Clubs are being formed for every type of hobby, sport, religion, or ethnic group. Smaller groups are breaking off from larger

ones. General-interest groups are becoming more specialized. And some groups are simply being duplicated.

8   At Rensselaer Polytechnic Institute, for example, the number of student organizations has increased from about 90 in 1996–97 to more than 120 today. Among the newest groups are the Malaysian Students Association, the Iranian Students Association, and even a club for something called Brazilian Jujitsu, a Latin-American martial art.

9   The number of clubs at Emory University has increased from 202 in 1997 to 281 last year. At Northwest Missouri State University, 25 new organizations have cropped up in the last two years. The College of New Jersey will have about 180 student groups this fall, up by 40 in the last two years. Salisbury State University adds about 10 new clubs a year, and the total is now up to about 100.

10   The proliferation of organizations, some observers say, is a sign that more students are becoming engaged in their campuses and that the student body is becoming increasingly diverse—ethnically, racially, religiously, culturally, and socially.

11   The growth is also the inevitable result of a generation of students who grew up on the Internet. At a time when it's easier than ever to find a national outlet for just about any student taste, Web hermits are seeking out campus groups as a way to find like-minded fellows.

12   But some observers worry that the division and multiplication of campus organizations are contributing to the Balkanization and segregation of student life.

13   In many ways, the growth of campus groups may be a response to what William A. Strauss, an expert on generational issues, calls the destruction of campus communities in the 1960's and 70's. During that time, many student groups became so politicized and radical that they lost their appeal.

14   By the time Generation X went to college, campuses lacked a sense of community. Students are now trying to create that community through small groups rather than large associations focused on a single objective, he says.

15   "Gen-Xers tend not to trust organizations that are too large," says Mr. Strauss, coauthor, with Neil Howe, of the new book, *Millennials Rising: The Next Great Generation* (Vintage).

16   When Virginia students finish registering for their clubs this year, officials estimate that there will be about 440 of them, up from 304 in 1996, for 17,000 undergraduate and graduate students.

17   At Virginia, a table was set aside for the all-inclusive Asian Student Union, but scattered throughout the activities fair were representatives from smaller groups, each rooted in a distinct region of the Asian continent: the Association of Indonesian Students, Chinese Students Association, Hong Kong Student Association, Indian Student Association, Japanese Club, Korean Students Association, Organization of Bangali Students, Taiwanese Student Association, Thai Students Association, and Vietnamese Student Association.

18   "It's amazing how they really cover their bases," said Elizabeth Carr, a freshman from Oakton, Va., who examined a map of the fair in search of clubs for women's volleyball, yoga, ballroom dancing, and community service.

19   Many college officials and students see the growth as a positive sign of the vibrancy of campus life.

20   "You no longer hear conversations about apathy occurring within the university community," says William W. Harmon, vice president for student affairs at Virginia. "You see a student population that is more active, and I think diversity has something to do with it in terms of the wide range of interests they bring to the university community."

21   Others, however, worry about what the trend says about society.

22   "The negative is not the proliferation, it's what it represents," says Arthur E. Levine, the president of Teachers College at Columbia University and a coauthor of *When Hope and Fear Collide: A Portrait of Today's College Student* (Jossey-Bass, 1998).

23   "It represents the multiplication of differences among people, and that leads to a lack of conversation and a growing sense of 'us' and 'them'. We're living on campuses that are increasingly segregated by more and more divisions, and the sad part is that colleges and universities aren't really talking about this."

24   The book was based on surveys and interviews with undergraduates and student-affairs officials between 1992 and 1997, and visits to 28 college campuses. It notes that campuses are growing more segregated as undergraduates "describe themselves in terms of their differences, not their commonalities," which is illustrated by what Mr. Levine calls the "mitotic nature" of student groups.

25   "As undergraduates search on campus for a place to call home, their clubs are dividing into smaller and smaller groups based on race, ethnicity, gender, and sexual orientation, just to name a few differentiations," the authors state in the book.

26   On one campus the authors visited, the undergraduate business club had splintered into an assortment of business clubs for women and for black, Korean, and gay and lesbian students, among others. According to a 1997 survey of student-affairs administrators, 8 percent of American colleges had 10 or more each of black and international-student groups on campus, 5 percent had 10 or more Asian-American groups, and 3 percent had 10 or more women's groups.

27   Brian Lejeune, a senior at the University of Virginia, thinks that students are segregating themselves. "The more specific you get, the more that happens," he says. "I like groups that are all about unity."

28   One Emory official says that the growth fulfills a need sparked by recent societal changes.

29   "This population of students has grown up in a society in which technology has put everything at their fingertips—they could get all the music they want without going to a music store, they could get all the information they need without going to a library—and that isolation is countered by these small microcommunities," says Karen M. Salisbury, assistant dean and director of student activities at Emory. "Institutions need to nurture and foster those communities."

30   One consequence of the expanding number of student organizations, college officials say, is that more groups are jockeying for space and money. "It does take away from the overall pie," says Ms. Salisbury. For example, a new radio station at Emory will share money that is allocated to all student media, meaning that the newspaper, the yearbook, and other organizations in that category will receive less.

31   At Virginia, the total amount allocated for student activities, which comes from students' fees, has increased from about $494,000 in 1996 to $640,000 last year, says C. William Hancher, the student-activities business manager.

32   In 1996, 17,445 full-time undergraduate and graduate students at UVA paid $28 each per year in activities fees. This year, a projected 18,245 students will pay $39 each.

33   For now, students at campuses across the country are finding ways to justify the existence of, say, a dozen Christian fellowships on a single campus. At Virginia, nurses, athletes, and Chinese students all have their own Christian fellowship organizations. Others include the Grace Christian Fellowship, the Intervarsity Christian Fellowship, the Orthodox Christian Fellowship, the Reformed

University Fellowship, the University Christian Fellowship, and the Westminster Student Fellowship.

34   "It seems like you could say that one Christian group should be enough," says Greg Thompson, the campus minister for the Reformed University Fellowship. But he says that the word "reformed" denotes a particular theological distinction.

35   Mr. Thompson puts a spiritual spin on the theories behind the proliferation of student organizations. "Culturally, we're fragmented," he says. "Families are not working, people spend too much time watching television, and so people hunger for community."

36   "We're creatures who crave meaning in life, and we look for ways to find significance in what we do," adds David Decosimo, a member of the fellowship and a senior at Virginia, whose interdisciplinary major combines intellectual history, sociology, and literature. "When a group gets to be too big, people feel like they're not a significant player."

37   Then again, there could be a simpler explanation, he says. "People might be looking at something to put on their resume. Why be a member of one group when you could create your own and be president?"

38   Christopher Yuskaitis had that in the back of his mind when he helped form the university's premedicine chapter of the American Medical Students Association last spring, even though the university already had a long-established honor society for premed students and a premed newsletter.

39   "It looks good on your resume to say that you're a founder and president of an organization, and that's important if you're going to med school," acknowledged Mr. Yuskaitis, a junior who transferred from the University of Florida, which had a chapter. But he said his main motivation was to meet other students with a common interest and to help others in the premed program.

40   Going into the fair, the group only had 10 members, but more than 250 students had signed up on the mailing list at the event.

41   Students looking for economics organizations may have been overwhelmed by the choices: the Adam Smith Economic Society, the Economics Club, an entrepreneurs' club, a finance club, and a marketing association.

42   Asked how the Economics Club differs from the Adam Smith Economics Society, Laura Bell, a senior and co-treasurer of the former, threw up her arms in bewilderment: "We were here first!"

43   The Economics Club started about four or five years ago and aims to help economics majors and prospective majors succeed in the program and find jobs.

44   The Adam Smith Economics Society, which began last spring, is more of an intellectual club for students to debate economic theories, said Scott Melchior, a sophomore and the group's founder.

45   Aside from the difference in the club's purpose, Mr. Melchior said he wanted to run his own group, rather than join an existing club and have to wait before climbing up the ranks.

46   "It's hard to get into leadership roles your first year, or to have ideas and plan activities and get really involved if you join an established group," Mr. Melchior said.

47   Kwok-Hin Wong, a member of the Hong Kong Students Association, which formed in 1995, says that international students from Hong Kong need their own distinct club, since the culture is different from that of the students who belong to the Chinese Students Association. For example, the native language of the students in the Hong Kong Students Association is Cantonese, while members of the Chinese Students Association speak Mandarin.

48   Not everyone who browsed the student-activities fair found the perfect match. A rebellious Brandon Joyce said he wasn't interested in any of the groups, so, four hours into the fair, he decided to start his own—one that satirized the vast array of interests that were represented at the event.

49   Mr. Joyce scrounged a table, found a big cardboard box, and with makeshift paint mixed from beet juice, created a sign that read, "PERSONALITY DISEASE."

50   "I wanted to form a group to put all the rotten apples together and put students on the road to degeneration," joked Mr. Joyce, a sixth-year senior and philosophy major.

51   More than 20 names were on the mailing list. Among Mr. Joyce's pitches: "If you're interested in sex, drugs, and rock 'n' roll, sign up." Mr. Joyce said.

52   Apparently, he didn't see the table for ROX—the Society for All Things Rock 'n' Roll.

Reading: Discussing the Text

1. According to Reisberg's sources, the explosion in the number of student organizations shows that "more students are becoming engaged in their campuses" (paragraph 10). How true do you find that idea?

2. In what ways is *balkanization* an appropriate word for the profusion of clubs?
3. Reisberg notes that some "see the growth as a positive sign of the vibrancy of campus life." To what extent do you agree?
4. Arthur Levine believes "We're living on campuses that are increasingly segregated by more and more divisions." What evidence can you find to support or refute that statement?

Writing: Brief Response

1. The paragraphs in the article are very short, as befits a newspaper. To what extent does that hinder or facilitate your reading?
2. Summarize Reisberg's article in one paragraph, beginning with a sentence that contains his main point.

Writing: Extended Response

1. Using your campus as your subject, analyze how it tries to foster a sense of community: What kind of community? What are its values? How successfully does it achieve that sense of community? Write an essay analyzing what you have discovered.
2. According to Levine's research, college students "describe themselves in terms of their differences, not their commonalities." Using your own experience, interviews, and research, test out that statement as it may apply to your own campus. How accurate is it?

Black Men and Public Space

Brent Staples

Brent Staples escaped the life filled with the crime and violence that killed his younger brother, a cocaine dealer dead at the age of 22. It's a life he writes about in his memoir, Parallel Time: Growing Up in Black and White *(1994), where he also writes about the life he moved into, the predominantly white world of the university and journalism. The memoir is now available in paperback and has been hailed as one of the best coming-of-age books in recent years. Thanks to his own intelligence and persistence as well as university scholarships, Staples holds an MA and PhD in psychology from the University of*

Chicago. A former reporter for the Chicago Sun-Times, *Staples became the assistant metropolitan editor of the* New York Times, *the editor of the* New York Times Book Review, *and now writes on politics and culture for* Times *editorial Board. The essay reprinted here was first published in* Harper's *in 1986. He's still whistling.*

Before You Read   On a scale of 1 to 10 (with 10 as the highest) rate the extent to which you are affected by street crime.

1   **M**y first victim was a woman—white, well-dressed, probably in her early twenties. I came upon her late one evening on a deserted street in Hyde Park, a relatively affluent neighborhood in an otherwise mean, impoverished section of Chicago. As I swung onto the avenue behind her, there seemed to be a discreet, uninflammatory distance between us. Not so. She cast back a worried glance. To her, the youngish black man—a broad 6 feet 2 inches with a beard and billowing hair, both hands shoved into the pockets of a bulky military jacket—seemed menacingly close. After a few more quick glimpses, she picked up her pace and was soon running in earnest. Within seconds she disappeared into a cross street.

2   That was more than a decade ago. I was 22 years old, a graduate student newly arrived at the University of Chicago. It was in the echo of that terrified woman's footfalls that I first began to know the unwieldy inheritance I'd come into—the ability to alter public space in ugly ways. It was clear that she thought herself the quarry of a mugger, a rapist, or worse. Suffering a bout of insomnia, however, I was stalking sleep, not defenseless wayfarers. As a softy who is scarcely able to take a knife to a raw chicken—let alone hold one to a person's throat—I was surprised, embarrassed, and dismayed all at once. Her flight made me feel like an accomplice in tyranny. It also made it clear that I was indistinguishable from the muggers who occasionally seeped into the area from the surrounding ghetto. That first encounter, and those that followed, signified that a vast, unnerving gulf lay between nighttime pedestrians—particularly women—and me. And I soon gathered that being perceived as dangerous is a hazard in itself. I only needed to turn a corner into a dicey situation, or crowd some frightened, armed person in a foyer somewhere, or make an errant move after being pulled over by a

policeman. Where fear and weapons meet—and they often do in urban America—there is always the possibility of death.

3   In that first year, my first away from my hometown, I was to become thoroughly familiar with the language of fear. At dark, shadowy intersections, I could cross in front of a car stopped at a traffic light and elicit the *thunk, thunk, thunk, thunk* of the driver—black, white, male, or female—hammering down the door locks. On less traveled streets after dark, I grew accustomed to but never comfortable with people crossing to the other side of the street rather than pass me. Then there were the standard unpleasantries with policemen, doormen, bouncers, cabdrivers, and others whose business it is to screen out troublesome individuals *before* there is any nastiness.

4   I moved to New York nearly two years ago and I have remained an avid night walker. In central Manhattan, the near-constant crowd cover minimizes tense one-on-one street encounters. Elsewhere—in SoHo, for example, where sidewalks are narrow and tightly spaced buildings shut out the sky—things can get very taut indeed.

5   After dark, on the warrenlike streets of Brooklyn where I live, I often see women who fear the worst from me. They seem to have set their faces on neutral, and with their purse straps strung across their chests bandolier-style, they forge ahead as though bracing themselves against being tackled. I understand, of course, that the danger they perceive is not a hallucination. Women are particularly vulnerable to street violence, and young black males are drastically overrepresented among the perpetrators of that violence. Yet these truths are no solace against the kind of alienation that comes of being ever the suspect, a fearsome entity with whom pedestrians avoid making eye contact.

6   It is not altogether clear to me how I reached the ripe old age of 22 without being conscious of the lethality nighttime pedestrians attributed to me. Perhaps it was because in Chester, Pennsylvania, the small, angry industrial town where I came of age in the 1960s, I was scarcely noticeable against a backdrop of gang warfare, street knifings, and murders. I grew up one of the good boys, had perhaps a half-dozen fistfights. In retrospect, my shyness of combat has clear sources.

7   As a boy, I saw countless tough guys locked away; I have since buried several, too. They were babies, really—a teenage cousin, a brother of 22, a childhood friend in his mid-twenties—all gone

down in episodes of bravado played out in the streets. I came to doubt the virtues of intimidation early on. I chose, perhaps unconsciously, to remain a shadow—timid, but a survivor.

8   The fearsomeness mistakenly attributed to me in public places often has a perilous flavor. The most frightening of these confusions occurred in the late 1970s and early 1980s, when I worked as a journalist in Chicago. One day, rushing into the office of a magazine I was writing for with a deadline story in hand, I was mistaken for a burglar. The office manager called security and, with an ad hoc posse, pursued me through the labyrinthine halls, nearly to my editor's door. I had no way of proving who I was. I could only move briskly toward the company of someone who knew me.

9   Another time I was on assignment for a local paper and killing time before an interview. I entered a jewelry store on the city's affluent Near North Side. The proprietor excused herself and returned with an enormous red Doberman pinscher straining at the end of a leash. She stood, the dog extended toward me, silent to my questions, her eyes bulging nearly out of her head. I took a cursory look around, nodded, and bade her good night.

10   Relatively speaking, however, I never fared as badly as another black male journalist. He went to nearby Waukegan, Illinois, a couple of summers ago to work on a story about a murderer who was born there. Mistaking the reporter for the killer, police officers hauled him from his car at gunpoint and but for his press credentials would probably have tried to book him. Such episodes are not uncommon. Black men trade tales like this all the time.

11   Over the years, I learned to smother the rage I felt at so often being taken for a criminal. Not to do so would surely have led to madness. I now take precautions to make myself less threatening. I move about with care, particularly late in the evening. I give a wide berth to nervous people on subway platforms during the wee hours, particularly when I have exchanged business clothes for jeans. If I happen to be entering a building behind some people who appear skittish, I may walk by, letting them clear the lobby before I return, so as not to seem to be following them. I have been calm and extremely congenial on those rare occasions when I've been pulled over by the police.

12   And on late-evening constitutionals I employ what has proved to be an excellent tension-reducing measure: I whistle melodies from

Beethoven and Vivaldi and the more popular classical composers. Even steely New Yorkers hunching toward nighttime destinations seem to relax, and occasionally they even join in the tune. Virtually everybody seems to sense that a mugger wouldn't be warbling bright, sunny selections from Vivaldi's *Four Seasons*. It is my equivalent of the cowbell that hikers wear when they know they are in bear country.

Reading: Discussing the Text

1. Reread the first two paragraphs, comparing Staples's reaction to that of his fellow pedestrians. How effective are they as an introduction to the essay?
2. Staples uses examples in paragraphs 8 to 10. What do all three have in common? To what extent is the conclusion he draws from them a valid one?
3. Toward the end of the essay Staples states, "Over the years, I learned to smother the rage I felt at so often being taken for a criminal." To what extent is he right to feel rage? To "smother" it?
4. Who are the "victims" in Staples's essay? What are they victims of?

Writing: Brief Response

1. Take a few moments to write down the various ways you identify yourself and others identify you, not only by how you look but also by what your wear, own, say. Which one is the most important and why?
2. Considering the essay as a whole, how effective do you find Staples's "tension-reducing device" with which he concludes his essay?

Writing: Extended Response

1. Consider an experience you have had in which someone assumed you were someone or something that you are not. Keep Staples's essay in mind, and write an essay in which you analyze the experience rather than simply relate what you felt. What caused your reaction? The other person's? What larger issue might your experience represent?
2. In a sense, any first-person narrative is fiction in that the *I* of the narrative may or may not resemble the real person. Think of the *I* of Staples's essay as a character in fiction, and analyze the degree to which Staples is able to make himself "real."

Two Ways to Belong in America

Bharati Mukherjee

You will find out much about Bharati Mukherjee as you read the essay that follows. What she does not say, however, is that she is the author of six novels, several short story collections, and two nonfiction books. Her seventh novel, Desirable Daughters *was published in 2002. Her essay also does not mention the numerous awards she has received, among them the 1988 National Book Critics' Circle Award (for her collection* The Middleman and Other Stories*) as well as Guggenheim and Canada Council grants and fellowships. Born and educated in India, Mukherjee was awarded a scholarship to the University of Iowa, where she earned a MFA in Creative Writing and a PhD in English and Comparative Literature. She now teaches at the University of California, Berkeley. Much of Mukherjee's writing focuses on the experiences of immigrants. That is also the focus of the essay included here, one that appeared in the Op-Ed section of the* New York Times *on September 22, 1996, a time when the U.S. Congress, along with many states, was considering bills that would severely curtail the benefits of legal immigrants.*

Before You Read   Look up the key terms Mukherjee uses—*emigrant, immigrant, expatriate, green card.*

1   This is a tale of two sisters from Calcutta, Mira and Bharati, who have lived in the United States for some 35 years, but who find themselves on different sides in the current debate over the status of immigrants. I am an American citizen and she is not. I am moved that thousands of long-term residents are finally taking the oath of citizenship. She is not.

2   Mira arrived in Detroit in 1960 to study child psychology and pre-school education. I followed her a year later to study creative writing at the University of Iowa. When we left India, we were almost identical in appearance and attitude. We dressed alike, in saris; we expressed identical views on politics, social issues, love

and marriage in the same Calcutta convent-school accent. We would endure our two years in America, secure our degrees, then return to India to marry the grooms of our father's choosing.

3   Instead, Mira married an Indian student in 1962 who was getting his business administration degree at Wayne State University. They soon acquired the labor certifications necessary for the green card of hassle-free residence and employment.

4   Mira still lives in Detroit, works in the Southfield, Mich., school system, and has become nationally recognized for her contributions in the fields of pre-school education and parent-teacher relationships. After 36 years as a legal immigrant in this country, she clings passionately to her Indian citizenship and hopes to go home to India when she retires.

5   In Iowa City in 1963, I married a fellow student, an American of Canadian parentage. Because of the accident of his North Dakota birth, I bypassed labor-certification requirements and the race-related "quota" system that favored the applicant's country of origin over his or her merit. I was prepared for (and even welcomed) the emotional strain that came with marrying outside my ethnic community. In 33 years of marriage, we have lived in every part of North America. By choosing a husband who was not my father's selection, I was opting for fluidity, self-invention, blue jeans and T-shirts, and renouncing 3,000 years (at least) of caste-observant, "pure culture" marriage in the Mukherjee family. My books have often been read as unapologetic (and in some quarters overenthusiastic) texts for cultural and psychological "mongrelization." It's a word I celebrate.

6   Mira and I have stayed sisterly close by phone. In our regular Sunday morning conversations, we are unguardedly affectionate. I am her only blood relative on this continent. We expect to see each other through the looming crises of aging and ill health without being asked. Long before Vice President Gore's "Citizenship U.S.A." drive, we'd had our polite arguments over the ethics of retaining an overseas citizenship while expecting the permanent protection and economic benefits that come with living and working in America.

7   Like well-raised sisters, we never said what was really on our minds, but we probably pitied one another. She, for the lack of structure in my life, the erasure of Indianness, the absence of an unvarying daily core. I, for the narrowness of her perspective, her

uninvolvement with the mythic depths or the superficial pop culture of this society. But, now, with the scapegoating of "aliens" (documented or illegal) on the increase, and the targeting of long-term legal immigrants like Mira for new scrutiny and new self-consciousness, she and I find ourselves unable to maintain the same polite discretion. We were always unacknowledged adversaries, and we are now, more than ever, sisters.

8   "I feel used," Mira raged on the phone the other night. "I feel manipulated and discarded. This is such an unfair way to treat a person who was invited to stay and work here because of her talent. My employer went to the I.N.S. and petitioned for the labor certification. For over 30 years, I've invested my creativity and professional skills into the improvement of *this* country's pre-school system. I've obeyed all the rules, I've paid my taxes, I love my work, I love my students, I love the friends I've made. How dare America now change its rules in midstream? If America wants to make new rules curtailing benefits of legal immigrants, they should apply only to immigrants who arrive after those rules are already in place."

9   To my ears, it sounded like the description of a long-enduring, comfortable yet loveless marriage, without risk or recklessness. Have we the right to demand, and to expect, that we be loved? (That, to me, is the subtext of the arguments by immigration advocates.) My sister is an expatriate, professionally generous and creative, socially courteous and gracious, and that's as far as her Americanization can go. She is here to maintain an identity, not to transform it.

10   I asked her if she would follow the example of others who have decided to become citizens because of the anti-immigration bills in Congress. And here, she surprised me. "If America wants to play the manipulative game, I'll play it too," she snapped. "I'll become a U.S. citizen for now, then change back to Indian when I'm ready to go home. I feel some kind of irrational attachment to India that I don't to America. Until all this hysteria against legal immigrants, I was totally happy. Having my green card meant I could visit any place in the world I wanted to and then come back to a job that's satisfying and that I do very well."

11   In one family, from two sisters alike as peas in a pod, there could not be a wider divergence of immigrant experience. America spoke to me—I embraced the demotion from expatriate aristocrat

to immigrant nobody, surrendering those thousands of years of "pure culture," the saris, the delightfully accented English. She retained them all. Which of us is the freak?

12   Mira's voice, I realize, is the voice not just of the immigrant South Asian community but of an immigrant community of the millions who have stayed rooted in one job, one city, one house, one ancestral culture, one cuisine, for the entirety of their productive years. She speaks for greater numbers than I possibly can. Only the fluency of her English and the anger, rather than fear, born of confidence from her education, differentiate her from the seamstresses, the domestics, the technicians, the shop owners, the millions of hard-working but effectively silenced documented immigrants as well as their less fortunate "illegal" brothers and sisters.

13   Nearly 20 years ago, when I was living in my husband's ancestral homeland of Canada, I was always well-employed but never allowed to feel part of the local Quebec or larger Canadian society. Then, through a Green Paper that invited a national referendum on the unwanted side effects of "nontraditional" immigration, the Government officially turned against its immigrant communities, particularly those from South Asia.

14   I felt then the same sense of betrayal that Mira feels now. I will never forget the pain of that sudden turning, and the casual racist outbursts the Green Paper elicited. That sense of betrayal had its desired effect and drove me, and thousands like me, from the country.

15   Mira and I differ, however, in the ways in which we hope to interact with the country that we have chosen to live in. She is happier to live in America as expatriate Indian than as an immigrant American. I need to feel like a part of the community I have adopted (as I tried to feel in Canada as well). I need to put roots down, to vote and make the difference that I can. The price that the immigrant willingly pays, and that the exile avoids, is the trauma of self-transformation.

Reading: Discussing the Text

1. Mukherjee uses her experience as an immigrant to highlight elements of the American culture and values. How accurate are her conclusions?
2. Indian culture may be unfamiliar to you. What aspects of it does Mukherjee bring out? What values are involved?

3. Mukherjee is careful to point out her sister's contribution to the United States. What, as an expatriate, does the sister *not* contribute?
4. The essay deals with a number of topics—the "trauma of self-transformation" (paragraph 15), the injustice of the proposed laws, the concept of citizenship, the plight of the immigrant, the question of what it means to hold a green card. What do you find to be the essay's major focus and what is Mukherjee saying about that subject?

Writing: Brief Response

1. Write a page or two that records your associations with the word *immigrant*. Based upon those associations, what one-sentence generalization can you infer?
2. List all the rights you are entitled to as a citizen, and then rank them in order of their importance. Which is the most important and why?

Writing: Extended Response

1. Use the library or Internet to research the present state of benefits granted to legal immigrants. Given that information, write an essay supporting your view of those benefits—fair or unfair (to whom?). Somewhere in between?
2. Mukherjee describes her Americanization as the "trauma of self-transformation" (paragraph 15). Think of someone in your classes or neighborhood or family who immigrated to the United States, and interview the person to find out if the same term is appropriate. You will then have information to compare to Mukherjee's experience and to evaluate it. Is her term accurate?

What Is an American?

Edward L. Hudgins

Edward Hudgins has spent most of his career working for the government and with non-profit institutions devoted to influencing governmental decisions. After finishing his BA at the University of Maryland, he earned an MA from American University and a PhD from Catholic University. Living and working in Washington, D.C., he has appeared before Congress on many occasions to testify on matters related to his specialties—agriculture, pharmaceuticals, space, transportation, and labor, all in terms of present and proposed regulations that would affect them. Formerly senior economist for the Joint Economic Committee of the U.S. Congress, Hudgins has held directorships with the Heritage Foundation, served as Director of the Regulatory Studies for the Cato Institute, and is now the Washington Director of The Objectivist Center, an organization "dedicated to promoting a culture of reason, individualism, achievement, and freedom." Hudgins has edited a number of books that appeal to anyone interested in governmental regulation, including Mail at the Millennium: Will the Post Office Go Private *(2001),* Space: The Free-Market Frontier *(2002), and* The Case for Nafta *(1993). As you might suspect, Hudgins is passionate about America, which is evident in his piece published by the Cato Institute, dated July 3–4, 1998.*

Before You Read   Take some time to read the *Declaration of Independence* and jot down the qualities it values.

1   We celebrate July Fourth as the day the Declaration of Independence created the United States. But in my heart I also honor July 15. On that day in 1930 Giustino DiCamillo, my grandfather, arrived here with my grandma, aunts and an uncle to start their lives as Americans. My mom was born the next year.

2   I never had the chance to hear my grandpop's deepest thoughts about his extraordinary journey and rich, long life, which ended when I was fairly young. But one way I can understand his character, and the character of my country, is to reflect on the question, "What is an American?"

3   An American is anyone who loves life enough to want the best that it has to offer. Americans are not automatically satisfied with their current situation. My grandpop wanted to be more than a poor, landless tenant farmer, no better off than his ancestors. Americans look to more than the next meal; they look to the future, the long term, a better tomorrow.

4   An American is anyone who understands that to achieve the best in life requires action, exertion, effort. Americans aren't idle daydreamers; they take the initiative. Fortune did not fall into my grandpop's hands. He had traveled to America several times before

1930 to find work, establish himself, and make it possible to bring over the family. He toiled for years to achieve his dream, but achieve it he did.

5   An American is anyone who understands the need to use one's mind and wits to meet life's challenges. How would grandpop secure the money necessary for his first trip to America? Where would he find a job and a place to stay? You don't need college to know that you have to use your brain as well as your brawn to make your way in America.

6   An American is anyone who understands that achieving the best in life requires risks. Immigrants have no assurance of success in a new land with different habits, institutions and language. They leave friends, relatives and familiar places, often risking their lives to cross oceans and hostile country to reach their new homes. But they, like all Americans, understand that the timid achieve nothing and forgo even that which sustains us through the worst of times: hope.

7   The nature of Americans explains the precious opportunity that has drawn millions to these shores. The Declaration states that all men are endowed "with certain unalienable rights, that among these are life, liberty and the pursuit of happiness."

8   Americans seek economic prosperity, leaving behind the resentment in other countries that is aimed at those who better their material condition. Throughout the world and throughout history, millions of individuals have endured poverty with dignity. But there is no inherent dignity in poverty. Individuals came to America to farm their own farms and run their own enterprises. My grandpop found work on streetcar lines so he could buy a house and provide a better life for his family.

9   Americans seek personal liberty, to live as they see fit, to worship as they please. Americans seek freedom from the use of power wielded arbitrarily by whoever holds the political sword. My grandpop no doubt did not want to be at Mussolini's mercy.

10   The Declaration—and the Constitution that followed it—created a political regime for individuals who wished to be united with their countrymen not essentially by a common language, ethnic background, or other accident of birth. Americans are united by a love of liberty, respect for the freedom of others, and an insistence on their own rights as set forth in the Declaration.

11   Unfortunately, the American spirit has eroded. Our forbearers would look with sadness at the servile and envious character of

many of our citizens and policymakers. But the good news is that there are millions of Americans around the world, living in every country. Many of them will never make it here to the United States. But they are Americans, just as my grandpop was an American before he ever left Italy. And just as millions discovered America in the past, we can rediscover what it means to be an American. The principles of this country are no mere abstractions; they are written in the hearts of all true Americans. And it is the spirit of America, the spirit of my grandfather, that we should honor on July Fourth.

Reading: Discussing the Text

1. What does Hudgins' example of his grandfather add to the essay?
2. Hudgins states that Americans are "united by a love of liberty, respect for the freedom of others and an insistence on their own rights as set forth in the Declaration." How accurate do you find his views?
3. The essay celebrates the Fourth of July and therefore fits the genre of patriotic writing intended to rouse the audience's emotions, inspire their ideals, and reinforce their concept of citizenship. How well does Hudgins succeed?
4. Consider some of the negative aspects of being an American. What are they? To what extent would the essay have been stronger had Hudgins included and countered them?

Writing: Brief Response

1. Think about the ways in which the Fourth of July is celebrated where you live. What values are involved and how are they shown?
2. Consider the words *grandfather* and *grandpop*. What reasons can you think of for Hudgins' choice of the latter?

Writing: Extended Response

1. Use your library or the Internet to get an overview of what the United States was like in 1930, the time at which Hudgins' grandfather brought his family to this country. Analyze the essay in terms of the importance of 1930 to Hudgins' views of American values.
2. Write a "What It Means to be an American" essay, viewing the subject from the perspective of an ethnicity you are familiar with, such as African American, Native American, Italian American. Use examples from your own experience and research so that you avoid a personal narrative and, instead, support more general, analytical points.

COMPARING THE SELECTIONS

1. In a sense, Brent Staples, Henry Han Xi Lau, and Bharati Mukherjee all analyze their experiences of being outside of "mainstream" America. Of the three, who deals most successfully with being an "outsider"? You will need to define your key terms, such as *outsider* and *success*.

2. Leo Reisberg analyzes the proliferation of clubs on college and university campuses. To what extent, if any, does that proliferation run counter to Edward L. Hudgins concept of being an American? Support your view by using evidence from both of the essays.

3. Reread the interview with Naomi Wolf together with Hudgins' essay. Given that Wolf would probably be characterized as a liberal and Hudgins as a conservative, it's likely that they have different ideas about what it means to be an American. Think about your own ideas on the subject and write an essay explaining how well the two writers fit them.

4. Henry Han Xi Lau and Leo Reisberg explore the tension between maintaining a sense of identity and having a sense of community. Consider how that tension plays out in your own life, together with what Lau and Reisberg have to say about it. Drawing on their essays and your own experience, analyze what you believe to be the right balance.

Relationships 2

Introduction

If you have a close-knit family, you are used to one of the most literal meanings of *relationships,* that of one family member to another. Pinning it down, however, may involve you in a tangle; though short of the old song "I'm My Own Grandpa," explanations such as " 'Uncle' Charlie is your great-aunt's first cousin" quickly become complex. That complexity increases when stepmothers or stepfathers and their children join a family or leave it, for our language lacks a precise word for who's who. Ex-stepmother? Former half-brother? Neither really works.

Our language hasn't quite caught up with the times, but even without political correctness, it's trying. Think of a term for two single people who share their lives but are not married. *Lover* can imply a somewhat temporary state, *roommate* doesn't get at a sense of intimacy, *significant other* is a bureaucratic label, and *partner* has echoes of law firms and other businesses. Longer descriptions aren't much better—*the person I'm living with* still lacks precision.

This kind of search for the right word or term involves a knot of connotations. Think of all the words that a son or daughter uses for a parent: *Mother* has very different emotional overtones compared to *Mom, Mommy, Mama,* or *Momma,* just as *Father* is far from *Daddy, Pop, Papa,* or *Pappy.* Even animals join the confusion. *Pet* is a word that some people would like to see replaced by *animal companion,* so "Man's best friend" is recognized for the friendship provided. But while *animal companion* will also work for a cat, maybe a hamster, how about a snake or exotic creature? Not for most people.

No matter what the term, any relationship involves emotion. Just think of all the emotions you associate with your parents or siblings, emotions that can change over the years and usually span the whole range from love to hate. If you sat down to analyze your relationship with one of your parents, probably the first thoughts that would come to mind would be scenes or incidents, events that could represent the entire relationship at a given time. These kinds of thoughts would lead you naturally into narrative and example, relating and shaping what happened so that you can analyze and define the relationship between you and your mother or father, allowing the reader to respond as you did. That's what the writers of the selections in this chapter try to do.

As you read the essays that follow, read each first for its basic meaning:

> What is the relationship the author is writing about?
> How does that relationship affect the author?
> What conflict, if any, exists?
> How, if at all, is that conflict resolved?
> How would you characterize the writer's attitude toward the relationship: Is it sad? Angry? Bemused? Hurt? Confused? Analytic? What?
> What have you learned from the essay?

Then when you reread each selection, be aware of how the writer describes the relationship:

> What examples or narratives does the writer use?
> What do they emphasize about the relationship?
> What descriptive language does the writer use?
> How does the writer involve your emotions?
> To what extent can you identify with the writer?
> How does the writer bring about that identification?

From the Nathaniel West novel *Miss Lonelyhearts* to "Dear Abby" to a best friend, advice on relationships surrounds us, and one such column is included in this chapter. Because parental ties are often the strongest ones, however, two essays examine how grown children think of their parents. Another tells of a crucial dinner, and one relates an encounter with a questionable furry companion.

My Mother

Amy Tan

You may be familiar with Amy Tan's work if you have seen the film or read the book The Joy Luck Club. *As a novel, it not only was a finalist for the National Book Award but also set the 1989 record for the number of weeks a hardcover edition was listed as a best-seller in the* New York Times Book Review. *The novel takes a hard look at the relationship between mothers and daughters, particularly those who are Chinese and Chinese American. Families and their languages are likely subjects for Tan. Born in Oakland, California, she graduated from high school in Switzerland and holds an MA in linguistics from San Jose State University. Author of numerous short stories published in mainstream as well as small press magazines, and two children's books—*The Moon Lady *(1992) and* The Chinese Siamese Cat *(1994)—she is best known for her novels, the most recent of which are* The Kitchen God's Wife *(1991) and* The Hundred Secret Senses *(1995). "My Mother" was published in the December 24 and 31, 2001, fiction issue of the* New Yorker *in the section titled "Memory." As you will see in the following essay, Tan may be writing about a culture different from yours, but the conflicts are the same.*

Before You Read   Surely everyone has said something cruel to a parent. Try to remember such a time in your life and what you learned from it.

1   The most hateful words I have ever said to another human being were to my mother. I was sixteen at the time. They rose from the storm in my chest and I let them fall in a fury of hailstones: "I hate you. I wish I were dead." I waited for her to collapse, stricken by my cruel words, but she was still standing upright, her chin raised, her lips stretched in a crazy smile. "O.K., maybe I die," she said. "Then I no longer be your mother!"

2   We had many similar exchanges. Sometimes she actually tried to kill herself, by running into the street, holding a knife to her throat. She, too, had storms in her chest. And what she aimed at me was as fast and deadly as lightning bolts.

3   For days after our arguments, she would not speak to me. She tormented me, acted as if she had no feelings for me whatsoever. I was lost to her. And, because of that, I lost battle after battle, all of them: the times she criticized me, humiliated me in front of others, forbade me to do this or that without even listening to one good reason that it should be the other way. I swore to myself I would never forget these injustices. I would store them, harden my heart, make myself as impenetrable as she was.

4   I remember this now, because I am also remembering another time, just a couple of years ago. I was forty-seven, had become a different person by then, had gone on to be a fiction writer, someone who uses memory and imagination. In fact, I was writing a story about a girl and her mother when the phone rang.

5   It was my mother, and this surprised me. Had someone helped her make the call? For three years, she had been losing her mind to Alzheimer's disease. Early on, she forgot to lock her door. Then she forgot where she lived. She forgot who people were and what they had meant to her. Lately, she had been unable to remember many of her worries and sorrows.

6   "Amy," she said, and she began to speak quickly in Chinese. "Something is wrong with my mind. I think I'm going crazy."

7   I caught my breath. Usually she could barely speak more than two words at a time. "Don't worry," I started to say.

8   "It's true," she went on. "I feel like I can't remember many things. I can't remember what I did yesterday. I can't remember what happened a long time ago, what I did to you . . ." She spoke as a person might if she were drowning and had bobbed to the surface with the force of the will to live, only to see how far she had already drifted, how impossibly far she was from the shore.

9   She spoke frantically: "I know I did something to hurt you."

10   "You didn't," I said. "Really, don't worry."

11   "I did terrible things. But now I can't remember what. And I just want to tell you . . . I hope you can forget just as I've forgotten."

12   I tried to laugh, so that she wouldn't notice the cracks in my voice. "Really, don't worry."

13   "O.K., I just wanted you to know."

14   After we hung up, I cried, both happy and sad. I was again a sixteen-year-old, but the storm in my chest was gone.

15   My mother died six months later. But she had bequeathed to me her most healing words, those which are as open and eternal as a

clear blue sky. Together, we knew in our hearts what we should remember, what we can forget.

Reading: Discussing the Text

1. You have probably been told that the opening of an essay is crucial—
   it either hooks the reader or the essay doesn't get a nibble. How effective do you find Tan's first paragraph?
2. Given that the general subject of Tan's essay is a familiar one—arguments with parents are common—what evidence can you find that Tan
   is trying to make her experience connect with that of the reader?
3. Tan is careful to point out that her mother had been "losing her mind to
   Alzheimer's disease." In what ways is that fact important to the essay?
4. In what ways had Tan and her mother changed from the time established at the beginning of the essay? How important is that change?

Writing: Brief Response

1. Think of a good metaphor for *rage*. Write a paragraph or two analyzing your metaphor.
2. Tan's mother's "apology" is an odd one: "I did terrible things. But now
   I can't remember what. And I just want to tell you . . . I hope you can
   forget just as I've forgotten" (paragraph 11). To what extent do you
   find the apology sufficient?

Writing: Extended Response

1. Tan's essay emphasizes that it is important to know "in our hearts what
   we should remember, what we can forget" (paragraph 15). Test out the
   accuracy of that statement, using an historical event.
2. Throughout the essay, Tan uses a metaphor centered on the idea of a
   storm. Reread the essay, noting each time such language occurs. Write
   an essay in which you analyze the appropriateness of the metaphor.

Silk Parachute

John McPhee

If you were to look up a list of contemporary nonfiction writers, you could be guaranteed that John McPhee would be on it. And if they were ranked by excellence, he would be at or near the top. Author of more than 25 books, his subjects and interests vary widely. The Headmaster *(1966) is about just that,* The Curve of Binding Energy *(1974) focuses on nuclear energy and its hazards,* Coming into the Country *(1977) tells about Alaska and his travels there, and* Annals of a Former World *(2000), four volumes in one, describes the geological history of North America. A selection from his works has been collected in two volumes,* The John McPhee Reader *(1977) and* The Second John McPhee Reader *(1996). It's no wonder that his books have won numerous awards. In 1977, McPhee received the American Academy of Arts and Letters Award in Literature for his overall contribution to the field, and in 1999, he received a Pulitzer Prize. Born in Princeton, New Jersey, and educated at Princeton and Cambridge, McPhee is now the Ferris Professor of Journalism at Princeton University. After beginning his career at* Time, *he moved to the* New Yorker, *for which he still writes and where this essay first appeared in 1997. It was reprinted in the 1998 edition of* The Best American Essays, *edited by Cynthia Ozick, and tells of the acts and events that epitomize his relationship with his mother, some alleged and negative, some real and positive.*

Before You Read   Think about your childhood and an incident that you remember one way but someone close to you remembers quite differently. Who was right and why?

1   When your mother is ninety-nine years old, you have so many memories of her that they tend to overlap, intermingle, and blur. It is extremely difficult to single out one or two, impossible to remember any that exemplify the whole.

2   It has been alleged that when I was in college she heard that I had stayed up all night playing poker and wrote me a letter that used the word "shame" forty-two times. I do not recall this.

3   I do not recall being pulled out of my college room and into the church next door.

4   It has been alleged that on December 24, 1936, when I was five years old, she sent me to my room at or close to 7 P.M. for using four-letter words while trimming the Christmas tree. I do not recall that.

5   The assertion is absolutely false that when I came home from high school with an A-minus she demanded an explanation for the minus.

6   It has been alleged that she spoiled me with protectionism, because I was the youngest child and therefore the most vulnerable to attack from overhead—an assertion that I cannot confirm or confute, except to say that facts don't lie.

7   We lived only a few blocks from the elementary school and routinely ate lunch at home. It is reported that the following dialogue and ensuing action occurred on January 22, 1941:

8   "Eat your sandwich."

9   "I don't want to eat my sandwich."

10   "I made that sandwich, and you are going to eat it, Mister Man. You filled yourself up on penny candy on the way home, and now you're not hungry."

11   "I'm late. I have to go. I'll eat the sandwich on the way back to school."

12   "Promise?"

13   "Promise."

14   Allegedly, I went up the street with the sandwich in my hand and buried it in a snowbank in front of Dr. Wright's house. My mother, holding back the curtain in the window of the side door, was watching. She came out in the bitter cold, wearing only a light dress, ran to the snowbank, dug out the sandwich, chased me up Nassau Street, and rammed the sandwich down my throat, snow and all. I do not recall any detail of that story. I believe it to be a total fabrication.

15   There was the case of the missing Cracker Jack at Lindel's corner store. Flimsy evidence pointed to Mrs. McPhee's smallest child. It has been averred that she laid the guilt on with the following words: "Like mother, like son' is a saying so true, the world will judge largely of mother by you." It has been asserted that she immediately repeated that proverb three times, and also recited it on other occasions too numerous to count. I have absolutely no recol-

lection of her saying that about the Cracker Jack or any other controlled substance.

16   We have now covered everything even faintly unsavory that has
been reported about this person in ninety-nine years, and even
those items are a collection of rumors, half-truths, prevarications,
false allegations, inaccuracies, innuendos, and canards.

17   This is the mother who—when Alfred Knopf wrote her twenty-
two-year-old son a letter saying, "The readers' reports in the case of
your manuscript would not be very helpful, and I think might discourage you completely"—said, "Don't listen to Alfred Knopf. Who
does Alfred Knopf think he is, anyway? Someone should go in there
and k-nock his block off." To the best of my recollection, that is
what she said.

18   I also recall her taking me, on or about March 8, my birthday, to
the theater in New York every year, beginning in childhood. I
remember those journeys as if they were today. I remember
A Connecticut Yankee. Wednesday, March 8, 1944. Evidently, my
father had written for the tickets, because she and I sat in the last
row of the second balcony. Mother knew what to do about that.
She gave me for my birthday an elegant spyglass, sufficient in
power to bring the Connecticut Yankee back from Vermont. I sat
there watching the play through my telescope, drawing as many
guffaws from the surrounding audience as the comedy on the stage.

19   On one of those theater days—when I was eleven or twelve—I
asked her if we could start for the city early and go out to La
Guardia Field to see the comings and goings of airplanes. The temperature was well below the freeze point and the March winds
were so blustery that the wind-chill factor was forty below zero. Or
seemed to be. My mother figured out how to take the subway to a
stop in Jackson Heights and a bus from there—a feat I am unable to
duplicate to this day. At La Guardia, she accompanied me to the
observation deck and stood there in the icy wind for at least an
hour, maybe two, while I, spellbound, watched the DC-3s coming
in on final, their wings flapping in the gusts. When we at last left
the observation deck, we went downstairs into the terminal, where
she bought me what appeared to be a black rubber ball but on
closer inspection was a pair of hollow hemispheres hinged on one
side and folded together. They contained a silk parachute. Opposite
the hinge, each hemisphere had a small nib. A piece of string

wrapped round and round the two nibs kept the ball closed. If you threw it high into the air, the string unwound and the parachute blossomed. If you sent it up with a tennis racket, you could put it into the clouds. Not until the development of the ten-megabyte hard disk would the world ever know such a fabulous toy. Folded just so, the parachute never failed. Always, it floated back to you— silkily, beautifully—to start over and float back again. Even if you abused it, whacked it really hard—gracefully, lightly, it floated back to you.

Reading: Discussing the Text

1. In a sense, the essay compares two sets of memories—those that are "alleged" and those that McPhee recalls. What do the "alleged" ones suggest about McPhee's mother?
2. What do the memories that McPhee recalls suggest about her?
3. Comparing the two sets of memories, why might McPhee call the first group "a collection of rumors, half truths, prevarications, false allegations, inaccuracies, innuendos, and canards"? (paragraph 16)
4. Reread the last paragraph, paying particular attention to the silk parachute. In what sense can it be considered a metaphor or symbol?

Writing: Brief Response

1. Choose one of McPhee's examples and explain how it is or is not effective.
2. Think of the structure of McPhee's essay as a road map. Drawing or writing about it, what does it look like?

Writing: Extended Response

1. Reread the essay, taking careful note of all the examples and what they signify. Write an essay arguing for what you find to be the relationship between McPhee and his mother.
2. Take a notebook with you into a busy place—cafeteria, grocery line, office, or some such—and observe (unobtrusively) two people who are interacting. What can you assume about their relationship? Who do they appear to be? The result will be a speculative essay based upon examples and inference.

The Mysteries of Tortellini

Kristina Streeter

According to Paul Auster's introduction to I Thought My Father Was God, *what ended up as Kristina Streeter's essay began "by accident." Auster, a novelist, had just been interviewed on National Public Radio and received an invitation to be a regular on NPR's* Weekend All Things Considered, *where he would "tell stories." When he balked at the idea, his wife suggested what became* The National Story Project. *Auster invited listeners to send in their stories, which "had to be true, and they had to be short, but there would be no restrictions as to subject matter or style . . . anecdotes that revealed the mysterious and unknowable forces at work in our lives . . . true stories that sounded like fiction." He received more than four thousand entries. Auster read many on the radio and has collected 179 in the anthology mentioned above, published in 2001. Kristina Streeter's essay appears in a section titled "Love" and is one of the pieces Auster calls "dispatches, reports from the front lines of personal experience." Streeter lives in California where she is the Creative Service Manager for the Napa Vintners Association, an organization formed to promote wines of the Napa Valley. As you will see, she has come a long way.*

Before You Read   What attitudes do you associate with the words "classically trained professional chef"?

1   Brian and I were a few months into our relationship, and I still hadn't cooked for him. He was a classically trained professional chef, and that intimidated the hell out of me. I was an appreciative audience, though, and would try anything he prepared for me when he came to my house with his wok and knives and sauté pans to seduce me with his cooking. But the thought of cooking for a chef terrified me. Mostly because the foods I knew how to make involved cans and jars and a pound of meat, your choice, which you threw into one pot and called a meal. Casserole. Lasagna. Or my roommate's specialty: pork chops smothered in cream-of-mushroom soup. Standard fare from our southern Ohio upbringing. But definitely not something to serve a California chef.

2   But I was beginning to feel guilty. So one Wednesday, after he had cooked one of his meals for me, I announced that I would make dinner for him Saturday night. He looked impressed and said that he would be over at seven o'clock.

3   I bought an Italian cookbook at the drugstore and found a recipe that looked doable: tortellini. From scratch.

4   Saturday afternoon, I made the filling. No problem. I made the dough, starting with the egg in the well of flour, which magically transformed into a mound of dough. I began to feel pretty confident. Even cocky, if the truth be told.

5   "Keryn, where's that rolling pin?" I called out to my roommate, who had promised to disappear for the evening.

6   "What rolling pin?" she yelled from the living room.

7   "You know," I said, "the wooden one."

8   "We don't have a rolling pin," she called out.

9   Stopping to close my eyes, I remembered where that pin was. In my mother's kitchen. Two thousand miles away. And it was 6:30 P.M.

10   I glanced around the kitchen, swearing under my breath. My eyes lit on a bottle of wine I had bought to go with dinner. Not as good as my mother's rolling pin, since it had only one handle, but it would have to do. I rolled as best I could, breaking into a sweat even though the air conditioner was going. I then cut the dough with a water glass, and from there I seemed to be back on track. I covered a baking sheet with tortellini, properly filled and twisted into shape.

11   Just as I was finishing, the doorbell rang. I slammed the tray of pasta into the fridge and greeted my dinner guest, flour dusting my clothes, my face shiny and flushed. He had brought along a bottle of sparkling wine and a rose to celebrate the occasion.

12   A glass of champagne later, I was collected enough to begin cooking the tortellini. The pot of water began to boil. He watched with interest as I pulled the baking sheet out of the refrigerator, and his eyes popped when he saw the rows of tiny twisted shapes. "You made that? By hand? I don't even make that, and I have a pasta machine."

13   I dropped the pasta into the boiling water, then served them. They looked beautiful. We sat down, and I watched as he put one in his mouth and chewed. And chewed. And chewed. I tried one. They were as dense as a pencil eraser.

14   It was over. I knew it. I had had a good thing going, and now he'd survive the meal, then beg off early with a headache and disappear into the summer evening, his box of knives and pans never to spend the night in my apartment again.

15   But he ate them. Every last one of them, admitting only that, yes, they were a little thick, but really not bad. So I confessed the story of the rolling pin. He didn't laugh. His look told me that this guy was the one.

16   When people ask us when we knew it was the real thing, Brian says, "The first time she cooked for me. She made me tortellini—from scratch." And I say, "The first time I cooked for him—he ate my tortellini."

Reading: Discussing the Text

1. How would you characterize Streeter's approach to preparing the meal?
2. What motives are involved in Streeter's thinking that she has to cook for Brian?
3. Who was the more surprised by the tortellini and why?
4. In what ways is the title of the essay appropriate?

Writing: Brief Response

1. Compare your initial response to the idea of a "classically trained professional chef" to the Brian you know from the essay. Write a brief entry comparing the two.
2. Streeter describes the tortellini as "dense as a pencil eraser." What other metaphors can you think of for a similar tough chew?

Writing: Extended Response

1. Reread the essay the way you would read a short story, noting how Streeter builds suspense and how she uses foreshadowing. Look up those devices in a handbook of literary terms and write an essay in which you analyze and evaluate her use of those literary devices.
2. Preparing and cooking a meal has a long history of significance, one that is most apparent in holiday celebrations. Chose a particular celebratory meal and analyze its significance.

Drama King Wants His Queen Back

Carolyn Hax

*Advice columns and books fill the pages of the newspapers and maga-
zines and weigh down the racks of bookstores, reaching the point
where the* New York Times Book Review *now lists a separate category of advice and "how-to" best-sellers. The "Dear Abbys" and their
soap-operalike concerns have been around a long time, but Carolyn
Hax and her "Tell Me About It" column is relatively recent, syndicated in 1998 by the Washingington Post Writers Group. As her biography at the Group's Web site points out, Hax's advice is aimed at
readers under 30 and their "stupid teen-age stunts" or, as she prefers
it, "learning experiences." For qualifications, she states that her "'expertise' is in bad dates, school pressures, strict parents, dubious decisions, new marriages and combination skin." Though she graduated
from Harvard, she believes her parents were the "best part of [her] education" and tries to share that education with her readers by being
"supportive, demanding, maddening, funny, serious when it counts
and virtually bromide-free." You'll be able to tell something about her
tone by the title of her first book,* Tell Me About It: Lying, Sulking,
Getting Fat . . . and 56 Other Things NOT To Do While Looking for
Love *(2002). The column below is reprinted from the January 17,
2002,* New Orleans Times-Picayune.

Before You Read   What advice columns do you know about?
Read? Why do you read them?

1   **D**ear Carolyn: Five years ago, in the carefree days of freshman
year, I was introduced to "Bob," and he seemed nice. On our first
date, he took a ring from my right hand and put it on my ring fin-
ger, telling me that would have to do until he got a real one for me.
That intrigued yet bothered me. Imagine my shock when several of
my female friends later approached me, telling me he was hitting
on them, singing love songs and asking them on dates—while still

dating me. I broke it off, then got back together with him. This happened three times in two months.

2   I was hurt by his inability to stay faithful, so I broke it off completely and did not speak to him again until two years later, when I heard he nearly committed suicide by OD'ing. When asked why, he said it was because he made a stupid mistake cheating on me. I forgave him, then introduced him into my acting group at church; he had a marvelous talent for acting, but just stopped coming one night, no note or call.

3   Now he's trying to come back into my life again. My older friends have advised me to stay away from him, but Bob is talking to the friends he and I shared, and now THEY think I should date Bob again. I don't want to. I have flat-out told Bob no. I also replaced my cell phone and told my friends not to give him my new number, but I have reason to believe they have. I know I've put myself into this position, but how can I get out again?

L.

4   **DEAR L:** The English slanguage fails us here, doesn't it—"drama king" just sits there.

5   Whatever you call Broadway Bob, he's highly manipulative, which makes him highly bad news. Bad news comes in countless forms and can be sneaky as hell, but know this: Good news will never, ever try to pin blame for its suicide attempt on you. If manipulative people were vampires, this would be the jugular vein of sympathy, fear and guilt.

6   But you have your own weakness here—*your* taste for drama, apparently oft-indulged. His ring schtick, the freshman infidelity wars, the breakups, his overdose—arranged *especially* for *you!!*—the shared call to the stage, his recruiting your friends to his cause . . . you're distressed by it now, of course, but on some level digging it, too. Call it "bothered," yet "intrigued."

7   You've already done what it takes to shake Bob—starts with N, ends with O—but it only works if you stick to it. (And you rethink some of those "friends.") Ignoring his attempt to charm you is behavioral garlic and holy water: When he senses he's failed to intrigue you, he'll go bother somebody else.

8   Still, you're in for a lot more Bobs unless you recognize you're a sucker for them. Your internal alarm is working; knowing yourself better will help you, next time, to resist your urge to ignore it.

• • • •

9   **HI CAROLYN:** Guy asks me out. We go to dinner. Check comes. Who pays?

10   I say that, even if Guy DIVES for the check, I should at least offer to pay something. I feel kinda snotty just sitting there, expecting Guy to pick up the tab. My friend (who has read every book ever published about dating and the mind of the single man) says that men go out on dates expecting to pay, and not really wanting us to offer. What's the protocol?

Not-a-mooch

11   **DEAR NOT-A-MOOCH:** So—it's a matter of heeding a friend who has read every book ever published about dating and the mind of the single man, or, respecting your own instincts.

12   Tough one there.

13   (Rub face.)

14   (Cry.)

15   Your friend will impress a guy whose philosophy on women is most likely to be voted Most Likely to Turn Up Verbatim in a Book About Dating and the Mind of the Single Man. The two of them will most likely be perfect for each other. To the extent that perfect exists; I believe there's a whole chapter on that. Somewhere.

16   You will impress a guy who thinks it's pretty cool that you offered to pay even though he asked you out and so the etiquette is that he pays. And you will, with any luck, like each other enough to find out whether there are other traits you admire in each other, like decency, generosity, courage to trust your instincts . . . vs. advice from a column . . . I was never going to win this one, was I.

17   Be you. You will alienate only the men who don't like you, which is kind of the point, don't you think?

Reading: Discussing the Text

1. L.'s letter describes her situation in some detail. To what extent do you believe her?
2. How would you characterize L. and "Bob's" relationship?
3. Hax's response finds fault on both sides but tries to be positive. How accurate is her interpretation? Her advice?
4. Reread the biographical sketch that precedes the column. To what extent does the Hax you find in her response to Not-a-mooch fit what she says about herself?

Writing: Brief Response

1. Is Carolyn Hax someone you would like to meet? Why or why not?
2. What advice would you give to L. and why?

Writing: Extended Response

1. Your local newspaper probably carries an advice column or two, as do many "women's" or "men's" magazines. If there is one column that you particularly like, gather together several examples of it to form an opinion about the advisor. Your essay will use examples from the person's responses to support your opinion.
2. You can take those same columns and analyze kinds of problems posed by the letter-writers. What do you find to be the purpose of the questions and answers? Is it to entertain? To provide a willing ear? A soft shoulder? A sounding board? What?

That Charlie

Daniel Pinkwater

You might be familiar with Daniel Pinkwater from listening to National Public Radio, where he frequently reads his work on the program All Things Considered. *Or perhaps as a child you might have read one of his many children's books, books that began with* The Terrible Roar *(1970), include a number of Werewolf Club tales, along with those of Big Bob, and continue, some 80 books later, with* Mush: A Dog from Space *(2002). His titles are often intriguing, such as* The Snarkout Boys and the Avocado of Death *(1982) or* Attile the Pun *(1994), and his books are often about animals—hogs, a moose, a polar bear, a lion, and, of course, various dogs. His biography on the pzone Web site describes his office that "contains a desk and a big old leather couch with a dog on it. The dog, 'a great monstrous brute,' came home with Daniel from the pound." His experience with Charlie is quite different. The essay is from Pinkwater's collection* Chicago Days/Hoboken Nights *(1991).*

Before You Read   To understand Pinkwater's language more fully, look up a brief biography of Charlemagne and use an unabridged dictionary to find the full meaning of *gauntlet.*

1   My friend Magda invited me to come along and help her pick out a cat at Friends of Felines in Greenwich Village. It was a four story building, FULL of cats. The smell was astonishing.

2   The old lady in charge wandered around with a big stainless steel bowl ladling out blobs of ground-up hearts and gizzards, not paying much attention to us, as we inspected what seemed to be hundreds of cats.

3   On the second floor, I saw a Maine Coon cat, every bit as impressive as Charlemagne, the first Maine Coon cat I'd ever seen— actually the only one I'd ever seen other than my own coon cat, Zoe—and in her case, I'd taken it on faith that she was the genuine article. She didn't have the fierce unearthly look that first attracted me to Charlemagne. But this cat did.

4   "Look at this, Magda!" I said. "Take him! A Maine Coon cat!"

5   "I had a red cat in mind," Magda said.

6   "But look at this guy. He's terrific!"

7   Magda stubbornly refused to see the virtue of the bulky, ringleted, tiny-eared, big-footed, fiery-eyed beast. She found a marmalade cat in the last cage on the top floor, and went downstairs to fill out papers. The old lady dumped Magda's cat into a box, and I walked her to the subway.

8   Then I went back to Friends of Felines.

9   "That long-haired cat on the second floor," I said.

10   "Charlie? He's a Maine Coon cat, you know," the old lady said. "Want to take him home?"

11   I noticed that the old lady put on heavy leather and chain-mail gauntlets when she took Charlie out of his cage.

12   "How come the gloves?" I asked her.

13   "It's policy," she said. "Always use these."

14   "You didn't use them with Magda's cat."

15   "Just forgot, that's all," the old lady said. "Now, Charlie, you be a good boy—and don't come back!" she said to the cat.

16   I took Charlie home, and introduced him to Zoe. Without a moment's hesitation, he made to kill her. This was not a feint or a

threatening display. It was a lunge. Zoe neatly got out of Charlie's way, by hopping up onto the windowsill.

17   Charlie appeared to lose interest in Zoe, and went around sniffing, acquainting himself with his new home. Zoe eyed him from the windowsill.

18   Suddenly, Charlie flew from the floor to the windowsill, and actually pushed Zoe hard enough to shatter the glass. What followed remains as a series of flashlight pictures in my mind. Zoe, astonished, passing through the smashing windowpane. Shards of glass in midair. Zoe vanishing. Charlie, methodically chipping away at Zoe's paws, which were desperately clinging to the edge of the outside sill, two stories above the street.

19   It seemed that less than a second had passed. I had stood frozen. Now I acted. I shouted. Charlie looked my way. This gave Zoe a chance to haul herself up onto the sill, and into the room. She dropped behind a radiator. In the same moment, I had picked up the nearest object and hurled it at Charlie. It was a plastic cottage-cheese container—one-pint size—full of royal purple ink. It whacked against the window frame, and burst open, drenching Charlie, who then hopped down and came straight for me. He wrapped himself around my foot, and sank teeth and claws through my sneaker.

20   When I shook him off, red blood was oozing through the white canvas. Now Charlie stood his ground, making a puddle of purple ink, waiting for my next move. He eyed me steadily. Zoe had the sense to stay behind her radiator.

21   My next move was to calm the cat down. I spoke to him. He seemed to soften a little. I approached and reached out a hand, tentatively. He raked it, leaving bloody stripes.

22   I began shouting for help, and my upstairs neighbor appeared.

23   This is what met his eyes. Me, faced off in the middle of the room with a soggy, shapeless, enraged creature. Blood and pools of purple something all over. The window, smashed.

24   "What the hell is it?" he asked.

25   "It's a cat."

26   He looked at the broken window. "How did it get in?"

27   "Just help me catch it."

28   It took maybe an hour until we were able to pounce on Charlie, and successfully shove him into his box. An hour after that, my wounds bandaged, I was in front of Friends of Felines. The old lady

was still there. I could see her through the windows, moving around with her bowl of slop. I rapped on the door until she finally heard me and let me in.

29   "I brought him back," I said.

30   "I'm not surprised," she said. "That Charlie is such a bad boy. He always comes back."

31   She opened the box, and Charlie stepped out and rubbed his head against her, purring. The ink had dried, and he was a beautiful shade of purple. The old lady didn't seem to notice. She was cuddling him and saying, "Charlie, you bad boy. You always come back."

Reading: Discussing the Text

1. In what sense is the name of the adoption organization ironic?
2. Find several examples of Pinkwater using understatement. How effectively docs he use it?
3. How effective a conclusion is the last paragraph?
4. Who won?

Writing: Brief Response

1. Write a brief entry analyzing what you find to be the ideal relationship between yourself and an animal you have known.
2. Use an unabridged dictionary to get a full definition of *pet*. In what ways can the term be an objectionable one?

Writing: Extended Response

1. Use the library or Internet to research the many ways animals work for humans, selecting one to write an informative essay.
2. People choose to live with dogs or cats for any number of reasons. Think through your own experience and do some research to discover some of those reasons. Then write a paper that argues for the most important one.

Lawless Friendships

Mary Cantwell

Growing up with her parents in New England and then moving to Manhattan, where she began her career as a writer, Mary Cantwell has learned a great deal about relationships and written about what she has learned. First working as a writer and editor of Vogue *and* Mademoiselle, *she married, had children, divorced, and became a member of the* New York Times *Editorial Board, on which she still serves. Her book* Manhattan Memoir *(2000) brings together her three earlier volumes:* American Girl: Scenes from a Small-Town Childhood; Manhattan, When I Was Young; *and* Speaking with Strangers. *Together, the three memoirs trace a complex series of relationships, but the essay that follows focuses on one—the relationship between friends. It is reprinted from the* New York Times Magazine, *where it was published on March 17, 1996. On the last page of the magazine, the* Times *regularly runs short essays under the heading "Lives," which is where Cantwell's piece appeared.*

Before You Read   *Friend* is a word that can apply to a casual acquaintance or the sort of person Cantwell describes, someone who is an important part of your life. What are the qualities of a good friend?

1   We were sitting on a sea wall one summer afternoon, laughing about a future that we envisioned as countless days in porch rockers, reminiscing and complaining about our dentures, when suddenly she said, "I can't imagine growing old without you." I was touched, but also startled. Ruthie and I had spent our lives together, separated by 200 miles and often many months, but always able to pick up a conversation as if space and time had never interrupted it. Still, we were undemonstrative, unsentimental, closemouthed really. Even in silence, we could always hear what the other was saying. "I can't imagine growing old without you." It was the only instance in which one of us had articulated what both of us had

always known: that the glue that bound us was as powerful as that which binds parent to child, husband to wife.

2   Ruthie is not going to grow old with me, or with anyone. She died in September, and all I could think of were Wordsworth's lines about Lucy: "But she is in her grave, and oh,/The difference to me!"

3   "She was my sister," I said, crying, to her husband. "No, she was more than a sister. She was. . . ." And then I stopped. I did not know how to explain, not even to myself, what she was to me. "Father," "mother," "wife," "husband," "child": all evoke similar resonances. But not "friend." Friend has many definitions, and no two are ever alike. I am reminded of F. Scott Fitzgerald's remark about there being all kinds of love in the world, but never the same love twice. There is never the same friend either.

4   Wordsworth and Fitzgerald come naturally when I think about Ruthie because we were both much given to reading. When we were 12 our Christmas presents to each other were identical copies of Elizabeth Barrett Browning's "Sonnets From the Portuguese." E.B.B., we said in our also identical inscriptions, had "helped us so much"—we who were still years from tabulating "How do I love thee." But already we had found magic in words, though seldom the same words. "You must read this," she'd say, pushing Tom Robbins at me. "God forbid," I'd moan, and respond with Bruce Chatwin.

5   Long after that solemn exchange of the sonnets, it was another book, or rather a line from a poem, that linked me to a second friend. Acquaintances at the time, we were in a jewelry store looking for elephant-hair bracelets, the rage at the moment. Trying one on, she said, "Whoever comes to shroud me, do not harm," and I continued, "that subtle wreath of hair, which crowns my arm." I do not recall our mentioning Donne, or any other poet, ever again. But a chain had been forged, and it lasted until she died. Or, to be precise, almost until she died. If we had been "domestic partners," I might have had official leave to give up work, be with her 24 hours a day. But with our friendship unsanctioned by sexual connection, we were outside the law's protection.

6   But, then, friendship is essentially lawless. There are no rules, only expectations. Realized, they are all the more valued because they are freely given. Unrealized, their lack usually occasions only a few tears. Saying, "This person is no longer my friend" rarely en-

tails the same devastation as saying, "This person is no longer my husband."

7   Yet it can, because "friend" covers degrees of affection ranging from that which emerges from constant (and often mindless) proximity to that which emerges from the deepest consonances of thought and character. I shall never forget the desolation in the voice of a very old man speaking of a lost companion. "There is no one left with whom I can talk about Diaghilev," he said. A culture, an esthetic was concentrated in those 12 words, and so was the sorrow of someone who had lost not only his friend but a good part of his world.

8   Friendship is lawless, too, in that it is the rogue elephant of emotions. It crashes into relationships, splinters intimacy. A parent is jealous of a child's cherished schoolteacher; a wife, of her husband's buddy; a husband, of his wife's old pal. What do these people—the teacher, the buddy, the pal—have that they haven't got? It's not physical attraction. Physical attraction would be understandable, if painful to accept. But it is not as powerful as two psyches touching and employing a lingua franca all their own.

9   They touch in different ways. One friend and I have been through a marriage apiece, reams of gossip and countless conversations about the difficulty of finding a decent lipstick. Yet in the end, we always come back to our work. Work is our passion, its language our language, and if we have both maintained our footing on some rather perilous ladders, I believe we owe our stubborn balance as much to each other as to ourselves.

10   We employed a different vocabulary, my friend who will never grow old and I. It started small—we met, literally, as babies—and over the years grew to encompass the pleasures and pains of a lifetime. Today I can scarcely bear the terrible singularity of my memories. Now no one but I knows what it was to be chased around a bandstand on an autumn afternoon by two little boys bent on kissing us. No one but I remembers our scary trip along Fifth Avenue on a snowy December day, Ruthie determined to drive me to my wedding and I certain she'd get us killed en route. No one but I remembers how at midnight after lobster dinners we would surreptitiously hurl the empty shells into the harbor. Returning them, we intoned, "to the deep whence they come." Yes, I remember. Sometimes I even laugh. But I laugh alone and, oh, the difference to me.

Reading: Discussing the Text

1. Essays such as Cantwell's can slip into straight narrative—"Let me tell you about my friend who died"—but Cantwell balances narrative with analysis, exploring what *friend* means. Which of her generalizations strikes you as true and why?
2. In what ways is the title of the essay appropriate?
3. Cantwell's essay contains many literary allusions: Wordsworth, Fitzgerald, Elizabeth Barrett Browning, Tom Robbins, Bruce Chatwin, and John Donne. To what extent do they add to the essay?
4. Cantwell calls friendship the "rogue elephant of emotions" (paragraph 8). In what ways is that description apt?

Writing: Brief Response

1. Read the full text of Wordsworth's "Lucy." Aside from the last line, how is the poem connected to Cantwell's essay?
2. Use the Internet or your library to look up a short biography of Diaghilev. What culture or esthetic did he represent?

Writing: Extended Response

1. Obviously, there's much to be said about the value of the kind of friendship Cantwell describes, but casual friendships also have a lot to offer. Write an essay in praise of casual friendships, or, if you prefer, argue against them.
2. Cantwell describes herself and her close friend as "undemonstrative, unsentimental, closemouthed, really," implying that much of the "glue that bound" them had little to do with what they revealed to each other. Write an essay in which you analyze Cantwell's friendship and what it was based upon.

COMPARING THE SELECTIONS

1. Both Amy Tan and John McPhee describe events that tell a great deal about their relationship to their mothers. Compare those events and what they suggest about those relationships. How do they differ? What do they have in common? Use your answers to determine which of the two is the more effective and why.

2. Humor sets the tone for the essays by Daniel Pinkwater and John McPhee, but the humor is quite different. You might begin by doing some research on humor and the nature of comedy so that you are more aware of their characteristics and types. Then reread the essays, noting examples of the type of humor used by each writer. What differences do you note? What similarities? Which writer is the better humorist?

3. If you had been Kristina Streeter and had just finished chewing your way through the tortellini, you might have had the urge to write Carolyn Hax for advice. Put yourself in Streeter's position and write to Hax; then place yourself in Hax's spot and answer Streeter.

4. Mary Cantwell and Amy Tan both describe relationships that are strong and lasting, but there the similarity ends. Tan's bond to her mother is largely negative, while Cantwell's association with her friend is positive. Yet the essays together lend themselves to defining the nature of strong connections. What are the characteristics of those relationships? What values are involved? What conflicts? What benefits? Use examples from the essays and your own experience so that you can write an essay in which you define what an ideal relationship should be.

Scenes and Places

3

Introduction

"Where are you from?" or "Where do you live?" probably rank as the two most common questions asked of someone you meet for the first time, and they are questions that emphasize the importance of the American concept of *place* and the scenes that may occur there. Place is a concept that carries over into the college or university curriculum in courses such as "The Urban Novel," "Southern Literature," "The Literature of the American West" and, most obviously, to fields such as anthropology, geology, political science, and the like. But more importantly the notion of place lives within us, taking many forms. It may be our general associations with a particular event or a region of the country or our neighborhoods, or it may be a particular scene triggered by an odor: a dry yet musty sniff of chalk may bring to mind a classroom; the sharp salt scent of the sea may evoke a picnic at the beach; the smell of a toasted marshmallow may bring back a range of memories—anything from goo on one's fingers to the acrid smoke of a camp fire.

Such scenes and places can be intensely subjective, which is why they lend themselves well to being described in the personal essay. There, the writer's task is to recreate what is essentially a private impression, give it shape and meaning, and then convey it to a general audience in such a way that the reader can understand and feel what the writer felt. Yet a place or scene can also be written about quite objectively. Think, for instance, of a news article or an accident report. The more dramatic the facts, the harder it is to read without replaying the scene in one's head. Then there's that area between subjective and objective, one occupied by writers of pieces such as press releases, public relations, and travel articles, where the facts are present but colored by the writers' views. For travel writers, for example, recreating the scene is vital, for the writer wants to persuade the reader that the place is or is not worth a visit. Subjective or objective, no matter what the perspective or subject, essays that focus on scenes and places depend heavily on examples and on the senses, calling upon sight, smell, touch, sound, and motion to convey the place or scene in mind.

As you read the essays that follow, read each first for its basic meaning:

What is the author writing about?

If it's a place, what does it look like?

How would you characterize the writer's attitude toward that place: Is it admiring? Sorrowful? Amused? Fearful? What?

Within that place, does the writer emphasize a particular scene? If so, what reasons can you think of for that emphasis?

Then when you reread each essay, be on the lookout for how the writer uses example and description:

To what senses does the essay appeal?

What examples stand out?

To what extent does the writer depend on detail?

How effective is the description?

Does it bring the place or scene to life?

How does the writer want you to respond?

The essays that follow will take you to a variety of places—a farm (of sorts) in upstate New York, a Latino neighborhood in Tucson, a resort town in Florida, a cemetery in Mississippi, a monument in Boston, and an island on a man-made lake in Wyoming.

The Phony Farm

Laura Cunningham

Laura Shaine Cunningham describes herself as having "a typical writer's personal history: atypical." Growing up in the Bronx in New York City, she was one of "seven people in three rooms," an experience she describes in her book Sleeping Arrangements *(1989). She continues that tale in* A Place in the Country *(2000), which tells of her search that ends with the farm of this essay. A playwright, journalist, and writer of both fiction and nonfiction, Cunningham's work has been published in the* Atlantic Monthly, *the* New Yorker, *and* Vogue, *among other journals. The essay below appeared as a food article in the* New York Times Magazine *in 1991, where it introduced several recipes including Roast Goose with Sour Grapes and $700 Tomato Salad. You'll understand the titles as you read the essay.*

Before You Read   Look up the words *irony* and *phony* in a dictionary, plugging in some examples from your own experience to flesh out the definitions.

1   Ours is the little farm that couldn't. The idea was "to live off the land," not that the land would live off us. But that is what happened: My husband and I stagger, lugging 50-pound sacks of chow, dragging water buckets with our chapped hands out to a crowd of 45 fat animals who do little but exist in a digestive trance. I cannot even call these animals decorative as they waddle from one meal to the next. How did I, a city person, get stuck running a salad bar for useless animals?

2   The fantasy: We would raise the food for our table. I imagined I would pass platters of young vegetables and fresh chèvre along with the modest message: "Our own." We began with "our own" kitchen garden, a disaster from which we learned nothing. After a season of rototilling, fertilizing, fencing and back-dislocating labor, we produced "the $700 tomato." It was a good tomato, a golden tomato, spared by the now-gentrified groundhogs who left their dental impressions on all the other tomatoes.

3   The goats came next. We had always loved goat cheese and imagined a few dainty dairy goats would supply us with chèvre or at least feta cheese, whilst cavorting as adorable pets. Thus, I accepted delivery of two demented goat sisters, Lulu and Lulubelle.

4   While I knew goats didn't simply extrude neat white logs of Montrachet, I had not known the complex processes that led to cheese; that the "goat person" must become involved with milking platforms and teat problems and, most significantly, must orchestrate the sexual liaisons of the goats. Goats won't give milk unless they have been mated, and in our town, mating meant a date with Bucky. Bucky was the only male goat around, horned and whiskered with an odor that seemed visible. On his initial conjugal visit, he and "the girls" kicked up such a fuss that they did $2,000 worth of damage to the barn before eating the windowsills. The romance was canceled.

5   My mistake. My penance: the lifelong care of Lulu and Lulubelle. In exchange for room and board (literal in their case), Lulu and Lulubelle occasionally entertain us with a goat frolic on our front lawn. They bang heads and perform a few choreographed moves, which recall some Dionysian rite, as we watch in a drunken stupor from the porch. Most of the time, the girls simply munch and relieve themselves.

6   Then came the dream of fresh eggs, gathered warm in the mornings, a dream that gave way to the reality of 38 irritable Rhode Island Red hens sulking in their expensively maintained nests. After several hundred dollars worth of chicken feed, there was, one morning, an egg—brown, silky and warm under the hen who almost took my hand off when I reached in to get at it. Thinking "scrambled," I headed off with a heavy glove.

7   Hens, I soon learned, are cranky creatures, who seem to suffer some form of poultry PMS: they have frequent layoffs. Even the rooster has let us down. We expected him, in addition to keeping our eggs fertile, to wake us with his proud crow. But on Phony Farm (as we call our spread), the rooster sleeps late and must be shaken awake at noon. But some days, I do have enough eggs to prepare a soufflé or other fanciful egg dish—and fresh whites do rise higher—if I have the strength to hold a whisk.

8   With the chickens came the geese, who make the least sense of all. We ordered them on impulse from the poultry mail-order catalogue when we read the listing: Toulouse goslings.

9   Goslings. The word itself had a nursery-rhyme appeal, which lulled me into acceptance of the five chartreuse fuzzed baby geese, who soon quacked and snacked their way into 20-pound fatties. My gaggle, as I am forced to refer to them, are now too fat to fly, and they too have settled in for the duration. For a time, I labored under the delusion they would fly south for the winter, giving me a break. I had seen a documentary, "Flight of the Snow Geese," and thought of taping it for my geese. Instead, I tried to teach them to fly, with the result that they fly about as well as I do—skidding a few feet down to their turquoise plastic kiddie swimming pool.

10   I became resigned to running a kind of spa for Toulouse geese, but my husband had other ideas. With a Jack Nicholson glint in his eye, he hissed, "Christmas is coming and the goose is getting fat." I was appalled. How could he consider roasting an animal that had imprinted on me as Mother Goose?

11   "It's not murder," he said, "it's agriculture." But it was too late. The goslings had come to me with eggshell still on their heads. They had followed me to a nearby pond (where neighbors assured me I could relocate them: "Once they hit that water, they'll never leave.") but when I left, so did they. I turned around and saw the single-file, goony gray heads raised above the high grass, seeking only to walk in my footsteps.

12   And I had to admit I was touched. For life. Even though the only male, Arnold (named for Schwarzenegger) turns mean in his sexual season, hissing and honking. He has even, when I turned my back on him, goosed me. Their gosling coronas of fuzz gone, their voices raucous, the geese have become kind of repulsive pets. And the other day, we learned the really bad news: They live to be 40.

13   So on Friday nights, before leaving the city I can make a dash to buy my "farm-fresh fare." Having telephone ordered ahead, I can pick up my anonymous goose from a prime meat market, and find "fresh laid" eggs and natural goat cheese at the fancy food emporium. I do get some eggs from my own chickens, but seldom enough for a weekend menu of gougère and soufflé puddings—so I fill out with the store-bought ($2.50 a *half* dozen). I am happy to report that at least the egg whites inflate along with the price.

14   And my own eggs, which cost $300 each if you include such high-ticket items as henhouses, are still the best—better than eggs that run $1.39 for a cardboard carton. (The premium $5-a-dozen eggs are nice compromise candidates.) But the best news is that I can roast a

goose, baste it, enjoy the aroma and know: *It's not Arnold.* Arnold is outside, in the kiddie pool, having incestuous sex with his sisters. Like Californians, geese seem to prefer to mate in water.

Reading: Discussing the Text

1. As you read "The Phony Farm," you were probably struck by the contrast between what Cunningham expected and the reality she later faced, a contrast that provides a skeleton for the essay as a whole, serving as its structure. What are those contrasts? Which one do you find particularly appealing and why?
2. Jot down any association you have with the word *farm.* Looking at your list, what words fit Cunningham's idea of a farm? How can Cunningham's place be considered a farm? In what sense is it "phony"?
3. Even though trying to explain what is comic often removes the humor, what incident or example strikes you as the most amusing? What details make it so?
4. Reread the essay, looking for clues to the character of the writer, writing down each one. Consider your list: How would you describe her? How might she describe herself?

Writing: Brief Response

1. Memory often distorts reality. A place you might remember from childhood now probably looks quite different, or a scene you recall may change radically upon hearing someone else's version. Think about your memory of a place or scene and its new reality, briefly analyzing what you learned from the comparison.
2. What places are most important to you? List as many as you can, and then select one and explain what it symbolizes to you.

Writing: Extended Response

1. Cunningham expected a "perfect" farm, an idyllic version of what a farm is, not what this one turned out to be. The contrast between what she expected and what happened is an example of situational irony. Look through your local newspaper to find another example, and write an essay in which you both describe and analyze it.
2. *Phony* is a word that can describe almost anything—a place, a mannerism, tone of voice, person, situation, even a war. Think about what you consider *phony,* and write an essay in which you define your meaning of the word and support your definition with examples.

El Hoyo

Mario Suarez

When Mario Suarez returned from four years in the Navy, he enrolled at the University of Arizona and found himself taking freshman English. The essay that follows was written for that class and so impressed his teacher, Ruth Keenan, that she not only encouraged him to take other writing courses but also to submit "El Hoyo" to The Arizona Quarterly, *where it was published. That was a long time ago (1947), but it started Suarez on a successful writing career; it is a rare anthology of Chicano literature that doesn't include at least one of Suarez's works.*

Before You Read   Consider what provides you with a sense of community. Perhaps it is your family, friends, neighborhood, region.

1   From the center of downtown Tucson the ground slopes gently away to Main Street, drops a few feet, and then rolls to the banks of the Santa Cruz River. Here lies the section of the city known as El Hoyo. Why it is called El Hoyo is not very clear. In no sense is it a hole as its name would imply; it is simply the river's immediate valley. Its inhabitants are chicanos who raise hell on Saturday night and listen to Padre Estanislao on Sunday morning. While the term *chicano* is the short way of saying Mexicano, it is not restricted to the paisanos who came from old Mexico with the territory or the last famine to work for the railroad, labor, sing, and go on relief. Chicano is the easy way of referring to everybody: Pablo Gutíerrez married the Chinese grocer's daughter and now runs a meat department; his sons are chicanos. So are the sons of Killer Jones who threw a fight in Harlem and fled to El Hoyo to marry Cristina Mendez. And so are all of them. However, it is doubtful that all these spiritual sons of Mexico live in El Hoyo because they love each other—many fight and bicker constantly. It is doubtful they live in El Hoyo because of its scenic beauty—it is everything but beautiful. Its houses are simple affairs of unplastered adobe, wood, and abandoned car parts. Its narrow streets are mostly clearings

which have, in time, acquired names. Except for some tall trees, which nobody has ever cared to identify, nurse, or destroy, the main things known to grow in the general area are weeds, garbage piles, dark-eyed chavalos, and dogs. And it is doubtful that the chicanos live in El Hoyo because it is safe—many times the Santa Cruz has risen and inundated the area.

2   In other respects living in El Hoyo has its advantages. If one is born with weakness for acquiring bills, El Hoyo is where the collectors are less likely to find you. If one has acquired the habit of listening to Octavio Perea's Mexican Hour in the wee hours of the morning with the radio on at full blast, El Hoyo is where you are less likely to be reported to the authorities. Besides, Perea is very popular and sooner or later to everyone "Smoke in the Eyes" is dedicated between the pinto beans and white flour commercials. If one, for any reason whatever, comes on an extended period of hard times, where, if not in El Hoyo, are the neighbors more willing to offer solace? When Teofila Malacara's house burned to the ground with all her belongings and two children, a benevolent gentleman carried through the gesture that made tolerable her burden. He made a list of 500 names and solicited from each a dollar. At the end of a month he turned over to the tearful but grateful señora $100 in cold cash and then accompanied her on a short vacation. When the new manager of a local store decided that no more chicanas were to work behind the counters, it was the chicanos of El Hoyo who, on taking their individually small but collectively great buying power elsewhere, drove the manager out and the girls returned to their jobs. When the Mexican Army was en route to Baja California and the chicanos found out that the enlisted men ate only at infrequent intervals, it was El Hoyo's chicanos who crusaded across town with pots of beans and trays of tortillas to meet the train. When someone gets married, celebrating is not restricted to the immediate friends of the couple. Everybody is invited. Anything calls for a celebration and a celebration calls for anything. On Memorial Day there are no less than half a dozen good fights at the Riverside Dance Hall. On Mexican Independence Day more than one flag is sworn allegiance to amid cheers for the queen.

3   And El Hoyo is something more. It is this something more which brought Felipe Suarez back from the wars after having killed a score of Japanese with his body resembling a patchwork quilt to marry Julia Armijo. It brought Joe Zepeda, a gunner, . . . back to compose

boleros. He has a metal plate for a skull. Perhaps El Hoyo is proof that those people exist, and perhaps exist best, who have as yet failed to observe the more popular modes of human conduct. Perhaps the humble appearance of El Hoyo justifies the indifferent shrug of those made aware of its existence. Perhaps El Hoyo's simplicity motivates an occasional chicano to move away from its narrow streets, babbling comadres, and shrieking children to deny the bloodwell from which he springs and to claim the blood of a conquistador while his hair is straight and his face beardless. Yet El Hoyo is not an outpost of a few families against the world. It fights for no causes except those which soothe its immediate angers. It laughs and cries with the same amount of passion in times of plenty and of want.

4   Perhaps El Hoyo, its inhabitants, and its essence can best be explained by telling a bit about a dish called capirotada. Its origin is uncertain. But, according to the time and the circumstance, it is made of old, new, or hard bread. It is softened with water and then cooked with peanuts, raisins, onions, cheese, and panocha. It is fired with sherry wine. Then it is served hot, cold, or just "on the weather" as they say in El Hoyo. The Sermeños like it one way, the Garcias another, and the Ortegas still another. While it might differ greatly from one home to another, nevertheless it is still capirotada. And so it is with El Hoyo's chicanos. While being divided from within and from without, like the capirotada, they remain chicanos.

Reading: Discussing the Text

1. While some essays are structured so that they begin with the general and then move into the particulars, you'll see that Suarez does just the opposite, the narrative moving from the examples to generalizations. Write down the examples he uses. What generalizations does he draw from them?

2. Take another look at the examples Suarez uses to describe El Hoyo and you'll notice that they can be divided into two categories, negative and positive. Which group predominates? What reasons can you think of for that emphasis?

3. Assuming that you are unfamiliar with the neighborhood Suarez describes, how does he recreate it so that you see it as Suarez does? What details stand out and why?

4. The essay ends with a definition of capirotada that then becomes a metaphor for El Hoyo's residents. In what ways is the metaphor apt or not?

Writing: Brief Response

1. Write a notebook entry explaining why you would or would not like to live in El Hoyo.
2. Think of a metaphor that would work for your neighborhood or for one of your classes. Write a paragraph or two developing your comparison.

Writing: Extended Response

1. Write an essay in which you describe your neighborhood or one that you know well in such a way that you recreate it for readers who are not familiar with it. Like Suarez, you can include people who exemplify it. If, like Suarez, you choose to imply a thesis, make sure that every detail supports it. Write out a thesis statement even if you decide not to use it.
2. Take your reader to a place or event that you know well though your reader may not. It might be a favorite hangout or a concert or a particular game you attended or played in. The point, like Suarez's, is to analyze for the reader the sense of community the place creates.

Key West

Joy Williams

It's not often that a good writer of fiction and nonfiction also writes travel guides, but that's what Joy Williams did when she wrote the first edition of The Florida Keys *(1987). Now in its ninth edition (2000), the book is far more than a where-to-go-and-what-to-see travel guide, reflecting Williams' deep interest in history, the environment, and wildlife. Those are topics Williams often addresses in her nonfiction, most recently collected in* Ill Nature: Rants and Reflections on Humans and Other Animals *(2002). The same comic and often bleak voice is heard in her fiction: her short stories, collected in* Taking Care *(1982) and* Escapes *(1990); and novels,* State of Grace *(1973), The*

Changeling *(1978),* Breaking and Entering *(1988), and* The Quick and the Dead *(2001). Bizarre is a word often used to describe Williams' fiction, which is possibly what she finds appealing about Key West. The essay that follows is from the 2000 edition of* The Florida Keys: A History and Guide *where it introduces Williams' section on the town.*

Before You Read   What do you want to know about a place before you visit it?

1   Wallace Stevens wrote "her mind had bound me round," and he was speaking of Key West. This peculiar and unlikely town does have a mind quite of her own, with attitudes and habits that can either charm or exasperate, seduce or dismay the new acquaintance. Her posturing and fancifulness, her seedy tropicality and zany eclecticism make her an urbane, freewheeling, lighthearted, and eccentric town. She is still an odd town, actually odd; rather dirty and with little dignity; excessive, even unnatural. The town can look somewhat like old New England, but with a decidedly unpuritanical cast. Jonathan Edwards would never have slept here. The Navy is a presence, certainly, owning a good quarter of the town as well as two thirds of the waterfront (though the waterfront holdings are increasingly being excessed and sold off) and all of Boca Chica, but it is not a highly visible one from land. From the air and water the extent of its holdings is clearly seen—the piers and berths, the housing, the ammunition dumps, the runways, the radar towers. In the early 1980s, when the military began pulling out of Key West, the former mayor water-skied to Cuba in an attempt to get the Navy to stay in full force by demonstrating how close that island was to our shores. It took him six hours and ten minutes. Key West, being Key West, didn't even think it a particularly strange thing to do.

2   Homosexuals, who probably command another quarter of the town in terms of real estate and influence, are more visible, providing a sleek and somewhat mordant glaze to the town. Tennessee Williams came to Key West in the 1940s, attracted by the sailors, who all seemed "to be walking to the tune of Managua,

Nicaragua," and was influential in introducing the town to artistic gays. Many of the shops, guest houses, and dance halls are owned by gays, and much of the town's restoration is attributable to them. They continue to provide much of the gloss and sophistication of Key West.

3   One knows where the city lies in a geographic sense. Forty-five miles north of the Tropic of Cancer. Closer to Cuba at 90 miles than it is to Miami at almost 150. Due south of Cleveland, Ohio. (Cleveland, Ohio!) A glittering, balmy, perhaps not terribly legitimate rock beneath vast sea skies. Key West's economy over the years has been based on a curious and volatile array of occupations: wrecking, shrimping, fishing, and smuggling. In the 1970s certainly most of the money that came into Key West was drug money, but things have quieted down considerably in that regard. Now the money comes from real estate. And things are changing fast.

4   Key West has been compromised by the successful marketing of her as "Paradise." Of course, she was never paradise and the word is now uttered with more of an ironic, grim twist. She was simply strangely unique and that uniqueness is becoming more and more stylized, increasingly fabricated, maintained by expensive contrivance. Key West is a tourist town—one and a half million people visit each year but still, still she is a town of contrast and contradiction, threat and carelessness and charm. The bars should be sampled, of course, and the reef investigated. The forts and the galleries should be visited. One should dance or stand on one of the balconies that line Duval and watch the prowl of the street. The beaches should be duly attended and a tan obtained. The yellowtail should be eaten, and conch fritters and Key lime pie and, if you're lucky, guava duff. *Café con leche* or the intense little energizing espresso called *bucce* must be bought from the window of a Cuban grocery. The flowers and trees should be puzzled over and appreciated and their lovely names said aloud. Jacaranda. Bougainvillea. Poinciana. Frangipani. One should be in the water and travel over and on the water as much as possible. And, when one is on land, one must assuredly walk. Stroll, linger, wander. For Key West is a walking town, and a bicycling one too. Architectural surprises are around every corner, and other interesting sights less classifiable.

Reading: Discussing the Text

1. Like many essays, this one is structured around contrasts, or as Williams puts it, Key West is "a town of contrast and contradiction" (paragraph 4). Reread the essay, writing down the contrasts. Which strikes you as particularly noteworthy and why?

2. Williams also deals with the effects of those comparisons, stating that Key West has "attitudes and habits that can either charm or exasperate, seduce or dismay the new acquaintance" (paragraph 1). Review the essay, noting which facts fall in each category. Given that Key West is a tourist town, what tourists would be put off by the descriptions? To what extent is Williams being fair to those tourists? To Key West?

3. Key West, according to Williams is "odd." Look up the word in an unabridged dictionary and explain the degree to which Williams' claim is an accurate one.

4. A recent Key West advertising campaign adopted as a slogan, "Come as you are!" To what extent does that invitation fit Williams' description?

Writing: Brief Response

1. What associations do you have with resorts or tourist towns in Florida? Write them down and then rethink Williams' description. Write a paragraph or two on the greatest difference between the two.

2. Williams' essay is also an introduction to the 110 pages that follow. How successful is it? Explain why or why not you would read on.

Writing: Extended Response

1. Williams maintains that "Key West has been compromised by the successful marketing of her as 'Paradise,'" implying that advertising can create a rosy and misleading impression. Take a close look at some of the promotional materials your college publishes (try the first few pages of the catalogue), and using that as your source material, analyze the accuracy of the impression it creates.

2. Travel writers have a formidable job. They must be accurate while at the same time conveying atmosphere and second-guessing their readers' attitudes, tastes, and interests. Reread the essay, looking for examples you can use in an essay that evaluates the degree to which Williams succeeds.

A Love That Transcends Sadness

Willie Morris

Willie Morris's career is a model for anyone who works on a college newspaper. Editor of the University of Texas's Daily Texan, *Morris went on to become a Rhodes scholar and then edit the* Texas Observer. *In 1963 Morris moved to New York and became editor-in-chief of* Harper's. *Returning to his native Mississippi in 1980 as writer-in-residence at the University of Mississippi, Morris continued to write essays, fiction, and journalistic nonfiction. His autobiographical works—notably* North Toward Home *(1967) and* New York Days *(1993)—reveal the central role of place in his works. Though Morris thought of himself as "an American writer who happens to have come from the South," the South figures largely in his works as some of their titles reveal:* Yazoo: Integration in a Deep-Southern Town *(1971),* Good Old Boy *(1971),* The Last of the Southern Girls *(1973),* Homecomings *(1989),* The Ghosts of Medgar Evers *(1998). The essay that follows was published in* Parade *in 1981 and describes a rather permanent place—a graveyard.*

Before You Read   List the emotions you associate with graveyards, noting which are positive, which negative.

1   Not too long ago, in a small Southern town where I live, I was invited by friends to go with them and their children to the cemetery to help choose their burial plot. My friends are in the heartiest prime of life and do not anticipate departing the Lord's earth immediately, and hence, far from being funereal, our search had an adventurous mood to it, like picking out a Christmas tree. It was that hour before twilight, and the marvelous old graveyard with its cedars and magnolias and flowering glades sang with the Mississippi springtime. The honeysuckled air was an affirmation of the tugs and tremors of living. My companions had spent all their lives in the town, and the names on even the oldest stones were as familiar to them as the people they saw everyday. "Location," the

man of the family said, laughing. "As the real-estate magnates say, we want *location*."

2   At last they found a plot in the most venerable section which was to their liking, having spurned a shady spot which I had recommended under a giant oak. I know the caretaker would soon have to come to this place of their choice with a long, thin steel rod, shoving it into the ground every few inches to see if it struck forgotten coffins. If not, this plot was theirs. Our quest had been a tentative success, and we retired elsewhere to celebrate.

3   Their humor coincided with mine, for I am no stranger to graveyards. With rare exceptions, ever since my childhood, they have suffused me not with foreboding but with a sense of belonging and, as I grow older, with a curious, ineffable tenderness. My dog Pete and I go out into the cemeteries, not only to escape the telephone, and those living beings who place more demands on us than the dead ever would, but to feel a continuity with the flow of the generations. "Living," William Faulkner wrote, "is a process of getting ready to be dead for a long time."

4   I have never been lonely in a cemetery. They are perfect places to observe the slow changing of the seasons, and to absorb human history—the tragedies and anguishes, the violences and treacheries, and always the guilts and sorrows of vanished people. In a preternatural quiet, one can almost hear the palpable, long-ago voices.

5   I like especially the small-town cemeteries of America where the children come for picnics and games, as we did when I was growing up—wandering among the stones on our own, with no adults about, to regard the mystery and inevitability of death, on its terms and ours. I remember we would watch the funerals from afar in a hushed awe, and I believe that was when I became obsessed not with death itself but with the singular community of death and life together—and life's secrets, life's fears, life's surprises. Later, in high school, as I waited on a hill to play the echo to taps on my trumpet for the Korean War dead, the tableau below with its shining black hearse and the coffin enshrouded with the flag and the gathering mourners was like a folk drama, with the earth as its stage.

6   The great urban cemeteries of New York City always filled me with horror, the mile after mile of crowded tombstones which no one ever seemed to visit, as if one could *find* anyone in there even if he wished to. Likewise, the suburban cemeteries of this generation with their carefully manicured lawns and bronze plaques

embedded in the ground, all imbued with affluence and artifice, are much too remote for me. My favorites have always been in the old, established places where people honor the long dead and the new graves are in proximity with the most ancient. The churchyard cemeteries of England haunted me with the eternal rhythms of time. In one of these, years ago as a student at Oxford, I found this inscription:

> *Here lies Johnny Kongapod,*
> *Have mercy on him, gracious God,*
> *As he would on You if he was God,*
> *And You were Johnny Kongapod*

7   Equally magnetic were the graveyards of eastern Long Island, with their patina of the past touched ever so mellowly with the present. The cemetery of Wainscott, Long Island, only a few hundred yards from the Atlantic Ocean, surrounded the schoolhouse. I would watch the children playing at recess among the graves. Later I discovered a man and his wife juxtaposed under identical stones. On the wife's tomb was "Rest in Peace." On the man's at the same level, was "No Comment." I admired the audacity of that.

8   But it is the graveyards of Mississippi which are the most moving for me, having to do, I believe, with my belonging here. They spring from the earth itself, and beckon me time and again. The crumbling stones of my people evoke in me the terrible enigmas of living. In a small Civil War cemetery which I came across recently, the markers stretching away in a misty haze, it occurred to me that most of these boys had never even had a girl friend. I have found a remote graveyard in the hills with photographs on many of the stones, some nearly one hundred years old, the women in bonnets and Sunday dresses, the men in overalls—"the short and simple annals of the poor." I am drawn here to the tiny grave of a little girl. Her name was Fairy Jumper, and she lived from April 14, 1914 to Jan. 16, 1919. There is a miniature lamb at the top of the stone, and the words: "A fairer bud of promise never bloomed." There are no other Jumpers around her, and there she is, my Fairy, in a far corner of that country burial ground, so forlorn and alone that it is difficult to bear. It was in this cemetery on a bleak February noon that I caught sight of four men digging a grave in the hard, unyielding soil. After a time they gave up. After they left, a man

drove toward me in a battered truck. He wanted to know if some fellows had been working on the grave. Yes, I said, but they went away. "Well, I can't finish all by myself." Wordlessly, I helped him dig.

9   One lonesome, windswept afternoon my dog and I were sitting at the crest of a hill in the town cemetery. Down below us, the acres of empty land were covered with wildflowers. A new road was going in down there, the caretaker had told me; the area was large enough to accommodate the next three generations. "With the economy so bad," I had asked him, "how can you be *expanding?*" He had replied: "It comes in spurts. Not a one last week. Five put down the week before. It's a pretty steady business."

10   Sitting there now in the dappled sunshine, a middle-aged man and his middle-aged dog, gazing across at the untenanted terrain awaiting its dead, I thought of how each generation lives with its own exclusive solicitudes—the passions, the defeats, the victories, the sacrifices, the names and dates and the faces belong to each generation in its own passing, for much of everything except the most unforgettable is soon forgotten. And yet: though much is taken, much abides. I thought then of human beings, on this cinder of a planet out at the edge of the universe, not knowing where we came from, why we are here, or where we might go after death— and yet we still laugh, and cry, and feel, and love.

11   "All that we can know about those we have loved and lost," Thornton Wilder wrote, "is that they would wish us to remember them with a more intensified realization of their reality. What is essential does not die but clarifies. The highest tribute to the dead is not grief but gratitude."

Reading: Discussing the Text

1. For many, death, one might say, is a morbid subject, one to be avoided if not feared. Yet Morris's view is quite different. How would you characterize it? In what ways does it differ from your own views?

2. Reread paragraphs 1 and 2. What mood and atmosphere does Morris establish? How do they prepare you for what is to follow?

3. For Morris "it is the graveyards of Mississippi which are the most moving," yet he includes other geographical regions and specific cemeteries in his essay. In what ways do his comparisons support his point about Mississippi graveyards?

4. Morris's essay abounds with quotations and allusions. What are they? What pattern can you discern about their placement? What do they contribute to the essay?

Writing: Brief Response

1. Reconsider the list you made before you read Morris's essay. Write an entry in which you explain how the essay has (or has not) changed those associations.
2. Think about the extent to which your ideas coincide with the ones Morris describes. If they are similar, analyze why you identified with them; if they are different, explain the differences.

Writing: Extended Response

1. Think about other places or scenes that, like graveyards, have a long history of traditions and associations—a church (temple or mosque), a battle site, or monument. Choosing the one you find the most compelling or interesting, what do you note about it? Write an essay in which you analyze its effect and significance.
2. The concept of region is important to Morris, as epitomized in Southern graveyards. What place do you find represents your region of the country? Or perhaps a certain spot symbolizes your neighborhood or city. Write an essay explaining the ways in which that place stands for the larger whole.

MIT Begins to Rebuild Hope

David Eisen

When you read the article by David Eisen, keep in mind that Boston, where the story appeared in the Boston Herald, *isn't that far from New York City, and September 14, 2001, when the memorial was dedicated, isn't that long after September 11, 2001. The memorial was built out of wood, with the idea that it would not be permanent, and it*

*stands next to the chapel on the campus of the Massachusetts Institute
of Technology. David Eisen, who writes on architectural matters for
the* Boston Herald, *was so impressed by it that he wrote the story that
follows, which appeared on September 23, 2001. Beyond the Boston
area, Eisen is probably best known for his book* Fun with Architecture:
The Metropolitan Museum of Art/Architectural Guidebook *(1992),
which also contains 35 rubber stamps and an inkpad. Aimed at a
young audience, the book encourages its readers to duplicate various
types of constructions, ancient to modern, as well as to create to their
own.*

Before You Read   What images of the destroyed World Trade
Center do you remember? Jot them down in a brief list.

1   The faces are burned indelibly into our memories—red with
blood, covered in dust, streaked with tears. The victims of last
week's terrorist attack are memorialized in countless news-stand
and TV images.

2   At MIT, faculty and students have created a different kind of
memorial. Doing what people have done for thousands of years,
they have used architecture to create a place for community and
compassion in the face of the violence that surrounds us.

3   Their design starts with the realization that images of architecture
as well as of people have helped shape our memories of these
events. A fragment of the all-too familiar World Trade Center facade
becomes a focal element, allowing us to engage the horror of the
towers' destruction. The memorial evokes such deep emotions because the center's architecture, despite its banality, has been imbued with such deep and lasting meaning.

4   For the extremists, the World Trade Center represented everything that they feared. Those twin 110-story monoliths standing
aloof at the southern tip of Manhattan were a perfect symbol of
American cultural and financial might. Identically striped packages
of high-rise real estate, they stood apart from the swarm of humanity that surrounded and inhabited them. They became the ultimate
expression of American arrogance.

5   Reduced to twisted shards rising so improbably from the debris,
the facades become another sort of symbol—of American vulnera-

bility. Unlike the faces in the photos, whose expressions speak of personal pain and anguish, those tortured fragments speak of a universal sense of loss. They bear witness to what was destroyed—lives, innocence, prestige.

6   The Massachusetts Institute of Technology memorial pulls from the jumble of Trade Center images one pure moment as the focus for our thoughts and feelings, its small segment of re-created facade lining a quiet courtyard near the MIT chapel. It is a place of tranquility on an active urban campus separated by an existing brick wall from the noise and traffic of Massachusetts Avenue near Memorial Drive. Seen out of context, the facade has the power and simplicity of an abstract sculpture. It is connected perhaps only subconsciously to those postcards and TV images.

7   The Reflecting Wall, as it is called, was built within 72 hours of the tragedy. Architecture department faculty members John Fernandez and Helene Lipstadt provided design guidance, MIT carpenters put it together from plywood and paint, and an enormous number of students and staff helped with their enthusiasm and ideas. The ethnically and religiously diverse MIT community, usually focused on the enduring truths of science, refocused on the enduring truths of the human spirit.

8   The facade section, so familiar from photos, has been subtly but meaningfully transformed in this new setting. The vertical structural columns once a quarter of a mile tall have become a line of silent sentinels guarding us in our time of need. The windows, through which terrified victims dropped to their deaths, are now niches to receive our flowers and prayers. We can reach out to them and their loved ones as we try to comprehend their plight.

9   The ground in front has been layered with flickering candles and notes on scraps of paper—the flames and debris of the World Trade Center Plaza recalled as images of faith instead of fear. Slots in the memorial facade receive personal messages in a way that the hard, cold, corporate original never could.

10   Moments of pleasure and pain begin and end so quickly, leaving us with nothing but memories. Photographers, writers, anchors, and architects all help reconfigure those memories and reveal their meaning. At the MIT Reflecting Wall, memories of devastation and despair have been shaped into a beacon of hope—that peace will

prevail over war, love over hate, and rational response over irrational reaction. At this little memorial the work of rebuilding our shattered world has begun.

Reading: Discussing the Text

1. Reread the selection, noting every contrast. What is being compared? What is the point of the comparisons?
2. Eisen's article emphasizes the idea of transformation. Underline any sentence related to that idea. What point do they add up to?
3. According to Eisen, the memorial is a "place for community and compassion." Where else in the article are those two qualities brought out? Are the links sufficient?
4. In what ways is the title "The Reflecting Wall" an appropriate one for the memorial?

Writing: Brief Response

1. Compare the description of the memorial with the images you jotted down before you read the article. Write a brief entry about the comparison.
2. Briefly explain whether you agree with Eisen that the memorial is a "beacon of hope."

Writing: Extended Response

1. More than likely, your hometown or your campus has more than one memorial. Put together a list of what's available, and then choose one to analyze, using Eisen's article as a guide to what to look for.
2. Using your library or the Internet, do some research on the controversy surrounding the selection of the Viet Nam Memorial in Washington, DC. Write an essay defending your position on the matter.

Island

Gretel Ehrlich

It's hard to think of the one best word to describe Gretel Ehrlich. She began her career as a documentary filmmaker, a job that introduced her to Wyoming where she now lives and writes and works on her ranch. Author of novels, poetry, essays, and general nonfiction, her work has appeared in journals as diverse as Atlantic *and* Outside, *and her books range in subject from Wyoming as in* The Solace of Open Spaces *(1986) to Greenland in* This Cold Heaven *(2001), and from being struck by lightning—twice—described in* A Match to the Heart/One Woman's Story of Being Struck by Lightning *(1995) to being an American Buddhist in China, the focus of* Questions of Heaven *(1988). As the essay that follows can attest, no matter what she writes about she has a keen sense of place and uses it to explore both exterior and interior landscapes. It was published in her collection of essays* Islands, The Universe, Home *(1991).*

Before You Read   It's probably fair to say that all of us have busy lives yet have some way of stepping away from the busyness to reflect. Where do you go?

1   I come to this island because I have to. Only geography can frame my mind, only water can make my body stop. I come, not for solitude—I've had enough of that in my life—but for the discipline an island imposes, the way it shapes the movement of thoughts.

2   Humpbacked, willow-fringed, the island is the size of a boat, roughly eighty-five feet by twenty, and lies on the eastern edge of a small man-made lake on our Wyoming ranch. I call this island Alcatraz because I once mistook a rare whooping crane that had alighted in the lower field for a pelican, and that's what the Spanish *alcatraz* means: pelican. But the name was also a joking reference to the prison island I threatened to send my saddle horse to if he was bad, though in fact *my* Alcatraz was his favorite spot on the ranch to graze.

3   Now Blue is dead, and I have the island to myself. Some days, Rusty, my thirteen-year-old working dog, accompanies me, sitting when I sit, taking in the view. But a view is something our minds make of a place, it is a physical frame around natural fact, a two-way transmission during which the land shapes our eyes and our eyes cut the land into "scapes."

4   I sit to sweep the mind. Leaves, which I think of as a tree's discontinuous skin, keep falling as if mocking my attempts to see past my own skin, past the rueful, cantankerous, despairing, laughing racket in my head.

5   At water's edge the tiny leaves of wild rose are burned a rusty magenta, and their fruit, still unpicked by birds, hangs like drops of blood. Sun on water is bright: a blind that keeps my mind from wandering. The ripples are grooves the needle of memory makes, then they are the lines between which music is written—quintets of bird song and wind. The dam bank is a long thigh holding all restlessness in.

6   To think of an island as a singular speck or a monument to human isolation is missing the point. Islands beget islands: a terrestrial island is surrounded by an island of water, which is surrounded by an island of air, all of which makes up our island universe. That's how the mind works too: one idea unspools into a million concentric thoughts. To sit on an island, then, is not a way of disconnecting ourselves but, rather, a way we can understand relatedness.

7   Today the island is covered with duck down. It is the time of year when mallards molt. The old, battered flight feathers from the previous spring are discarded, and during the two or three weeks it takes for the new ones to grow in, they can't fly. The males, having lost their iridescent plumage, perform military maneuvers on the water, all dressed in the same drab uniform.

8   Another definition of the word "island" is "the small isolated space between the lines in a fingerprint," between the lines that mark each of us as being unique. An island, then, can stand for all that occurs between thoughts, feathers, fingerprints, and lives, although, like the space between tree branches and leaves, for example, it is part of how a thing is shaped. Without that space, trees, rooms, ducks, and imaginations would collapse.

9   Now it's January, and winter is a new moon that skates the sky, pushing mercury down into its tube. In the middle of the night the temperature drops to thirty-two below zero. Finally, the cold

breaks, and soon the groundhog will cast a shadow, but not here. Solitude has become a reflex: when I look at the lake no reflection appears. Yet there are unseen presences. Looking up after drinking from a creek, I see who I'm not: far up on a rock ledge, a mountain lion, paws crossed, has been watching me.

10 Later in the month, snow on the lake melts off, and the dendritic cracks in ice reappear. The lake is a gray brain I pose questions to. Somewhere in my reading I come on a reference to the island of Reil. It is the name given to the central lobe of the cerebral hemisphere deep in the lateral tissue, the place where the division between left and right brain occurs, between what the neurobiologist Francisco Varela calls "the net and the tree."

11 To separate out thoughts into islands is the peculiar way we humans have of knowing something, of locating ourselves on the planet and in society. We string events into temporal arrangements like pearls or archipelagos. While waiting out winter, I listen to my mind switch from logic to intuition, from tree to net, the one unbalancing the other so no dictatorships can stay.

12 Now snow collapses into itself under bright sun with a sound like muffled laughter. My young friend Will, aged nineteen, who is suffering from brain cancer, believes in the laughing cure, the mango cure, the Molokai cure, the lobster cure—eating what pleases him when he can eat, traveling to island paradises when he can walk, astonished by the reversal of expectation that a life must last a certain number of years.

13 In the evening I watch six ravens make a playground of the sky. They fly in pairs, the ones on the left, for no reason, doing rolls like stunt pilots. Under them, the self-regulating planet moves and the landscape changes—fall to winter, winter to spring, suffering its own terminal diseases in such a way that I know nothing is unseasonal, no death is unnatural, nothing escapes a raven's acrobatic glee.

Reading: Discussing the Text

1. Throughout the essay Ehrlich gives several definitions of *island*. Summarize each one and note its paragraph number. What pattern can you discern to the order in which the definitions are presented?

2. In a way, the essay is an extended analogy that compares two landscapes, one physical, exterior and one mental, interior. Reread the essay, noting each comparison. In what ways do they structure the essay?

3. Ehrlich states, "I come to this island because I have to," because "it shapes the movement of thoughts." Given the essay as a whole, what image can you think of that best describes that movement? In what ways is the image appropriate?
4. The last two paragraphs conclude the essay with mention of 19-year-old Will, six ravens, and the "self-regulating planet." What point is Ehrlich making? How does it relate to her concept of islands?

Writing: Brief Response

1. Take a few moments to write down the words you associate with *island*. Write a brief entry explaining how your associations do or do not relate to Ehrlich's view.
2. Reread the essay, writing down any verbs or comparisons that strike you as particularly effective. Choose one and explain why it works well.

Writing: Extended Response

1. For Ehrlich, the island is a place that "shapes the movement of thoughts," an apt phrase to describe the spot where she is able to step back from the "racket" in her head and think about more general, universal ideas. Write an essay in which you analyze the value of introspection.
2. Ehrlich points out a paradox, that "To sit on an island . . . is not a way of disconnecting ourselves but, rather, a way we can understand relatedness." Consider other places or events that struck you as a paradox. Perhaps you felt calm in the middle of chaos (or chaotic in the middle of calm), something like the stillness that occurs in the eye of a hurricane. Write an essay in which you describe and analyze the scene or event and why it is a paradox.

COMPARING THE SELECTIONS

1. The essays by Willie Morris and Gretel Ehrlich are classic meditative pieces, each using a place as a departure point for introspection, each revealing as much about the thinker as about the scene. Both also deal with similar ideas—the meaning of death. Which do you find the more effective and why?

2. Although different in tone and effect, Laura Cunningham's "Phony Farm" and Joy Williams' "Key West" attempt to describe an unfamiliar place in such a way that it comes alive for the reader. Reread both essays looking for the details and examples each author uses. Assuming you have never seen a farm like Cunningham's or Williams' Key West, which of the two writers is the more successful in recreating an unfamiliar scene?

3. A graveyard, a slum, a tourist town are all places that many people have negative associations with, yet they are the main focus of the essays by Willie Morris, Mario Suarez, and Joy Williams. As you review each essay, notice the ways in which the writers counter those negative ideas. Which author has the tougher job and why? Which one deals with them the most effectively and how?

4. David Eisen and Mario Suarez both write about places that represent "community and compassion." Write an essay in which you compare what the writers mean by the terms, using examples from the selections to defend your opinion as to which of the two does a better job giving meaning to those abstractions.

Work

4

Introduction

In one of his more unusual equations, Albert Einstein hypothesized "If A is a success in life, then A equals x plus y plus z. Work is x; y is play; and z is keeping your mouth shut." But writers never keep their mouths shut, and much of what they write focuses on work and play. Chapter 5 will take up some of the ways we spend our leisure time—such as going to movies, watching television, or listening to music—but in this chapter, you'll find the world of work.

As a culture, we've come a long way from the ideal of work as embodied in the Puritan ethic, though elements of it still cling to us like moss. The Puritans believed that hard work led to spiritual and material success and was therefore good for you. Leisure, no matter what form it may take, must be earned. Sounds familiar. As a child, you may have been told that you could play or watch television after you had finished your homework. And as adults, we may feel guilty about a day spent lazing around in bed, not working.

Work, of course, occupies much of our lives. As a college student, you not only have homework but probably an outside job as well, and many students think of their education as job-related, majoring in business or education, or taking courses that are pre-med or pre-law. In the past, choosing a career (even as a homemaker) was often a lifetime decision, but now, more and more people take longer to make a choice—spending a year or more out of college or after graduation to explore options—and more and more are changing careers after 20 years or so.

Before you read the works in this chapter, consider your own experience with and attitudes toward work and leisure. What is the difference between a job and a career? What has been your work experience? What feelings do you associate with work? How do you spend your leisure time? What part does it play in your life? Ten years from now, what job do you think you will have? How will you use your free time?

If you were to write an essay that took up one of those questions, you would probably find yourself analyzing your subject, perhaps using narrative and example to explain about a job you have had or want to have. You would also draw upon description, and perhaps persuasion, trying to convince your reader to take a particular action or hold a specific opinion.

As you read the essays that follow, read each first for its basic meaning:

> What experience is the author writing about?
> Who are the main characters in the piece?
> What is the author's attitude toward that experience? Toward the characters?
> What do you think the author wants you to understand, think?
> How relevant is the piece to your own experience?

Then when you reread each selection, be aware of the techniques the writer uses to clarify and emphasize various points:

> What examples or narratives does the writer use?
> What do they emphasize about the subject?
> What descriptive language does the writer use?
> How does the writer involve your emotions?
> How are you encouraged to identify with what the writer has to say?
> How does the writer bring about that identification?

Two of the essays focus on first jobs, two analyze what work really means, and two combine work and leisure in the form of volunteer work.

Legal Aide

Lorrie Moore

Lorrie Moore's writing career probably began early on, but she was 19 when she won Seventeen's *fiction contest. At the time, she was a student at St. Lawrence University, where she majored in English and earned her BA. She then moved to New York City to work as a legal aide, a job her essay describes as "exquisitely wrong." Recognizing that wrongness, she decided on graduate school, earning an MFA from Cornell University. While there, her short fiction appeared in* Ms., Fiction International, *and* Story Quarterly. *Her MFA thesis, a collection of stories, was published as* Self-Help *(1985). Since then, her short stories have been published in many magazines, including* Harper's, *the* Paris Review, Rolling Stone, *the* New Yorker, *and* Gentlemen's Quarterly, *and have appeared in the collections* Like Life *(1990) and* Birds of America *(1998). In addition to short fiction, Moore has written two novels—*Anagrams *(1986) and* Who Will Run the Frog Hospital *(1994)—though her most recent work is a children's book,* The Forgotten Helper: A Christmas Story *(2000). Moore now teaches at the University of Wisconsin, worlds away from Manhattan and life as a legal aide. Her essay was published in the* New Yorker, *April 23 and 30, 2001.*

Before You Read   Moore uses the term *middle-class poverty.* What examples can you think of to illustrate the term?

1   In the nineteen-seventies, a new para-profession was getting a foothold in urban law firms—that of the legal assistant, or paralegal—and some college graduates, uncertain how to pay the rent or fund their art, were venturing into this day job. In New York, these jobs paid slightly better than entry-level publishing positions but involved a level of exploitation that had actually caused the paralegals at one prominent Manhattan firm to strike. Upon graduation from college, fresh from editing the school literary magazine, perplexed at the number of people I knew going in an automatic fashion to law school (when I asked them what it was a lawyer did

exactly, none of them could say), I entered this strange professional racket. I would find out what a lawyer did exactly. Others I knew at the time who also embarked on this pursuit included a woman with a just completed master's thesis on Carlyle's "Sartor Resartus" (who promptly used her employer's legal services to change her last name from Schmunk) and a high-school teacher with a deep case of burnout.

2   Paralegals did not type! This was a kind of rallying cry. Nonetheless, I often coveted the jobs of the secretaries who did, for if they stayed after five they were paid overtime, and the kind of mindless typing they did looked restful to me. I, meanwhile, had to organize documents—which fell under the category of "exhibit preparation"—and, murmuring into a Dictaphone, to digest depositions into a kind of telegraphic code ("W can't recall Palm Too din. w/ Stutz"), reducing the testimony of deposed witnesses to what was optimistically called its "essence." I also had to make the occasional and terrifying court appearance to get an adjournment on a motion. This is now almost always done by attorneys, but in the seventies Manhattan paralegals were a cheap substitute. "In this city you would make more money as a paraplegic than as a paralegal," I was continually told by one of the associates.

3   I was twenty-one and mute with shyness. Up until this point in my life I had lived only in tiny towns in northern New York. The midsized, midtown firm I worked for comprised a dozen lawyers, all Jewish, all men, with names like Ira and Julian, which to a provincial ear did not even properly sound like boys' names. The staff was not Jewish: the goyim served, grumblingly and winkingly; everyone smoked and drank too much coffee. My boss, the senior partner, had apparently made his name with some big case for Sears, Roebuck in the nineteen-forties, and he had coasted on this reputation for years. With his money he bought antiquarian books, boxes of which he ripped open hungrily when they arrived, as well as some Calder prints, which he displayed in the firm's lobby and which made a big impression on me. His clients still tended to be department stores, and the case he had me working on involved the firing of the chairman of Bonwit Teller, whose makeup counters I dreamily visited during lunch hours. My boss was alternately tetchy and expansive; he spoke loudly and crazily, as all bosses, in my experience from summer jobs, did. By the time I came on

board, he was also a little hard of hearing. When after two years I told him I was leaving for graduate school in writing, he thought I'd said "riding" and made a crack about horses.

4   But this is what my first real job brought me: my first gay friend, my first African-American friend, and what I thought of as my first grownup friend (a lawyer fifteen years my senior who remains my friend to this day). And though I envied the chicly dressed young women who worked in the Pace Gallery and at Cambridge University Press, housed in the same building and sharing the elevators, my own exquisitely wrong job did bring me, for a brief period, a life in Manhattan—improvised, lonely, exhilarating. I lived on Eighteenth Street and First Avenue, above a restaurant, and was always broke, though it was middle-class poverty—temporary, part of youth and art, more a game to be played than a true condition. It produced in me an eccentric economy. Tired from work and fearful of the subways at night, I would get into a cab and say, "Give me a dollar-fifty's worth, please," then hop out at Murray Hill. I had one suit, which I wore all week: the jacket on Monday with slacks, the skirt on Tuesday with a blouse, the jacket and skirt together—at last!—on Wednesday, and so on. I ate hamburgers but not cheeseburgers, which cost ten cents more. Still, I spent twenty-five dollars to see Bette Midler on Broadway, and another twenty-five dollars to see Liza Minnelli at Carnegie Hall. I was like a fourteen-year-old gay boy escaped to the bright, big city from the farm—which is perhaps what, in my heart, given even the slimmest of paychecks, I continue to be.

Reading: Discussing the Text

1. The first paragraph of the essay sets out Moore's reasons for becoming a paralegal. What are they? Which one is the most compelling?
2. To someone who "lived in tiny towns in northern New York," Manhattan could be overwhelming. What word best describes Moore's attitude toward Manhattan and why is that word apt?
3. One of the conflicts in Moore's essay is between insider and outsider. Reread the piece, tracing that conflict. How well does Moore communicate it?
4. Moore is careful to include both the positive and the negative aspects of her experience. What are they? To what extent does one outweigh the other?

Writing: Brief Response

1. How accurately does "middle-class poverty" describe Moore's situation?
2. Everything in the essay except for the last sentence is set in the 1970s. How effective is Moore's switch to the present?

Writing: Extended Response

1. At this point in your life, you have probably narrowed down your career choices to a short list. Pick the job that appeals to you most and write an essay in which you explain your interest.
2. Moore refers to herself at 21 as "mute with shyness." Write an essay in which you support or refute her claim, using the essay itself as your resource.

Ka-Ching

Margaret Atwood

Born in Ottawa, Canada, Margaret Atwood earned her BA from the University of Toronto and an AM from Radcliffe College. Though she has held many teaching positions as Writer-in-Residence, she is a writer who is difficult to categorize. Her published works include poetry, children's books, criticism, short stories, and, of course, novels. Most recently, her The Blind Assassin *(2000) won the coveted Booker Prize for the best novel in the United Kingdom, Republic of Ireland, and the Commonwealth, quite a feat given that there are 55 Commonwealth countries. She may be best known, however, for* The Handmaiden's Tale *(1985), a chilling fable set in the future that was made into a film by the same name. Not many writers have been awarded honorary degrees by Cambridge and Oxford, earned the Swedish Humour Association's International Humourous Writer Award, and have had their works translated into Catalan and Icelandic. Those of you who like to play with words would enjoy the "Anagram Corner" of Atwood's Web site <www.owtoad.com> where,*

*among other things, she explains that the O.W. Toad who owns the
copyright to Atwood's novels is an anagram of Margaret Atwood. The
following essay was published in the* New Yorker, *April 23 and 30,
2001.*

Before You Read   No matter what kind of job you may have or
have had, there was probably one part of it that you disliked intensely. What did you learn from it?

1   I'll pass over the mini-jobs of adolescence—the summer-camp
stints that were more like getting paid for having fun. I'll pass over,
too, the self-created pin-money generators—the puppet shows put
on for kids at office Christmas parties, the serigraph posters turned
out on the Ping-Pong table—and turn to my first real job. By "real
job," I mean one that had nothing to do with friends of my parents
or parents of my friends but was obtained in the adult manner, by
looking through the ads in newspapers and going in to be interviewed—one for which I was entirely unsuited, and that I wouldn't
have done except for the money. I was surprised when I got it, un-
derpaid while doing it, and frustrated in the performance of it, and
these qualities have remained linked, for me, to the ominous word
"job."

2   The year was 1962, the place was Toronto. It was summer, and I
was faced with the necessity of earning the difference between my
scholarship for the next year and what it would cost me to live. The
job was in the coffee shop of a small hotel on Avenue Road; it is
now in the process of being torn down, but at that time it was a
clean, well-lighted place, with booths along one side and a
counter—possibly marble—down the other. The booths were
served by a waitressing pro who lipsticked outside the lines, and
who thought I was a mutant. My job would be serving things at the
counter—coffee I would pour, toast I would create from bread,
milkshakes I would whip up in the obstetrical stainless-steel device
provided. ("Easy as pie," I was told.) I would also be running the
customers' money through the cash register—an opaque machine
with buttons to be pushed, little drawers that shot in and out, and a
neurotic system of locks.

3   I said I had never worked a cash register before. This delighted the manager, a plump, unctuous character out of some novel I hadn't yet read. He said the cash register, too, was easy as pie, and I would catch on to it in no time, as I was a smart girl with an M.A. He said I should go and get myself a white dress.

4   I didn't know what he meant by "white dress." I bought the first thing I could find on sale, a nylon afternoon number with daisies appliquéd onto the bodice. The waitress told me this would not do: I needed a dress like hers, a *uniform*. ("How dense can you be?" I overheard her saying.) I got the uniform, but I had to go through the first day in my nylon daisies.

5   This first humiliation set the tone. The coffee was easy enough— I just had to keep the Bunn filled—and the milkshakes were possible; few people wanted them anyway. The sandwiches and deep-fried shrimp were made at the back: all I had to do was order them over the intercom and bin the leftovers.

6   But the cash register was perverse. Its drawers would pop open for no reason, or it would ring eerily when I swore I was nowhere near it; or it would lock itself shut, and the queue of customers waiting to pay would lengthen and scowl as I wrestled and sweated. I kept expecting to be fired for incompetence, but the manager chortled more than ever. Occasionally, he would bring some man in a suit to view me. "She's got an M.A.," he would say, in a proud but pitying voice, and the two of them would stare at me and shake their heads.

7   An ex-boyfriend discovered my place of employment, and would also come to stare and shake his head, ordering a single coffee, taking an hour to drink it, leaving me a sardonic nickel tip. The Greek short-order cook decided I would be the perfect up-front woman for the restaurant he wanted to open: he would marry me and do the cooking, I would speak English to the clientele and work—was he mad?—the cash register. He divulged his bank balance, and demanded to meet my father so the two of them could close the deal. When I declined, he took to phoning me over the intercom to whisper blandishments, and to plying me with deep-fried shrimp. A girl as scrawny as myself, he pointed out, was unlikely to get such a good offer again.

8   Then the Shriners hit town, took over the hotel, and began calling for buckets of ice, or for doctors because they'd had heart at-

tacks: too much tricycle-riding in the hot sun was felling them in herds. I couldn't handle the responsibility, the cash register had betrayed me once too often, and the short-order cook was beginning to sing Frank Sinatra songs to me. I gave notice.

9   Only when I'd quit did the manager reveal his true stratagem: they'd wanted someone as inept as me because they suspected their real cashier of skimming the accounts, a procedure I was obviously too ignorant to ever figure out. "Too stunned," as the waitress put it. She was on the cashier's side, and had me fingered as a stoolie all along.

Reading: Discussing the Text

1. Atwood begins by defining various kinds of jobs, building up to a definition of a "real job." How accurate is that description?
2. Any good narrative involves conflict, often both external (such as Atwood versus the cash register) and internal (such as Atwood's self-confidence versus her frustration). Reread the essay noting all the conflicts involved. Which is the most effective and why?
3. In a sense, Atwood's' description of what happened to her at her job is a study of humiliation. To what extent do you agree with that assessment?
4. If you think of graduate school as preparation for a profession, then Atwood's essay can be analyzed as a conflict between classes—working class versus professional class. How valid is that claim?

Writing: Brief Response

1. Consider the jobs you have had. To what extent, if any, did they involve humiliation?
2. In the last paragraph, Atwood tells you that the waitress considered her a "stoolie." In what ways can that be true?

Writing: Extended Response

1. Atwood's use of humor is subtle and sharp. Take a close look at her word choice and examples to analyze the essay in terms of the humor Atwood uses and the effect it achieves.
2. It's possible to read Atwood's essay as a sort of fable, an introduction to the "real" world of work. Reread the essay, noting what would or

would not carry over to a more permanent kind of position. Then write an essay arguing for the degree to which the essay prepares a person for a job.

The Puritan Work Ethic

Brian Dean

The title of the article would lead you to believe that an earnest and straightforward essay follows, but that's hardly what Brian Dean delivers. Instead, you'll find a subversive analysis of what has come down to us as part of our cultural heritage. Dean believes that heritage has produced a curious by-product, one suggested by the title of his magazine Anxiety Culture. *The magazine is now defunct, but its spirit lives on in Web form <www.anxietyculture.com>, and there you'll read about what* Network News *calls the "anxieties encoded in the building blocks of mainstream culture." That culture in question is British and American. The titles of some of Dean's articles give you a good idea of his perspective—"Office Rat Maze," for example, and "The Beginning of the End of Work." You can find Dean's articles on his Web 'zine, and in various British publications such as the* Guardian, Idler, *and* In Business, *in which the following article first appeared.*

Before You Read   List as many reasons as you can think of to explain why people work.

1   Phil Laut, the American financial author, has defined hard work as "doing what you don't want to do," and suggests that to operate with integrity, you should forget work and do what you want. This revolutionary viewpoint directly opposes certain beliefs which have

become codified into our work ethic courtesy of the Puritans. Puritan sects were greatly over-represented among the early major industrialists (quoted in Ashton's *History of the Industrial Revolution*), and their belief that suffering is required to redeem our "original sin" as human beings became part of their work ethic. This is a notion which continues to underlie our attitude towards work even today.

2   This is why, in our society, work is closely related to, and often motivated by, guilt. To sweeten their view of work and provide positive motivation, the Puritans believed that honest toil, if persevered with, led to mundane and spiritual rewards. The modern equivalents of these archaic religious beliefs are:

  i. that hard work is the main causative factor in producing material wealth, and,
  ii. that hard work is character building and morally good.

The available statistics don't support the belief that hard work leads to wealth—for example, US government figures from the eighties showed the average savings of a person reaching retirement age in North America to be less than $500. This is the typical level of financial reward a person can expect for forty years of full-time hard work—based on government data for an entire generation of working Americans.

3   Whatever its correlation with material wealth, hard work is undoubtedly seen as virtuous—the greatest tribute paid to the deceased seems to be "worked hard all his/her life," although this epitaph sounds more appropriate for an item of machinery than a human being. There is, in fact, a lot of evidence to suggest that our work ethic is extreme and pathological in its effects. For example, a major UK survey (quoted recently by *The Guardian*) showed that 6 out of 10 British workers dislike their jobs, suffer insecurity and stress, fret over inadequate income, feel that their work isn't of use to society, and find themselves exhausted by the time they get home. A 1995 National Opinion Poll (NOP) revealed that 50% of British workers say work makes them depressed, and 43% have problems sleeping because of work. So unless you regard stress-related illness as character building, these findings don't really support the idea of work being morally uplifting.

4   The hard work ethic has also conditioned us to see happiness as something that must be earned through toil. In effect, this is saying you have to suffer in order to get happiness, or to put it another way, you must be unhappy to be happy. The underlying idea behind this insanity is that you are infinitely undeserving—that reward, ie happiness, will always be contingent upon the endurance of some unpleasant activity. The problem with this way of thinking is that it endlessly perpetuates itself—you can never totally relax because nobody ever comes along to say, once and for all, that you've worked enough (the religious beliefs which originally gave rise to this mindset don't permit you to relax until after you've died).

5   A popular cliché says "nothing worthwhile is easy." Another version of the same idea has been used as a political slogan: "if it isn't hurting, it isn't working." Beliefs like these don't only describe viewpoints, they also program our expectations. You are effectively programming yourself to experience hurt and hardship if you accept this idea of "no pain, no gain." How can you despise ease and laziness then not feel guilty when you take a rest? Try an alternative slogan: "anything worthwhile is best done without effort," or "if you can't enjoy it, don't do it."

6   According to classical economic theory, wealth is created from land, labour and capital. Increasingly though, information is becoming the primary source of wealth. If you drill for oil, you need precise information about where to drill. As knowledge-intensive markets grow in proportion to labour-intensive industry, information is overtaking labour (ie hard work) as an important wealth-creating factor. Employees in busy offices rush so much to get things done, that they never stop to consider if there is any point to it. Quality thinking and innovation don't usually result from hard work and stress. The human brain processes complex information better when the person is relaxed and happy (adrenaline addiction notwithstanding).

7   One futurist dream is that technology will eventually free people from the necessity of hard work. This doesn't mean that all-day leisure and enjoyment would be imposed—those who like being miserable could construct their own simulations of busy offices or noxious factories to work in. But for everybody else, drudgery and toil would be pointless and obsolete. The fact that we are nowhere

near manifesting such a dream has more to do with our attitudes and beliefs than with the current state of technology.

8   Currently there are alternatives to the 9–5 work culture (job-sharing, teleworking etc) which are forward-looking and advantageous to everybody (the *Institute of Manpower Studies* has found that employees who work "non-standard" hours tend to be more efficient, enthusiastic and committed), but which are still very rare. The Information Age is here, but in terms of work patterns we cling to the attitudes of a mechanical-industrial culture steeped in the Puritan ethic.

9   A strange effect of the "dark ages" view of work as atonement, is the idea that we should enjoy it, or at least try to look as if we're enjoying it. By happily accepting our punishment (ie daily hard work) we demonstrate our moral fibre. This also explains why (according to the US figures quoted above) the average person is prepared to work forty hours per week for no great financial reward—most people believe they don't deserve to be paid for enjoying themselves (even when the "enjoyment" is for appearances only).

10   In order to more deeply understand current attitudes to work, there is an interesting exercise you can try:—spend a whole day in bed for no particular reason (i.e., don't wait until you are ill or exhausted). Don't do anything, just lie in bed and doze all day, without feeling ashamed of your laziness. This could be the greatest challenge you have ever faced. The acceptance of laziness breaks the link between guilt and work which chains us to primitive patterns from the past.

Reading: Discussing the Text

1. Dean maintains, "Hard work is the main causative factor in producing material wealth." How valid are Dean's definitions of "hard work"? "Wealth"?

2. How credible is the evidence Dean provides to support the idea that "hard work is undoubtedly seen as virtuous" (paragraph 3)?

3. Dean describes the "futurist dream" as the belief that "technology will eventually free people from the necessity of hard work" (paragraph 7). How realistic do you find that "dream"?

4. According to Dean, "A strange effect of the 'dark ages' view of work as atonement, is the idea that we should enjoy it, or at least try to look as if we're enjoying it" (paragraph 9). Evaluate the validity of that claim.

Writing: Brief Response

1. Try the experiment that Dean describes in his last paragraph. What is the result?
2. How true do you find the idea that "the hard work ethic has also conditioned us to see happiness as something that must be earned through toil" (paragraph 4)?

Writing: Extended Response

1. Use your library or the Internet to research data about the United States population so you can update the "average savings of a person reaching retirement age." What do you find and what inferences do you draw?
2. If you prefer, research the topic of "job satisfaction," again using the United States as your focus. To what extent are Dean's claims valid?

The Work Ethic, Redefined

Virginia Postrel

Virginia Postrel began her writing career as a reporter for Inc. *and the* Wall Street Journal, *moving on first to become associate editor and then editor of* Reason, *a monthly magazine that provides news, opinion, analysis, and reviews that focus on politics and culture. She is now* Reason's *Editor-at-Large, a position that frees her to spend more time on her own work. Her book* The Future and Its Enemies *(1999) examines the ways in which traditional political polarities, such as conservative and liberal, fail to deal with the major issues of our present time. She is now at work on a new book,* Look and Feel, *one that argues that aesthetics are increasingly important to society and to business. In addition to writing a regular column, "The Economic Scene," for the* New York Times, *Postrel also contributes to* Forbes, IntellectualCapital, *and the* Wall Street Journal, *where this article appeared on September 4, 1998.*

Using an unabridged dictionary, look up *meritocracy*, *tacit*, *discretion*, and *quintessential*, as the words are important to your full understanding of the essay.

1   Monday is Labor Day, a holiday that harks back to the industrial revolution and honors the struggles of American workers. But the American workplace's downtrodden Everyman is no longer a cog in a machine, fighting to keep up with the inhuman pace of the assembly line. (Think of Charlie Chaplin in "Modern Times" or Lucy Ricardo stuffing candies in her mouth.) He's a cartoon cubicle dweller who loves technology and struggles against "time-wasting morons." Dilbert knows more than the boss does, and he craves the chance to use that knowledge. He dreams less of security than of meritocracy.

2   In other words, Labor Day isn't what it used to be. The value, and values, of American workers have changed dramatically over the past few decades. The shorthand phrase to describe the change is the "knowledge economy." While technically accurate, the description is misleading. Hearing it, people tend to assume that the economy rewards only the highly educated elite, and that there's no longer a place for Everyman. (Even Dilbert is an engineer.) But many economically valuable forms of knowledge aren't taught in school. They're valuable, in fact, because they're difficult to articulate and therefore to teach. Formal education may indicate the ability to acquire such tacit knowledge, but it doesn't convey the knowledge itself.

3   Consider the three groups of jobs identified by the Bureau of Labor Statistics as likely to be the fastest growing over the next decade. The first is "professional specialty occupations," projected to increase by nearly five million workers between 1996 and 2006. These jobs include such obvious areas as computers, engineering and health care, but also special-education teachers, social workers, physical-training instructors, musicians and designers. Next come technicians and related support positions, a smaller group that complements the first. Finally, there are service occupations, which include such fast-growing jobs as home health care aides, child care workers, and manicurists. (Bureau figures undoubtedly undercount

some of these jobs. The 1996 estimate of 43,000 manicurists equals the total number of free-standing nail salons, most of which employ at least four manicurists.) These three categories are projected to make up about 36% of the total work force by 2006, or about 54 million jobs, a jump from about 30% in 1996.

4   What all these jobs have in common, regardless of their educational requirements, are specific skills and a great deal of employee discretion. Many also reward the ability to interpret and respond to the unpredictable moods and actions of other people. In short, they all employ knowledge workers.

5   That knowledge may be gained in school or passed down through apprenticeship and custom. Whether caring for a sick elderly person, writing music for a TV commercial or repairing a photocopier, none of these employees can be constantly supervised or told in advance exactly how to do their jobs. All belong to "communities of practice," in which they share knowledge by recounting war stories and soliciting advice from people in similar jobs, though not necessarily with the same employer. In contrast to the traditional routines of factory work, such employees add value by their ability to handle the exceptional case.

6   Meanwhile, on the factory floor itself workers are increasingly expected to be innovative and alert. Gone are the days of Frederick W. Taylor's decree: "You are not supposed to think. There are other people paid for thinking around here." Nowadays, pretty much everyone gets paid for thinking.

7   Understood this way, the growth of the knowledge economy has important implications not only for management but also for personal character and public policy. If the quintessential American employee isn't an obedient (and probably resentful) factory worker, but a decision maker who must use good judgment, intelligence and charm, then we must reconsider what we mean by the "work ethic." The knowledge economy gives us not only the opportunity but the obligation to reunite work with independent thinking, self-expression and even joy. It challenges many deeply held assumptions about what work should be like and how it should be evaluated.

8   Most obviously, the knowledge economy upsets the old career order. It disrupts the "loyalty ethic" of Organization Man days, encouraging employees to be on the lookout for opportunities elsewhere and employers to shed workers when their skills are no

longer needed. Successful employees think of themselves as challenge-seeking professionals, moving from mission to mission, even when they stay for years in the same company.

9   By rewarding a different sort of person—resourceful rather than predictable, sensitive rather than muscular, creative rather than obedient—the knowledge economy essentially redistributes human capital. New virtues reap the benefits, but old virtues suffer. In a workplace where no one is a cog, each employee is special and therefore unequal. This insecurity troubles those who value stability above all, from Pat Buchanan on the right to Jeremy Rifkin on the left. They see only the dutiful worker bees hurt by the new economy, not the talented free spirits put down by the old.

10   The knowledge economy also discomfits those who equate the "work ethic" with a narrow range of industrial-era virtues: diligence, stoicism, patience, conformity. Particularly for conservatives, the idea that a job should be satisfying in itself is an uncomfortable one. They fear the consequences of allowing play to infect work.

11   Discipline is, of course, important. If work were completely rewarding in and of itself, no one would need to be paid. But striving to learn, to conquer new problems, and to find satisfaction is more likely to generate progress than is dutiful drudge work.

12   Ultimately, the knowledge economy will prove more upsetting to its fans on the left than to its critics on the right. With all its emphasis on messy discretion, unarticulated wisdom, and personal judgment, knowledge work fits uneasily into a legal order that requires every employee to be treated identically and every decision to be justified in words. Sit on a medical malpractice jury, as I did this summer, and you will hear countless questions that assume that the criteria for every decision—from equipment repair to medical procedures—must be specified in advance by some outside authority. Litigation punishes discretion.

13   So does employment law. Economic value may lie in the tacit knowledge and special qualities each individual brings to a job, but public policy treats "qualification" as an either-or proposition. The law forces employers to reduce complex individuals to a few easily documented traits and to govern them according to written, inflexible rules. It's safer to be consistent than sensible or humane.

14   Treating knowledge workers as interchangeable, unintelligent cogs isn't the fault of public policy alone. The halls are full of bad bosses, and old habits die hard. But as long as the law rewards

Catbert, the Evil H.R. Director, for cooking up conformist policies, Dilbert's struggle against time-wasting morons will go on.

Reading: Discussing the Text

1. The term *knowledge economy* is crucial to Postrel's main point. How well does she define it?
2. According to Postrel, the American worker has evolved from a "cog in a machine" to Dilbert who "dreams less of security than of meritocracy." To what extent does the new worker, as defined by Posterel, seem motivated by meritocracy?
3. Why are both conservatives and liberals suspicious of the knowledge economy? Is Postrel's evidence for that suspicion sufficient?
4. Postrel foresees a conflict between those who work in the knowledge economy and the law. What is the nature of that conflict? How realistic does it seem to be?

Writing: Brief Response

1. Write a brief entry explaining what Postrel means by her title. What is the "work ethic"? How does she redefine it?
2. Find an example or two of a Dilbert cartoon strip and use it to test Postrel's assertions about Dilbert.

Writing: Extended Response

1. Postrel quotes Frederick W. Taylor as saying, "You are not supposed to think. There are other people paid for thinking around here." Test that assertion against your own job experience.
2. Reread Postrel's essay, paying particular attention to what she calls tacit knowledge. Using her definition and examples as background, together with your own experience on the job and in college, write an essay in which you evaluate the usefulness of tacit knowledge.

Why Serve and Learn in Mexico?

The International Partnership for Service-Learning

Founded in 1982, the International Partnership for Service-Learning (IPS-L) is one of many non-profit organizations that offer undergraduate and graduate students an opportunity to work on their degrees, learn about a different culture, and contribute to that culture's sense of community. With programs in 13 different countries, IPS-L administers its own programs and coordinates some of its plans of study with affiliated universities in various countries. The organization believes in the hyphen between service *and* learning, *finding that joining the two: "(1) is a powerful means of learning, (2) addresses human needs that would otherwise remain unmet, (3) promotes intercultural/international literacy, (4) advances the personal growth of students as members of the community, (5) gives expression to the obligation of public and community service by educated people, and (6) sets academic institutions in right relationship to the larger society." What follows is what you would see if you brought up their Web site <www.ispl.org> and clicked on Mexico, then scrolled to the bottom of the page and clicked the "printer friendly version," which is an Acrobat file.*

Before You Read   What do you associate with the word *service*?

1 Why serve & learn in Mexico?

Located in Guadalajara in the state of Jalisco, the program is based at the Universidad Autónoma de Guadalajara. UAG is one of the leading universities of Mexico and was founded as Mexico's first private university more than 60 years ago on the principle of the obligation of those in higher education to serve their community.

Guadalajara is an historic city with roots both in the indigenous cultures and the earliest colonization of Mexico by Spain. It is also a contemporary cosmopolitan cultural center, noted for its beautiful public buildings, plazas, markets, arts and crafts, museums, and extensive murals by Orozco.

The state of Jalisco, in central Mexico, has a temperate climate virtually year round, and is in traveling distance of many of the main areas of Mexico.

Your intensive Spanish language studies, given in four-week modules so that you may move through three to four levels (US semesters) during a program, also involve studies of culture, social issues and literature, as well as field exercises. Your family homestay and community service will enhance your language learning.

Other studies give you a comprehensive view of Mexican history; social, political, and economic structures; and cultural issues dealing with class and the position of indigenous peoples.

Your community service will bring these studies alive, allowing you to link your studies to the social issues you are actually experiencing. Through the program you will come to know and appreciate the ethnic, cultural and regional variety which makes up the "many Mexicos."

Students wishing an experience of the diversity of Latin America may wish to consider spending a summer or semester in Mexico, and a summer or semester in Ecuador.

2   **Dates—semester / summer / year**

Semester, summer, and year-long programs are offered in Mexico.

> Summer 2001: June 13–August 10
> Fall 2001: August 14–December 7
> Spring 2002: January 8–May 17
> Summer 2002: June 12–August 9

3   **Program Design**

The program begins with intensive study and practice in written and spoken Spanish, an introduction to the academic studies, and an orientation to the culture and current conditions of Mexico. During the orientation and visits you will be introduced to your service agency. In the following weeks, you will continue your language and academic studies, and work approximately 20 hours per week in your service assignment.

4　**Academic Study**

The program is based at the Universidad Autónoma de Guadalajara, one of the leading universities of Mexico.

1. **Spanish Language**—On arrival, you will be given a language examination for placement in one of seven levels, from beginning to advanced. Each level is given in intensive four-week modules, each module equating with a US semester at that level. You may therefore move through as many as four modules (levels). Each module carries 3 semester credit hours. In all levels, the instruction uses materials from the culture of Mexico and Spanish/Latin American literature to illustrate characteristics of the society as well as to develop language skills. *3–12 semester credits; 3–6 summer credits.* Fall semester students may arrive early for intensive preparation in Spanish at an additional cost.

2. **Institutions in Mexican Society**—This course, taught in English and Spanish, and based primarily on the disciplines of sociology and economics, introduces you to the culture, conditions and issues of contemporary Mexico. The class meets for 3 hours each week and involves lectures by the professor and invited speakers, discussions, and reading and writing assignments. In addition, you meet regularly with the service coordinator to discuss the issues you encounter in your service. You will keep a journal and write a paper in English or Spanish on an issue facing the nation which is addressed by your service agency. *6 semester credits; 3 summer credits.*

Students staying for a second term (semester/summer) continue their service and Spanish studies, and choose from regular course offerings at the University, depending on Spanish proficiency.

5　**Service**

Some examples of service opportunities are: serving in a developing community; working with street children; assisting with children in special education programs; providing day care to children of prisoners or single mothers; teaching English; or working with Mexican social workers on programs designed to help the poor. Exact assignments depend on your language skills, skills and interests, as well as community needs.

6 **Housing**

Housing is with local families, arranged in advance through the University.

7 **Language of Instruction**

Academic studies are taught in both English and Spanish.

8 **Eligibility & Language Requirement**

The program welcomes students of any nation. To fulfill the academic requirements and be useful in your service assignment, English and romance language speakers must have completed at least 2 years of secondary school Spanish or 1 year of college/university Spanish. Students whose native language is structured very differently from Spanish should have completed 1.5–2 years of university study of Spanish and have facility in spoken Spanish. Students may arrive early for an intensive preparation course in Spanish at an additional cost.

9 **What Former Students Say about Service-Learning in Mexico**

"My boys at Casa Hogar have challenged me forever. I can no longer see any child—Mexican or of any other nationality—with the same eyes as I had before. My boys taught me to look deeper into each person before passing any judgments. They taught me that each person has a story to be told, a reason why they act like they do."

—Shana McGillivray, Pacific Lutheran University
Service: tutored boys at a school

10 **Costs / Financial Aid**

Summer 2001: $4,900
Fall 2001: $7,600
Spring 2002: $7,800
Full Year 2001–2002: $14,900
Summer 2002: $4,900

Fees include all instruction, room and board, service placement and supervision, administrative fees, and pre-departure materials.

Personal expenses include airfare, books, lunches when not with family, spending money, and local travel.

Students participating in 2 undergraduate IPS-L programs will have a $500 reduction in the cost of the second program.

11 **Application Deadline**

Applications are due two months before the start of the program.

Applications are reviewed as they are received. You will be notified of acceptance within two weeks of our receipt of your completed application. Early application is encouraged, as it gives our resident Program Directors time to arrange your housing and service placement. Late applications may be accepted if space is still available in a program. Students wishing to apply late should call The International Partnership before applying.

The International Partnership for Service-Learning
815 Second Avenue, Suite 315, New York, NY 10017 USA
Tel (212) 986-0989 Fax (212) 986-5039 pslny@aol.com www.ipsl.org

Reading: Discussing the Text

1. Reread the information, noting the topics covered. How complete is the information?
2. What would you want to know more about and why?
3. Compare the cost of a semester to what you are now paying. To what extent is the IPS-L program a good value?
4. IPS-L believes in "service-learning," the two vital components of the program. To what extent do the two receive equal emphasis?

Writing: Brief Response

1. If you were eligible and the tuition were not a problem, would you apply for this program? Write a brief entry explaining why or why not.
2. To what extent should service be part of an academic program? Write a brief entry stating your ideas on the subject.

Writing: Extended Response

1. The selection serves two purposes—to provide information and to interest prospective students. Write an essay in which you evaluate how well it achieves its dual purpose.

2. Using your own campus and choice of study as the subject, write your own version of IPS-L's description. Like IPS-L, you would want to explain and persuade.

The Volunteers

Peter Matthiessen

Hailed by the New York Times Book Review *as "Our greatest modern nature writer in the lyrical tradition," Peter Matthiessen helped found the* Paris Review *and is a winner of a National Book Award. Although he writes fiction, he may be best known for his essays and nonfiction that reflect his extensive travels and his interest in nature: South America in* The Cloud Forest *(1961); Africa in* The Tree Where Man Was Born *(1972), Sand (1981), African Silences (1991), and* Shadows of Africa *(1992); Nepal in* The Snow Leopard *(1978); and Siberia in* Baikal: Sacred Sea of Siberia *(1992). He also writes about people, places, and issues closer to home:* Wildlife in America *(1959),* In the Spirit of Crazy Horse *(1983),* Men's Lives: The Surfmen and Baymen of the South Fork *(1986). His focus is even closer in the essay that follows—one of the shelters for the people working at Ground Zero immediately after the attack of 9/11/01. It is reprinted from* Orion, *a journal centered on the environment, and focuses on a different kind of work.*

Before You Read   Use your library or the Internet to find out these exact locations in or near New York City: East Northport, Long Island; Jamaica, Long Island, Brooklyn, and (in Manhattan) Canal Street and the Javits Center on West 34th Street.

1   My blind son Lucas commutes each day by train and subway, changing trains at Jamaica on a round trip of almost four hours between East Northport, Long Island, and Brooklyn, where he runs a

clinic for drug and alcohol addiction. In early September of this year, he had lost his Seeing-Eye dog to an unexpected cancer and until the dog could be replaced had been obliged to change trains and navigate rail platforms and rough neighborhoods with a white cane. Always in need of a break by the weekend, he was mildly dismayed on the first Sunday after September 11 when his twelve-year-old son informed him that he wished to go that day to the disaster site at the World Trade Center to see what he could do to help.

2   Patiently Luke suggested to the child that such a journey would be in vain, since volunteers were no longer welcome at the site. But Joe was adamant, and the more his father listened, the clearer it became that he must honor his child's decision. A few years earlier, Luke's older boy had been run over and killed on the street in front of their house, and although no link has been established, Joe can be emotional and sometimes difficult. He can also be startlingly sweet and gentle, and in the end, his father was so touched by his impulse and moved by his determination that instead of pleading for his day off, he said, All right, let's go! And away they went by train to New York City.

3   Arriving on the subway from Penn Station at Canal Street, this well-intentioned pair was met by a blue line of police. Taken aback by a man with a white cane and a little boy guiding his elbow, the cops were naturally incredulous, and wasted no time sending them on their way. But seeing them start north again, one officer, touched, called after them that if they were serious, they could go register at the Jacob Javits Center on West 34th Street, where rescue efforts were being coordinated. I'll try to find you guys a ride, he said, and soon he did, flagging down a building inspector who was headed uptown and providing the delighted boy with an official escort.

4   At the Javits Center, the staff proved unwilling to expose a child to the grim atmosphere, but when his father took responsibility, saying Joe was serious and could handle it, the two were put to work at once in the medical personnel section, assembling "care packages" for the firemen, police, and other rescue workers—eye drops, throat lozenges, moist tissues for wiping the face, aspirin, granola bars and the like. Luke's hands quickly learned the separate items, and the two had assembled quite a stack when a police captain came over and asked Joe, Was this your idea, Son? When Joe acknowledged shyly that it was, the officer said, Well, you're the

youngest volunteer I've seen here and my hat's off to you. And he actually doffed his cap, reported Joe, with a proud smile in his voice which his father felt sure had lit up the whole room.

5   Meanwhile, a shift of iron workers from Ground Zero had arrived, and one man came straight to the medical group to request an aspirin. Hearing the precarious tone of this man's voice, Luke identified himself as a trained social worker and asked the man if it would help to talk. In tears, the man blurted, I've got to go home, I can't go back there! Apparently ashamed of his own frailty in the face of the dreadful conditions of his mission, he had wandered away, all but incoherent.

6   Even so, Luke felt grateful for the chance to offer help, and walking back to Penn Station that afternoon, he thanked his son for his excellent idea, saying, "That was one of the most worthwhile Sundays I have ever spent."

Reading: Discussing the Text

1. Matthiessen appeals to many emotions in this essay. Review the text, identifying what you felt and the details that lead to your response. What is the primary emotion the essay evokes?

2. What details in paragraph 1 does Matthiessen provide to set the emotional tone for the essay? Although Matthiessen's narrative rests on facts, they are presented in such a way that they play on the emotions. Discuss whether he goes overboard, tipping the tone from empathy to pity.

3. The idea of helping is one that runs throughout the essay, providing its backbone. Reread the essay, accounting for who is helping whom and how. In what ways are the responses to that aid believable or not?

4. The essay concludes with Luke saying, "That was one of the most worthwhile Sundays I have ever spent." What support does Matthiessen provide for that statement? Given that a conclusion should end an essay not just stop the narrative, how effective is the last sentence?

Writing: Brief Response

1. The spot where one was when hearing momentous news usually sears itself into memory. Describe where you were when you found out about what happened on September 11, 2001.

2. When Ground Zero was being cleared, many people went to see it. If you were one of them, explain why you went. If you were not, explain whether you would have gone to see the site and why.

Writing: Extended Response

1. Use your library or the Internet to research the controversy behind the statue memorializing the firefighters who died at the site of the World Trade Center. Write an essay defending your position on the controversy.

2. In many ways, the World Trade Center symbolized both New York City and the United States. If you live in an urban area, what building or site symbolizes your city? If you live in a rural area, what scene is most representative of it? Assume your reader is not familiar with your subject and explain the symbolism involved.

COMPARING THE SELECTIONS

1. The essays by Margaret Atwood and Lorrie Moore relate the authors' experiences with "first jobs." Reread both essays, noting the differences and similarities to determine who had the better experience and why.

2. In a sense, all volunteer work involves learning, often on several levels. Reread "Why Serve and Learn in Mexico?" and pay particular attention to the various kinds of learning involved. Then do the same for the essay by Peter Matthiessen. Assuming you were able to choose between the two, which would you find the more rewarding and why?

3. Brian Dean and Virginia Postrel present very different views of the work ethic. Using your own experience as a guide, which of the two is the more accurate and why?

4. All of the selections in this chapter deal with various forms of work. Using at least three of the selections as sources as well as your own experiences, analyze the various kinds of work you have done and expect to do so that you can define what work means to you. What role should it play in your life and why?

Popular Culture

5

Introduction

Popular culture encompasses all the forms of enjoyment that exist within a given society. What those forms may be varies from person to person. Some people may enjoy video games, others theme parks, but the vast majority of the public shares similar tastes in entertainment: they go to movies, watch television shows, read books, listen to music, drink sodas, eat at fast food restaurants. McDonald's hamburgers (or Wendy's or Burger King's) are as much a part of our popular culture as "Seinfeld" or "Law and Order."

If you think about music the idea of popular culture may become clearer. Most of us would agree that rap, blues, rock and roll, country western, soul, some jazz, and bluegrass fit the category, but opera and classical music do not, unless a song or melody becomes so popular that it has mass appeal, such as Ravel's "Bolero" or Pachabel's "Canon." And there are many crossovers. Consider singers. Placido Domingo, though an operatic tenor, has cut any number of albums of popular songs. What's popular, of course, changes with the times. The Big Band sound is now almost a thing of the past (though it may return), the name Rudy Vallee doesn't ring many bells, and even Frank Sinatra seems a bit old fashioned.

It can be informative and interesting to take a modern look at what was once in mainstream popular culture. Television shows such as "Howdy Doody," "American Bandstand," "Ozzie and Harriet," or "The Smothers Brothers" are now more interesting as cultural artifacts than as art or entertainment, though some old shows, such as "I Love Lucy," still have a strong following. Analyzing why that is so can lead to an interesting essay.

Take a few moments to jot down everything in the public sphere that you find entertaining. What films have you enjoyed recently? What television shows do you usually watch? What music do you listen to? What books do you read? What foods do you enjoy? What arcade or video games do you play? After you've completed your list, look at it again to see if each entry fits the category of popular culture. Consider what those entries have in common. The result will probably be a definition of your taste. And you will have thought through a number of causal relationships to reach that definition.

As you read the prose that follows, read each piece first for its basic meaning:

> What specific subject is the author writing about?
> What is the author's opinion about that subject?
> How accurate is the writer's analysis of the subject?
> What do you think the author wants you to understand, think, believe, feel?
> How relevant is the piece to your own experience?

Then when you reread each selection, be aware of the techniques the writer uses in writing about popular culture:

> What examples does the writer use?
> What comparisons or contrasts does the writer use?
> What do the examples and comparisons emphasize about the subject?
> What descriptive language does the writer use?
> How does the writer use cause and effect?
> How does the writer try to keep your interest?

You'll find that two of the pieces in this chapter are longer than most of the others in this book, but the length probably won't bother you as both focus on subjects you're likely to be very familiar with: the Beatles' George Harrison and the television show "Seinfeld." You'll also find essays on country music, fried chicken, and movies.

A Black Fan of Country Music Tells All

Lena Williams

Lena Williams started her career in journalism as a reporter for a radio station while she was a student at Howard University. After earning her BA at Howard, she entered the Columbia University Graduate School of Journalism, from which she received an MSc. She worked as a reporter while she was an intern at the Washington Post, *then as an associate editor at* Black Sports Magazine, *and has been on the staff of the* New York Times *since 1974, first as a clerk, then trainee, and now senior writer. She has written on civil rights, life styles, metropolitan news, and sports, winning various publishing awards along the way. An article she originally wrote for the* Times *in 1997 grew to the point where it is now a book,* It's the Little Things: the Everyday Interactions that Get under the Skin of Blacks and Whites *(2000). The essay that follows appeared on Sunday, June 19, 1994, in the* Times' *"Arts and Leisure" section's coverage of "Pop Music." The column was titled "Pop View."*

Before You Read   What names do you associate with country western music? What reasons can you find for its popularity?

1   I heard that Reba McEntire's new album, "Read My Mind," shot to No. 5 on the Billboard chart the first weekend of its release.

2   Well, she got my $11.95.

3   I'm a 40-something black woman who spent her youth in Washington, lip-syncing to the Supremes and slow dancing to the Temptations. Now I often come home to my Manhattan apartment and put on Vince Gill, Randy Travis or Reba. Consider me a fan of country music. So there. Deal with it.

4   For most of my adult life, I was a closet country music fan. I'd hide my Waylon Jennings and Willie Nelson albums between the dusty, psychedelic rock. I'd listen to Dolly Parton on my earphones, singing along softly, afraid my neighbors might mistake my imita-

tion twang for a cry for help. I'd enter a music store, looking over my shoulder in search of familiar faces and flip through the rhythm-and-blues section for about five minutes before sneaking off to the country aisle where I'd surreptitiously grab a Travis Tritt tape off the rack and make a beeline for the shortest cashier's line.

5   Just when I'd reached for my American Express card, I'd spot a tall, dark, handsome type in an Armani suit standing behind me with a puzzled look. What's he going to think? "The sister seems down, but what's she doing with that Dwight Yoakum CD?"

6   So now I'm publicly coming out of the closet and proclaiming my affection for country perennials like Ms. McEntire.

7   When I told a friend I was preparing this confessional, he offered a word of caution: "No self-respecting black person would ever admit to that in public."

8   I thought about his comment. As a child growing up in the 1950's, in a predominantly black community, I wasn't allowed to play country-and-western music in my house. Blacks weren't supposed to like country—or classical for that matter—but that's another story. Blacks' contribution to American music was in jazz, blues and funk. Country music was dismissed as poor white folks' blues and associated with regions of the nation that symbolized prejudice and racial bigotry. Even mainstream white America viewed country as lower class and less desirable, often poking fun at its twangy chords and bellyaching sentiments.

9   But I was always a cowgirl at heart. I liked country's wild side; its down-home, aw-shucks musicians with the yodel in their voices and the angst in their lyrics. I saw an honesty in country and its universal tales of love lost and found. Besides, the South didn't have a monopoly on racial hatred, and country artists, like everybody else, were stealing black music, so why should I hold it against country?

10   And while snickering at country, white America also demonstrated a similar cultural backwardness toward black music, be it gospel, ragtime or the blues. So I allowed country to enter my heart and my mind, in spite of its faults. Indeed, when prodded, some blacks who rejected country conceded that there was a spirituality that resounded in the music and that in its heartfelt sentiment, country was a lot like blues. Yet they could never bring themselves to spend hard-earned dollars on Hank Williams Jr.

11   The 1980's saw country (western was dropped, much to my chagrin) become mainstream. Suddenly there was country at the Copa and at Town Hall. WYNY-FM radio in New York now claims the largest audience of any country station, with more than one million listeners. Dolly Parton and Kenny Rogers became movie stars. Garth Brooks became an American phenomenon.

12   Wall Street investment bankers bought cowboy boots and hats and learned to do the two-step. And black and white artists like Patti LaBelle and Lyle Lovett and Natalie Cole and Ms. McEntire now sing duets and clearly admire one another's music.

13   Perhaps the nation's acceptance of country has something to do with an evolutionary change in the music. Country has got edge. It has acquired an attitude. Womens' voices have been given strength. Oh, the hardship and misery is still there. But the stuff about "standing by your man" has changed to a more assertive posture.

14   In "I Won't Stand in Line," a song on Ms. McEntire's new album, she makes it clear to a skirt-chasing lover that "I'd do almost anything just to make you mine, but I won't stand in line." That line alone makes me think of Aretha Franklin's "Respect."

15   One other thing: I don't like sad songs. I've cried enough for a lifetime. Country makes me laugh, always has. Maybe because it never took itself so seriously. Think about it. "Drop-Kick Me, Jesus, Through the Goal Posts of Life." "A Boy Named Sue."

16   Ms. McEntire serves up a humorous touch in "Why Haven't I Heard From You." "That thing they call the telephone/ Now there's one on every corner, in the back of every bar/ You can get one in your briefcase, on a plane or in your car/ So tell me why haven't I heard from you, darlin', honey, what is your excuse?" Call it Everywoman's lament.

17   Well it's off my chest; and it feels good.

18   I will no longer make excuses for my musical tastes. Not when millions are being made by performers exhorting listeners to "put your hands in the air and wave 'em like you just don't care."

19   Compare that with the haunting refrain of Ms. McEntire's "I Think His Name Was John," a song about a woman, a one-night stand and AIDS: "She lays all alone and cries herself to sleep/ 'Cause she let a stranger kill her hopes and her dreams/ And in the end when she was barely hanging on/ All she could say is she thinks his name was John."

Reading: Discussing the Text

1. How credible are the reasons Williams presents for liking country music?
2. Williams supports her thesis with examples from popular music, both country-western and black. Explain whether you find her evidence sufficient for her point.
3. Although the essay presents Williams' personal opinion and is subjective, she achieves a balance between the personal and the general. How does she do that?
4. Is the essay addressed primarily to a black or a white audience or both? What evidence can you find to support your view?

Writing: Brief Response

1. Write a brief entry explaining why you do or do not like country music.
2. How would you characterize your taste in music? Use your notebook to write a brief definition.

Writing: Extended Response

1. Williams' essay is an assertive defense of her taste in music. Write an essay in which you evaluate the essay's effectiveness. You might start by asking yourself questions such as, "Does she present enough evidence?" "Are her examples apt?" "Does she provide enough background for her explanations?"
2. Popular culture often contains movements or tastes that were once fringe. Think, for instance, of rap music or tattoos. For a topic pick something that was once out and is now in, and write an essay analyzing its evolution into the mainstream.

George Harrison, 1943–2001

Dave Laing and Penny Valentine

Some 40 years ago, the Beatles signed their first contract and started recording careers that quickly became a legend. While John Lennon and Paul McCartney, even Ringo Starr, were the better known of the group, it may be George Harrison who had the most interesting life, one described in the obituary that follows. It appeared in the Guardian, *one of the United Kingdom's most widely known dailies, on December 1, 2001. The authors are well known to England's popular music public. Dave Laing wrote* One Chart Wonders: Power and Meaning in Punk Rock *(1985) and, with Sarah Davis,* The Guerilla Guide to the Music Business *(2001), as well as edited, with Richard Newman,* Thirty Years of the Cambridge Folk Festival *(1994). Penny Valentine was a journalist, teacher, and author (with Vicki Wickham) of* Dancing with Demons *(2000), a biography of Dusty Springfield. Like Laing, she was often called on by the* Guardian *to write obituaries of popular figures from the music world. When she died in 2003, her own obituary, written by Richard Williams, hailed her as the "first woman to write about popular music as though it really mattered." Appropriately , that obituary also ran in the* Guardian.

Before You Read   Use your local newspaper (or a national one) to find several obituaries. Analyze them to form a full definition of the form. What are its characteristics?

1   By the time the Beatles released their first No 1 hit, "Please Please Me," in February 1963—and made their first appearance on ITV's *Thank Your Lucky Stars*—it was apparent that three members of the group had clearly defined personalities. John Lennon was the most acerbic, Ringo Starr was the joker in the pack, and Paul McCartney, smoothing ruffled feathers, was the public relations man.

2   Perhaps because of the way he had joined the group, George Harrison, who has died of cancer aged 58, was always the quietest Beatle, and the least easy to pigeonhole—although he would occasionally surprise journalists with a sudden, pithy, off-the-wall remark. He was, however, unquestionably the best looking, and certainly the most dapper, with those little collarless jackets, a la Pierre

Cardin, sitting comfortably on his shoulders, not a button under pressure.

3   Harrison's isolation was most noticeable on stage. The Beatles gravitated from church halls and Hamburg's red light district to a global fame greater than any British performers since Charlie Chaplin, but it was Lennon and McCartney who dominated. The early line-up saw McCartney, Lennon and Harrison strung out stage front, with Starr flailing his drumkit at the back. That style super-seded the daft foot movements of the Shadows, and became de rigueur for British 60s groups, but it started to fracture as the Beatles grew more successful.

4   From 1963, McCartney and Lennon wrote more of the songs, and it became more usual to see their two heads crowding round a single mike, providing lead vocal and back-up or chorus. Harrison, even when he was adding his voice to the mix, seemed stranded at the far side of the stage, even if he was the best musician and the motor of the band.

5   For the Beatles, he designed breaks and riffs. But for himself, he lacked—or rarely took—the opportunity to cut loose in the rockabilly style of his American hero, Carl Perkins. And with, and without, the Beatles, he was also an underrated songwriter. "Something" (1969) was a great song—even the Beatles' antithesis, Frank Sinatra, picked up on it—and "My Sweet Lord" (1970), while unconsciously plagiarised from Ronnie Mack's "He's So Fine," justifiably sold in its millions.

6   In 1971 came his New York concert for Bangladesh. That new country had been devastated by war and floods, and the event launched the vogue for celebrity rock fund-raising. It also resulted in a three-volume album, featuring Harrison with Ringo Starr, Bob Dylan, Eric Clapton, and Ravi Shankar, and put the stamp on Harrison's relationship with the Indian sub-continent that had be-gun when he effectively introduced the sitar to the Beatles in the mid-1960s.

7   The formula with the Beatles was that Harrison got to sing at least one number on each album, beginning with the Lennon and McCartney song "Do You Want To Know A Secret?" on the group's debut album, *Please Please Me*. Gradually, his own work began to feature. There was "Within You Without You," on *Sgt Pepper's Lonely Hearts Club Band* (1967), "Here Comes The Sun" and

"Something," on *Abbey Road* (1969), and "While My Guitar Gently Weeps," on *The White Album* (1968).

8   The youngest Beatle, Harrison was born in Wavertree, Liverpool, eight months after McCartney, two years after Lennon, and three years after Starr. He experienced his rock 'n' roll epiphany in 1956, when, on the verge of his teens, he cycled past an open window out of which was wafting Elvis Presley's "Heartbreak Hotel."

9   The son of a bus driver, he was educated at Dovedale primary school, where the young Lennon had gone, and, after passing the 11-plus, was awarded a place at the Liverpool Institute, one of the city's leading grammar schools. He met McCartney—also at the institute—on the bus to school. The pair became close friends. When, in 1957, McCartney linked up with Lennon in the Quarrymen skiffle group, he tried to persuade them to invite Harrison along. At first, Lennon resisted—he didn't want a 14-year-old in the band—but then relented after hearing Harrison play Bill Justis's rock instrumental, "Raunchy."

10   Lennon realised that having someone who could play guitar solos—and Harrison was already a more competent musician than McCartney or himself—would expand the group's ability to handle rock 'n' roll. The disapproval with which Lennon's guardian, his Auntie Mimi, greeted the new boy's teddy-boy style and thick Scouse accent may also have helped to change his mind.

11   Harrison's absorption into music took its toll on his school career, and he left the Liverpool Institute in 1959 with only one O-level, in art. By then, the Quarrymen had metamorphosed into the Silver Beatles. The following year, and by now the Beatles, they were booked to play for four months in a club on Hamburg's Reeperbahn. The trip was cut short when the 17-year-old Harrison was discovered to be under age, but the quintet (as it then was, with Pete Best on drums and Stuart Sutcliffe on guitar) had gelled into an arresting, idiosyncratic unit.

12   By 1962, and now managed by Brian Epstein, the Beatles had signed their recording contract with EMI. In those simple times, when the group was almost a proto-teeny bop band, fan sheets listed Harrison's pet likes as "hamburgers, the colour purple and friendly girls." When their record producer George Martin asked if there was anything they were unhappy with, Harrison managed: "Yes, I don't like your tie."

13   Although Harrison was a fine lead guitarist—and his understated work was influential on many later players—his most important influence on the Beatles was always concerned with the new sound textures he introduced. Chief among these was the sitar.

14   He had first heard the instrument during the filming of *Help!* (1965), the second Beatles movie. He was intrigued, and the instrument was to feature on the *Rubber Soul* album, being recorded at the Abbey Road studios. A string had broken on Harrison's sitar, and the Indian embassy had put him on to the Hampstead-based Asian Music Circle, where the Beatles were introduced to Ravi Shankar at the home of the circle's co-founder Patricia Angadi (obituary, July 17, 2001). Harrison briefly studied with Shankar in order to use the sitar in Beatle music. The two remained close friends, touring the United States together in 1974, and Shankar's recordings appeared on Dark Horse, the record label Harrison started in 1976.

15   Between 1967 and 1968, Harrison's interest in Indian music led to the group's entanglement with transcendental meditation, via the Maharishi Mahesh Yogi. When they headed east, Harrison was with his then wife Pattie Boyd—whom he had met on the set of the first Beatles film *A Hard Day's Night* (1964), and married in 1966, with Paul McCartney as best man. But the Indian trip was not a success, and, although Lennon and Yoko Ono used chanting Hare Krishna followers on their recording of Give Peace A Chance, it was Harrison alone who remained faithful to the Vedic tradition. He observed that one of his greatest thrills was seeing members of the London Hare Krishna Temple on Top Of The Pops, chanting the record he had produced with them.

16   He donated a Hertfordshire mansion—renamed Bhaktivedanta Manor—for use as a Hindu centre, and played concerts in support of that curious political manifestation, the Natural Law Party. He did, however, turn down the Maharishi's request that he, McCartney and Starr should stand in Liverpool in the 1992 general election.

17   By 1968, the Beatles were on a downward path. McCartney and Lennon were drifting apart, and both had antagonised Harrison, who walked off the set of their documentary, *Let It Be* (released in 1970), after an argument with McCartney. In March 1969, during a Fleet Street and police media blitz on drugs, youth, politics, and rock stars, Harrison and Boyd were fined for possessing cannabis.

That August, the group were in the recording studios for the last time together, to complete tracks for *Abbey Road*.

18   Harrison was the first Beatle to succeed as a solo artist. He had made two instrumental albums—*Wonderwall Music* and *Electronic Sound* (both 1969), while the group was still together. Then, in 1970, he co-produced the double album, *All Things Must Pass*. It sold 3m copies, and was his most commercially successful record, although a plagiarism suit over the song "My Sweet Lord" cost him almost $600,000 in the American courts.

19   He continued to write and record at a fast pace for the next few years, releasing the hit, "Give Me Love: Give Me Peace On Earth" (1973), and the albums, *Living In The Material World* (1973) and *Extra Texture* (1975). By the end of the 1970s, the Beatles partnership had been officially dissolved. Harrison's spiritual soft rock, meanwhile, had gone out of fashion and, for much of the next decade, he concentrated on a new career as a producer with Handmade Films, the company he had formed in 1979 with Denis O'Brien.

20   Their first success was Monty Python's *The Life Of Brian* (1979), which they took on after EMI decided it might incur charges of blasphemy. In 1980, there was *The Long Good Friday*, followed by *Time Bandits* (1981), *A Private Function* (1985), *Mona Lisa* (1986), and *Withnail And I* (1987). The failure of the appalling Madonna–Sean Penn vehicle, *Shanghai Surprise* (1986), heralded a downturn in the company's fortunes, and it was eventually wound up in acrimony, with Harrison winning a $11m lawsuit against his former partner.

21   After John Lennon's murder in 1980, Harrison composed a tribute song of his own, "All Those Years Ago," but his own recording career was not effectively rekindled until 1987. Then, he and Jeff Lynne, of the Electric Light Orchestra, co-produced the album *Cloud Nine*, which included two singles, "Got My Mind Set On You" and "When We Was Fab."

22   With Lynne, he also formed the Traveling Wilburys, with Bob Dylan, Roy Orbison, and Tom Petty. In 1992, the success of two of the group's albums encouraged Harrison to undertake his first international tour for 18 years.

23   In the 1980s and 1990s, he appeared in public infrequently, usually on Beatle-related occasions. He lived quietly in his restored

19th century mansion at Friars Park, Henley-on-Thames, with his second wife, Olivia, whom he married in 1978, and their son, Dhani, an idyllic life shaken only when a schizophrenic Beatles fan, Michael Abram, broke in in December 1999, and badly injured Harrison. He is survived by Olivia and Dhani.

24   George Harrison, guitarist, singer, songwriter, born February 25, 1943, died November 29 2001

Reading: Discussing the Text

1. The obituary is thoroughly British—written by a English authors about a British pop idol, and published in a British newspaper. What "non-American" words or phrases can you find? To what extent do they interfere with meaning?
2. Many obituaries are structured strictly by chronology, but Laing and Valentine's piece treats what happened more loosely. Trace their treatment of time throughout the selection. How effective is it?
3. In many people's minds, it's hard to separate George Harrison from the Beatles. Laing and Valentine's challenge is to keep the focus on Harrison and at the same time be fair to his involvement with the band. How well do they achieve that goal?
4. Obituaries are often straight factual pieces, but the one for George Harrison contains a fair amount of opinion. To what extent do those opinions add or detract from the obituary?

Writing: Brief Response

1. What one fact in the obituary do you find particularly interesting and why?
2. What part of Harrison's life would you like to know more about and why?

Writing: Extended Response

1. Choose a figure from popular culture, and then research that person's life so that you can write his or her obituary.
2. While the Beatles' popularity was phenomenal, it was also a long time ago. What individual or group has now achieved enormous popularity? Draw up a list and then pick one to focus upon and research. Write an essay in which you analyze the reasons behind the person or group's appeal.

Chicken Riddle

Jane and Michael Stern

It may seem odd to include an essay on fried chicken in a chapter headed "Popular Culture," but think about it. Food, particularly "American" food, is very much a part of our daily life, and not just for nourishment. We are the nation that invented fast food, making McDonald's as much of a target for those who oppose globalization as Texaco, and hamburgers, apple pie, hot dogs, and fried chicken have become symbols of our culture, both at home and abroad. Home is the turf for Jane and Michael Stern. Anyone who reads food magazines or watches morning television shows or browses the food titles at bookstores has already met the Sterns. They write the "Two for the Road" column for Gourmet *as well as the "Wish You Were Here" segment for the Web site* Epicurious, *and, over the years, they have written more than 20 books about American food. A new edition of* Roadfood *appeared in 2002, joining* Blue Plate Specials *and* Blue Ribbon Chefs *(1999),* Eat Your Way Across the U.S.A. *(1999), and* Chili Nation *(1999). Their quest for the perfect fried chicken led to the article that follows, reprinted from the January 2002* Gourmet.

Before You Read   Assuming you have sampled the dish at various restaurants and fast food places, what are the qualities of the perfect fried chicken platter?

1   This is a story about getting lost and eating chicken. When you drive around western North Carolina, it is good to do both.

2   For those of us accustomed to ordinary roads laid out with logic, traveling this part of the world can be mind-bending. It is a mysterious terrain of low blue clouds and mists that hug the hilltops, where people live in hidden hollers and where capillary roads thread past ancient wood cabins in the forest. Five hundred years ago, travelers would have said dragons live here. Today, even the spillover from corporate Winston-Salem, the lure of Dollywood, and traffic to the bustling discount furniture malls of Hickory and High Point have scarcely affected the landscape.

3   In these parts, extreme seclusion is a hallmark of the best places to eat. There is no such thing as an easy way to get anywhere worthwhile; driving directions to restaurants inevitably include rights and lefts at bent trees and abandoned smokehouses, as well as long climbs up ever-narrowing unmarked roads.

4   And so, 650 miles from home, we are in a familiar High Country state of being—profoundly lost and profoundly hungry. As the road twists among the hills, we drive past log homes with dilapidated recliners on their front porches, a man in overalls actually working his fields with a hand-pushed tiller, and signs nailed to tree trunks advertising a service that pads church pews.

5   Our goal is east of the mountains: **Keaton's,** a restaurant that appeared out of our good-eats tip file like the ace of hearts rising to the top of a magician's deck of cards. Recommended in a note from a reader, Keaton's food was described as "different than any chicken you've ever had . . . so good it almost makes you cry." The writer's passion was irresistible. We want chicken worth weeping over! With a box of Kleenex on the backseat and pockets packed with handkerchiefs, we were on our way.

6   Despite Rand McNally and MapQuest printouts and specific directions we acquire by calling Keaton's in advance, we find ourselves utterly disoriented as we veer off Highway 64 east of Statesville onto Woodleaf Road, miles from the interstate, past cattle farms and alongside wide open fields. And then we see a weather-beaten sign pointing to a dreary tan cinder-block building that boasts "Best Test by Taste Test." Okay by us; we like anything scientific.

7   Another sign says "Original Barbecue." But we smell no smoke. Slow-smoldering hickory wood is fundamental to barbecue in North Carolina, and its haze customarily envelops barbecue restaurants with a sweet aroma. But there is no pit in evidence here.

8   There are, however, a lot of house rules. Keaton's is big on telling customers how to behave. An electric banner-light display on the wall flashes "No Profanity . . . Keep Noise to a Minimum." Behind the counter, a large, handwritten sign says, "If Your Waiter or Waitress Takes Your Order and Gives You a Booth or Table Number and You Move and Don't Tell Anyone, There Will be a Delay in Your Food Order." We learn, furthermore, that no customer is allowed more than two beers or ten "uppers" (chicken breasts) per visit.

9   We stand up straight and slick back our unruly hair with wet palms. We enunciate politely to the lady behind the counter, giving her two orders that echo the one placed by the regular customer ahead of us in line, a strapping man who could have been the prototype for the folk song "John Henry." We ask for a pair of half chickens, "dipped," with sides of macaroni and cheese, baked beans, hot (i.e., spicy) coleslaw, and sweet iced tea.

10   We are given a table number and pointed toward the corresponding booth. We sit down, don't move, and try hard not to use profanity.

11   In less than five minutes, a waitress appears with two trays. She sets the food before us. Each meal is plated on Styrofoam and draped with a sheet of translucent Cut-Rite—an ingenious country variant of the glass dome that intensifies the intoxicating aroma of Cognac-infused pheasant. Here, when the wax paper is lifted, the sharp tang of barbecue sauce provides the olfactory rush. We have never seen chicken quite so pretty, glistening with a caramelized glaze that is crusty but not brittle, encasing meat that vents a savory steam when the surface is fractured.

12   The glaze is what makes Keaton's recipe unique. The pieces are peppered and salted, floured and panfried, at which point they are simply excellent country-style chicken. Then comes the "dip," the distinctive extra step developed by the late B.W. Keaton in 1953: Just-fried chicken is immersed in a bubbling vat of red sauce, a high-spiced, opaque potion similar to the one that graces High Country barbecued pork. The process takes only seconds, but the throbbing sauce permeates to the bone, making every shred of meat an exclamation point. You must eat it with your hands, pulling off crisp strips of sauce-glazed skin, worrying every joint to suck out all the flavor you possibly can. Each table is set not only with a fully loaded napkin dispenser, but with a stack of paper towels as well.

13   Dining amenities at Keaton's are picnic-primitive, and décor is minimal. The most interesting thing hanging on the paneled walls is a picture of the late Mr. Keaton, who looks to us like the culinary cognate of bluesman Muddy Waters. Dishes, cups, and flatware are disposable. Corn bread muffins, dinner rolls, and slices of homemade red velvet cake arrive in plastic wrap. All such rituals, like the formal rules of service in this back-roads chicken shack, make sense once you taste the food. Strict policies of civilized conduct are necessary to maintain order in a place where the natural result

of eating the chicken is a dining room spirit of jubilation verging on anarchy.

Reading: Discussing the Text

1. What reasons can you find for the Sterns' rather lengthy introduction (paragraphs 1–5)? What does it contribute to the essay?
2. Because the piece is written by two authors, they choose the pronoun *we* for their narrative. To what extent do you find it bothersome?
3. How would you describe the Sterns in relation to the restaurant? Are they outsiders? Tourists? Gourmands? Pretenders? What?
4. Any description of an off-the-beat restaurant has to try to be accurate yet also persuasive. How well do the Sterns achieve a balance?

Writing: Brief Response

1. Write a brief notebook entry describing your response to the "house rules."
2. Assuming you were in the area, would you go to Keaton's? Why or why not?

Writing: Extended Response

1. Reread the essay, thinking of Keaton's as a symbol. Write an essay in which you explain and analyze the values Keaton's stands for.
2. Fast food franchises dot almost every major entrance to any American city. List the most popular ones and then choose one to focus on in an essay that analyzes its appeal.

Cheerio Seinfeld

Joyce Millman

Think of the word critic, *and almost automatically you might plug in* film *or* theater *or* music *or* book, *but* television *would be far down the list, if it were on it at all. But television critic describes Joyce Millman's job. Starting as the popular music critic for a weekly Boston newspa-*

per, the Phoenix, *she switched to television, moved to California, and was hired as the TV critic for the San Francisco* Examiner. *She now works for* Salon, *a Web 'zine that describes itself as "an Internet media company that produces ten original content sites as well as two online communities."* Salon *is no ordinary site, as attested by its various awards, awards ranging from* Time's *"Web Site of the Year" (1996) to* Yahoo's *"Best Online Magazine" (2001). Millman's work has helped earn those awards. As Senior Editor/Television, she prepares the magazine's daily list of television programs, contributes to the Arts and Entertainment section, and writes a biweekly column. Her titles are as interesting as her columns, titles such as "Doc Hollywood" (on George Clooney and "ER") and "Married . . . with Hitmen" (on "The Sopranos"). The one reprinted here is from* Salon, *May 4, 1998, nine days before the last "Seinfeld."*

Before You Read   What is your favorite sitcom and why?

---

1   **I** didn't get "Seinfeld" at first. My review of the July 1989 pilot episode (which NBC was then calling "The Seinfeld Chronicles") was lukewarm: The shift from Seinfeld's comedy club scenes to the sitcom plot was shaky and too cute, George was just another whining Woody Allen knock-off, Kramer was vaguely unpleasant, yada, yada, yada. I half paid attention for a couple more weeks, then lost interest.

2   Everything changed, though, when I saw the one about the bad melon.

3   I don't remember what the main plot was, but there was this bit where Kramer and Elaine were in Jerry's apartment and he offered them some cantaloupe and they took a bite and did spit takes ("This melon *stinks!*"). Kramer heatedly urged Jerry to return the offending melon, but Jerry took a more nonchalant view: "Fruit's a gamble!" Now, you have to understand—my parents are militant fruit returners (I myself side with Jerry on this one), but I had never seen this particular quirk portrayed on TV before. I was awed by Seinfeld and co-creator/writer Larry David's brilliant grasp of, A) working-class Jewish craziness, and, B) the absurd humor of the deeply mundane.

4   Over the next few weeks, "Seinfeld" spoke to me as no sitcom ever had—an episode introducing Jerry's kvetching Uncle Leo; a knowing aside about the Three Stooges (my favorites!); an episode

set entirely in a Chinese restaurant that captured the misanthropy and predatory instinct that arises in big city folk when they have to wait for a table. The more I watched "Seinfeld," the more I knew: These are my people!

5   Of course, the key to the show's popularity (30 million viewers weekly at its height) has been that a lot of *other* viewers believe that Jerry, George, Elaine and Kramer are their people, too. But, when you come down to it, who among us has never felt persecuted or screwed over, has never worried that they were out of the loop, has never tried to get a "deal," has never obsessed over microscopic annoyances and imagined slights, has never been petty, selfish, vain, self-defeating or weak-willed? "Seinfeld" caught on because it expressed an undiluted pessimism rarely seen in sitcoms. It drew in people who had given up on TV comedies because of their by-the-numbers jokes and heavy-handed sentimentality. Faster, smarter, darker and more unpredictable than any other network sitcom around, "Seinfeld" was a gasp-for-breath funny portrayal of bad behavior.

6   Jerry, George, Elaine and Kramer were not particularly nice people. They were self-centered, irresponsible, commitment-phobic. For this, and for the dead-on way the show nailed the tribal codes of single, upper middle class (white) urbanites, some pundits called "Seinfeld" a glorification of '90s yuppiedom—which completely misses the point. "Seinfeld" was an *anti*-yuppie sitcom. Jerry and company were wish-fulfillment figures for baby-boomer viewers weary from shouldering adult responsibilities, from being *good*. While we struggled with the demands of marriage, parenthood and work, Jerry, George, Elaine and Kramer—who were probably in their mid-to-late 30s and early 40s (it was never made clear)—behaved like eternal teenagers. Unencumbered by spouses or kids, either unemployed or working at an adolescent's fantasy job (entertainer, New York Yankees executive), they mooched off each other, played board games, ate handfuls of cereal out of the box, schemed about how to get what they wanted—a date, a car, cable TV—with no strings attached. Fixated on the minutiae of life, "Seinfeld" was pure escapism for grown-ups, a weekly release from having to think about the big stuff.

7   Ironically, though, Jerry and his maturity-challenged pals never really got away with anything. And that was fine with us. We like to imagine ourselves as the most heroically overworked and stressed-out generation in history; we don't want to see cheating and sloth

rewarded (too much). In its twisted way, "Seinfeld" was a very moral show. The intricately plotted comeuppances that Seinfeld, David and their roster of uncommonly clever writers devised for this foursome were the comedic equivalent of biblical judgment.

8   Tangled webs of lies tightened around them. Temptation (like George's unforgettable pursuit of "the trifecta"—enjoying sex, food and TV at the same time) inevitably led to abject humiliation. Schemes undertaken to get even or gain the upper hand repeatedly backfired. There was a definite higher power at work in the "Seinfeld" universe. Call it karma, call it the vengeful God of Sunday school and superstitious grandmothers—either way, Jerry, George, Elaine and Kramer suffered the wrath of its punch lines. And anybody who has ever felt like the butt of some huge cosmic joke could identify.

9   As we await the end of the world as we know it (coming to NBC May 14), let's take a final look at the 10 reasons why "Seinfeld" was the greatest sitcom of all time.

1. **Because there were no Very Special Episodes.** Larry David's "No hugs" edict was never breached. "Seinfeld" was the one sitcom you could count on to never get treacly, to never get too big for its comedy britches and veer into Drama. Nobody learned a lesson here; nobody evolved. However, the characters did devolve, gloriously. Over the past two seasons, Jerry's fastidiousness became (in the words of Elaine) a "full-blown disorder." Meanwhile, Elaine's mid-life bitterness manifested itself in her blanket contempt for every other person on the planet (her superficial, mutually exploitative relationship with on again/off again beau David Puddy was a particularly inspired development). As for George. . . Where to begin? "Seinfeld" was fueled by a divine sourness that other sitcoms ("Drew Carey," "Just Shoot Me," "Lateline") have attempted to duplicate, with often crude results.

2. **Because a cast like this comes along as often as Halley's comet.** The characters may not have matured, but the actors did—even self-described non-actor Seinfeld got more relaxed and agile as the show went on. One of the pleasures of the past few seasons has been watching Seinfeld's fussy Jerry, Jason Alexander's neurotic George, Julia Louis-Dreyfus' acerbic Elaine and Michael Richards' screwy Kramer feeding off each others' madness with fine-tuned reactions and inflections.

"Seinfeld" was the quintessential ensemble comedy; no actor was more or less important than another. When the four of them were in a scene together, it was like watching a melting pot of comedic styles coming to a rolling boil. They *cooked*.

3. **Because it made us feel like insiders.** "Seinfeld" was the first sitcom to attain the fervid cult following and the cool, rock 'n' roll idol–like status of a "Monty Python" or a "Saturday Night Live." And that was because "Seinfeld" existed in its own universe and spoke its own language, but assumed we understood. "Seinfeld" rewarded viewers with secret club phrases ("the vault," "master of my domain," "Mulva," "spongeworthy," "No soup for you!"), recurring fringe characters and references to past episodes. It was a trivia buff's dream, a cult for people who usually don't go in for such foolishness. It was all an illusion, of course: Can the No. 1 comedy on TV really be called a cult favorite? But consider these newly minted additions to the "Seinfeld" lexicon: Festivus, Hellooo! "Serenity now," yada, yada, yada. After nine years, "Seinfeld" is still TV's biggest private joke.

4. **Because Jerry and Elaine aren't married (so far).** How refreshing "Seinfeld" was in the age of such misbegotten ratings ploys (and plot dead-ends) as Sam and Diane pairing off in "Cheers," Murphy Brown as a single mother, the "Mad About You" baby. Jerry and Elaine only rekindled their old sexual relationship once; realizing they still had no chemistry, they went back to being platonic pals. (Some misguided fans want "Seinfeld" to end with Jerry and Elaine getting married. How grisly is *that?*) Similarly, Louis-Dreyfus' two real-life pregnancies were not written into the show. In fact, her burgeoning belly wasn't even well-hidden the second time around—viewers were just expected to ignore Elaine's sudden fondness for smocks. OK, it *was* a little weird seeing a character pregnant with no explanation. But it was infinitely less horrible than the prospect of Elaine Benes as a mother.

5. **Because you didn't have to be Jewish to appreciate it, but it helped.** All those who believe that Jerry is the only Jewish character on "Seinfeld" raise your hands. The network asked for name changes (Kramer was originally called the more Semitic-sounding "Hoffman") and ethnic vagueness (the Costanzas are not supposed to be Jewish, but we know better). Still, "Seinfeld" was the most successful Jewish-centric sitcom

ever seen in prime time, from the guilt-tripping of Uncle Leo ("You couldn't say hello?"), to the deal-seeking of Jerry's father Morty, who was retired from the garment business (he designed the beltless trench coat), to the subtle Jewish pride signaled by Jerry's obsession with Superman (created by two Jews), to the use of rabbis, marble rye breads, anti-Semitism and Jewish singles dances as plot devices. A handful of detractors slammed "Seinfeld" for perpetuating Jewish "stereotypes." They obviously haven't met my family.

6. **Because of the food.** Every episode of "Seinfeld" included one or more eating scenes and, in many episodes, food played an essential role. There were muffin tops, mutton, Junior Mints, calzones, pudding skin, babka, gyros, crepes, cake, latte, paella, pastrami, mangos, Jujyfruits and Twix. Not to mention Snapple, the Soup Nazi, Kenny Rogers' Roasters, the big salad, Atomic Sub, Chinese takeout and, of course, cereal, lots and lots of cereal. During a decade of extreme diet-consciousness and food phobia, "Seinfeld" was an in-your-face celebration of gluttony.

7. **Because of Newman.** "Seinfeld" boasted the most impressive sideshow in sitcom history, featuring such well-cast and perfectly drawn supporting players as Jerry Stiller's bellicose Frank Costanza, John O'Hurley's long-winded J. Peterman and Estelle Harris' shrill Estelle Costanza. The biggest scene-stealer (in every way), though, was Wayne Knight as Kramer's friend Newman, the malicious postal worker. Knight, the Ironman of NBC (he's also a regular on "3rd Rock from the Sun"), was a hilarious all-purpose nemesis for Jerry: equal parts empty bluster, sinister greed and sniveling cowardice. He was the Sydney Greenstreet of sitcoms; the Soup Nazi episode, where he sucked up to the take-out food despot and proved to be the perfect Soup Nazi collaborator, was his finest half-hour. Also eminently praiseworthy: Barney Martin and Liz Sheridan as the easily-alarmed Seinfelds, Len Lesser as Uncle Leo, Sandy Baron as temperamental Jack Klompus, Patrick Warburton as dear, dim Puddy, Heidi Swedberg as the ill-fated Susan and Larry David (voice) and Lee Bear (body) as the blustery George Steinbrenner.

8. **Because it aimed high.** "Seinfeld" packed more dialogue, plot lines and scenes into a half-hour than most comedies tackled in a month. Furiously paced, more than a touch surreal and

strewn with dazzling verbal humor, "Seinfeld" was like watching a miniature classic screwball comedy every week. The prime example of how it all came together: the abstinence-from-onanism episode "The Contest," a frantic farce in which the word "masturbation" is never once uttered, but you know exactly what's going on. And the surprise ending, featuring Jerry's girlfriend of the week, Marla the Virgin (a pre-"Frasier" Jane Leeves), is a stroke (no pun intended) of genius.

9. **Because it aimed low.** "Seinfeld" frequently borrowed from Seinfeld and David's comedy idols, Abbott and Costello; Jerry and George's circular coffee shop conversations derive from "Who's on First?" And there were references aplenty to the Three Stooges, Jerry Lewis and Looney Tunes. "Seinfeld" was not above cartoony clowning, pratfalls, cheap sex jokes or sight gags. The prime example of how it all came together: the scene in "The Contest" where George visits his mother in the hospital and writhes in an agony of pent-up sexual energy while an attractive nurse spongebathes the young woman in the next bed.

10. **Because it's making a graceful exit.** The classic-episode quotient has been falling for the past couple of years (although I am partial to this season's "The Blood," where squeamish Jerry ends up receiving a transfusion from Kramer after a freak X-acto knife accident—"I can feel his blood inside me, borrowing things from my blood!"). Too many episodes felt sluggish, or were tied to pop cultural moments that had long passed ("Thelma and Louise," "Pulp Fiction"). You only have to look at the creaky "Murphy Brown" (finally calling it quits in this, its 10th year) or remember the last moribund seasons of "All in the Family" (when it was called "Archie Bunker's Place") to appreciate Jerry Seinfeld's desire to go out on top. This is the right decision, to end "Seinfeld" while it still matters, while it still has some life left in it. On the upside, "Seinfeld" is going to run forever in syndication. On the downside, there will never be another like it, ever. It was the master of its domain.

Reading: Discussing the Text

1. The critique appears to break into two parts, paragraphs 1–9 and the "10 reasons." To what extent is the break disruptive?
2. If the essay stopped after paragraph 8, what would be lost? Gained?

3. How convincing is the evidence Millman presents to support the idea of the show's universality?

4. The tenth reason also serves as the critique's conclusion. How effectively does it fulfill that role?

Writing: Brief Response

1. What support can you find for the show being a "glorification of 90s yuppiedom" (paragraph 6)?

2. What support can you find for the show being an anti-yuppie sitcom?

Writing: Extended Response

1. Choose a popular sitcom, and using Millman's critique as a rough guide, write your own evaluation of its appeal and success.

2. Millman portrays Jerry Seinfeld as a universal (albeit Jewish) figure. Reread the essay analyzing her evidence for that view and evaluating its validity.

Where Woman Was, There Gal Shall Be

Natalie Angier

An English major with a minor in physics and astronomy at Barnard College, Natalie Angier is a natural to write about science. She started her career as a writer with Discover, *became senior associate editor of the now defunct* Sassy, *moved to* Time, *covering news in science and the environment, and worked as a freelance editor and science writer while teaching at New York University's Graduate Program in Science and Environmental Reporting. She then joined the staff of the* New York Times *in 1991 and received a Pulitzer Prize "for her compelling and illuminating reports on a variety of scientific topics." Her essays have appeared in the* Atlantic, Parade, American Health, Discover, *and the* Washington Monthly, *among others. Her books also focus on science, particularly medicine and biology.* Natural Obsessions: Striving to Unlock the Deepest Secrets of the Cancer Cell

(1988) examines the world of cancer research; The Beauty of the
Beast *(1995) provides a new look at invertebrates; and* Woman: An
Intimate Geography *(1999), her latest, focuses on women's bodies
and biology. It was perhaps this last interest that led her to notice who
at what age is cast in various film roles. The selection that follows was
published in the* New York Times *on December 9, 2001, where it appeared in the Sunday section "The Week in Review."*

Before You Read   Make a list of five or so popular film stars,
both male and female, looking up their ages in an almanac or on the
Internet. What, if anything, does a comparison of their ages reveal?

1   William Shakespeare said that there are seven ages of man,
infant, schoolboy, lover, soldier, justice, pantaloon and second
childishness.

2   Goldie Hawn said that, in Hollywood, there are three ages of
woman: babe, district attorney and "Driving Miss Daisy."

3   So what happens to an actress's extra ages? Hollywood, ever resourceful, taketh from the woman and giveth to the man. And thus
it is that in the film industry, women seem to age and disappear
from view with the alacrity of movie calendar leaves flying off the
pages, while male stars are given indefinite tenure in those glorious
androgenic stages of "lover" and "soldier." Witness the surfeit of
over 45 actors appearing in the lineup of holiday movies (and this
is not an exhaustive list): Gene Hackman, who stars in *two* new
movies, is 71; Robert Redford, 64; Danny DeVito, 57; Steve Martin,
56; Kevin Kline, 54; Jeff Bridges, 52; William Macy, 51; Jeff
Goldblum, 49; and John Travolta, 47.

4   The men play heisters, dentists, architects, admirals, oenophiles,
fathers of young children, husbands of much younger wives: not a
pathetic pantaloon among them! And even when the male stars
play "mature" roles, the character is generally scripted as somebody
years younger than the actor's true candle count. Sure, Mr.
Hackman, as Joe Moore in "The Heist," is an "aging" master thief—
a fellow of, oh, 60, and certainly frisky enough to be married to the
luscious 38-year-old Rebecca Pidgeon.

5   As for the older actresses, well, there's Sissy Spacek, 50, in the
critically acclaimed "In the Bedroom," in a not exactly Ponce de

Leonic turn as a mother with a 21-year-old son; and Stockard Channing, 57, as a hard-bitten, dragon-ladyish boss in "The Business of Strangers"; and Maggie Smith, 66, as a grand-dame wizard in "Harry Potter," a character who is supposed to be what she appears to be: fully wizened.

6   "Hollywood has always bumped women into older age roles," said Katha Pollitt, a culture critic for The Nation and Slate. When older women appear at all on screen, they're not really older. Forty-year-olds play women in their 50's, 50-year-olds play grandmothers and then, poof, they disappear, except for one last go-round as the ancient survivor of The Titanic.

7   The actress Tyne Daly, said: "The experience of being an older woman is not exactly something that the guys in Hollywood spend a lot of time thinking about. As a culture, we just haven't studied women the way we have men and their changes and every little move they make."

8   Ms. Daly, 55, who plays the mother of 37-year-old Amy Brenneman on the television series "Judging Amy," is accustomed to being prematurely ripened as though with ethylene gas. "I skipped the uncomfortable middle years and went right to 60," she said. "I'm playing a nice little gray-haired lady."

9   The tendency for Hollywood to simultaneously add years to women and deduct them from men is not new, and it has led to some amusing and even biologically impossible casting choices. Angela Lansbury, at 37, played the mother to 34-year-old Laurence Harvey in 1962's "The Manchurian Candidate." In the 1990 production of "Hamlet," Glenn Close played Mom Gertrude to Mel Gibson's waffling prince; she was 43, he was 34. And then there was the 1959 movie "North by Northwest," in which Jessie Royce Landis, the actress who played Cary Grant's mother, was 11 months *younger* than Grant—meaning she somehow bore her son before she herself was even conceived.

10   The practice of chrono-bending is so common, in fact, that it can almost be reduced to a formula, rather as one dog year is estimated to equal seven human years. For the basic calculus let's use the classic older woman/younger man film, 1967's "The Graduate," in which the 36-year-old Anne Bancroft declares (between notably gritted teeth) to the 30-year-old Dustin Hoffman that, "I'm twice as old as you are." Hence, one Hollywood Annum—Gal Stars, or HAGS, equals about 1.8 Hollywood Annum—Male Stars, or HAMS.

11   That ratio is strikingly similar to a formula that has been offered to compute the standard age difference between an older alpha male, in Hollywood and elsewhere, and his trophy wife: she is half his age, plus seven.

12   So why are women HAGS and men HAMS?

13   The reasons are as familiar and flame retardant as Woody Allen's wardrobe. For one thing, it's easier to be a guy actor from the first whack of the clappers. Men constitute only 49 percent of the population, but, according to the Screen Actors Guild, they racked up 62 percent of all film and television roles last year, and that percentage only gets more lopsided for the older age cohorts.

14   In addition, the vast numbers of people working behind the screen are male. Most producers are male, most scriptwriters are male, and nearly all directors are male, each presumably harboring a pet fantasy of the good life. Which means that, if Jeff Goldblum, 49, is going to be cast with Anne Heche, 32, as he is in "Auggie Rose," it sure won't be as her father.

15   It is, of course, the chronic coupling of older men with much younger women that most bestows on aging male actors the aura of invincibility. Helen Hunt (b. 1963) fell for Jack Nicholson (b. 1937) in 1997's "As Good as It Gets." (Is that really as good as it gets?) A year later, Hallie Berrie, then 30, was paired with a grizzled Warren Beatty, 61. Laura Dern, 34, is in two new movies this season, and in each case her love interest—Mr. Martin in "Novocaine" and Mr. Macy in "Focus"—is over 50.

16   But the reverse scenario, an older woman with a younger man, remains rare. And when it does occur, it must be explained. In fact, it's usually the theme of the movie. For example, in the new film "The Simian Line," Lynn Redgrave, 58, plays an aging real estate broker who lives with a much younger lover, played by the 34-year-old Harry Connick Jr. Ms. Redgrave agonizes over the age difference; it defines her role. Yet in most reviews of "Novocaine" and "Auggie Rose," which opened the same day, the extreme age gaps between the men and the women they bed with is not so much as a wisp of an issue.

17   Except perhaps, for certain segments of the female audience. "Nobody has asked me what I want," said Ms. Pollitt, 52. "I'm sure the average 50-year-old woman does not want to see a movie about a 20-year-old woman and a man her husband's age, and I doubt that the 20-year-old woman wants to see that either."

Reading: Discussing the Text

1. How would you describe Angier's attitude toward her topic? Is she amused? Bitter? Annoyed? Enraged? What? What evidence can you find to support your view?
2. Reread the article noting anything that could be called ironic. What ironies do you uncover? How do they support Angier's main point?
3. What explanations does Angier provide for the inequalities she notes? To what extent are her explanations valid?
4. The article appeared in a section devoted to general news. What other sections of a newspaper might be appropriate for the piece and why?

Writing: Brief Response

1. How true is Goldie Hawn's statement that "in Hollywood there are three ages of woman: babe, district attorney and "Driving Miss Daisy" (paragraph 2)?
2. Take a look at the "what's showing" section of a recent newspaper, noting the movies and their stars. How well does Angier's point hold?

Writing: Extended Response

1. Angier confines her examination of films and actors to the United States. To what extent does her view apply to foreign films? To explore that question, select a country and then research what films were popular in the last year or so. What you discover may support or refute Angier's point, and provide a ready-made thesis for your essay.
2. Reread the essay, making a list of the male actors over 60. Choose one and research his career, paying particular attention to the approximate ages of the parts he played and how old he was when he played them. Did his "star appeal" remain constant? Did the roles change age with the actor? Did his "leading ladies" get younger? Your research may take you in a number of directions, but narrow your questions down to one, and use your research to answer it in your essay.

Why Don't We Like the Human Body?

Barbara Ehrenreich

Essayist, novelist, journalist, activist, Barbara Ehrenreich has written extensively on almost every imaginable subject, though politics and the media are her prime targets. A regular contributor to Time *and the* Nation *as well as numerous other magazines, her work also appears in the electronic magazine* Z, *and her voice is often heard on* Today, Nightline, *and* All Things Considered, *among other radio and television shows. For Ehrenreich, the writing process is anything but calm: "Each article, column, or even short review is a temporary obsession, characterized by frantic research and moments of wild mania, tempered with crushing self-doubt. Adding up to a heady, thrill-filled life." You can also identify her sense of humor from the titles of her collections of essays:* The Worst Years of Our lives: Irreverent Notes From a Decade of Greed *(1990) and* The Snarling Citizen *(1995). Her latest books, however, have a different tone:* Blood Rites: Origins and History of the Passions of War *(1997) and* Nickel and Dimed: On Not Getting By in America *(2001). In 1980, Ehrenreich shared the National Magazine Award for Excellence in Reporting, excellence also reflected in her numerous fellowships and honorary degrees. The essay that follows was published in* Time *in July, 1991.*

Before You Read   Think of the most violent movie you've seen recently. To what extent did it shock you?

1   There's something wrong when a $7 movie in the mall can leave you with post-traumatic stress syndrome. In the old days killers merely stalked and slashed and strangled. Today they flay their victims and stash the rotting, skinless corpses. Or they eat them filleted, with a glass of wine, or live and with the skin still on when there's no time to cook. It's not even the body count that matters anymore. What counts is the number of ways to trash the body: decapitation, dismemberment, impalings, and (ranging into the realm of the printed word) eye gougings, power drillings, and the application of hungry rodents to some poor victim's innards.

2   All right, terrible things do happen. Real life is filled with serial killers, mass murderers and sickos of all degrees. Much of the 20th century, it could be argued, has been devoted to ingenious production and disposal of human corpses. But the scary thing is not that eye gougings and vivisections and meals of human flesh may, occasionally, happen. The scary thing, the thing that ought to make the heart pound and the skin go cold and tingly, is that somehow we find this fun to watch.

3   There are some theories, of course. In what might be called the testosterone theory, a congenital error in the wiring of the male brain leads to a confusion between violence and sex. Men get off on hideous mayhem, and women, supposedly, cover their eyes. Then there's the raging puritan theory, which is based on the statistical fact that those who get slashed or eaten on the screen are usually guilty of a little fooling around themselves. It's only a tingle of rectitude we feel, according to this, when the bad girl finally gets hers. There's even an invidious comparison theory: we enjoy seeing other people get sautéed or chain-sawed because at least it's not happening to us.

4   The truth could be so much simpler that it's staring us in the face. There's always been a market for scary stories and vicarious acts of violence. But true horror can be bloodless, as in Henry James' matchless tale, *The Turn of the Screw*. Even reckless violence, as in the old-time western, need not debauch the human form. No, if offerings like *American Psycho* and *The Silence of the Lambs* have anything to tell us about ourselves, it must be that at this particular historical moment, we have come to hate the body.

5   Think about it. Only a couple of decades ago, we could conceive of better uses for the body than as a source of meat or leather. Sex, for example. Sex was considered a valid source of thrills even if both parties were alive and remained so throughout the act. Therapists urged us to "get in touch with our bodies"; feminists celebrated "our bodies, ourselves." Minimally, the body was a cuddly personal habitat that could be shared with special loved ones. Maximally, it was a powerhouse offering multiple orgasms and glowing mind-body epiphanies. Skin was something to massage or gently stroke.

6   Then, for good reasons or bad, we lost sex. It turned out to spread deadly viruses. It offended the born-again puritans. It led to messy entanglements that interfered with networking and power lunching. Since there was no way to undress for success, we switched in the mid-'80s to food. When we weren't eating, we were

watching food-porn starring Julia Child or working off calories on the Stairmaster. The body wasn't perfect, but it could, with effort and willpower, be turned into a lean, mean eating machine.

7   And then we lost food. First they took the red meat, the white bread and the Chocolate Decadence desserts. Then they came for the pink meat, the cheese, the butter, the tropical oils and, of course, the whipped cream. Finally, they wanted all protein abolished, all fat and uncomplex carbohydrates, leaving us with broccoli and Metamucil. Everything else, as we know, is transformed by our treacherous bodies into insidious, slow-acting toxins.

8   So no wonder we enjoy seeing the human body being shredded, quartered, flayed, filleted and dissolved in vats of acid. It let us down. No wonder we love heroes and megavillains like RoboCop and the Terminator, in whom all soft, unreliable tissue has been replaced by metal alloys. Or that we like reading (even, in articles deeply critical of the violence they manage to summarize) about diabolical new uses for human flesh. It's been, let's face it, a big disappointment. May as well feed it to the rats or to any cannibalistically inclined killer still reckless enough to indulge in red meat.

10   No, it's time for a truce with the soft and wayward flesh. Maybe violent imagery feeds the obsessions of real-life sickos. Or maybe, as some argue, it drains their sickness off into harmless fantasy. But surely it cheapens our sense of ourselves to think that others, even fictional others, could see us as little more than meat. And it's hard to believe all this carnage doesn't dull our response to the global wastage of human flesh in famine, flood and war.

11   We could start by admitting that our '70's-era expectations were absurdly high. The body is not a reliable source of ecstasy or transcendental insight. For most of our lives, it's a shambling, jury-rigged affair, filled with innate tensions, contradictions, broken springs. Hollywood could help by promoting better uses for the body, like real sex, by which I mean sex between people who are often wrinkled and overweight and sometimes even fond of each other. The health meanies could relax and acknowledge that one of the most marvelous functions of the body is, in fact, to absorb small doses of whipped cream and other illicit substances.

12   Then maybe we can start making friends with our bodies again. They need nurture and care, but they should also be good for a romp now and then, by which I mean something involving dancing or petting as opposed to dicing and flaying. But even "friends" is

another weirdly alienated image. The truth, which we have almost forgotten, is that Bodies "R" Us.

Reading: Discussing the Text

1. Given the amount of violence in popular culture and in the media, it's easy to become inured to it. We become harder to shock, yet that's what Ehrenreich wants to do to us with her first paragraph. How well does she succeed?
2. What reasons does Ehrenreich provide to support her claim that "we have come to hate the body" (paragraph 4)? Which seem the most valid and why?
3. Reread paragraphs 5 to 12. How serious is Ehrenreich?
4. Given her essay, how would you describe the person Ehrenreich appears to be? How informed is she? How credible?

Writing: Brief Response

1. To what extent do you believe Ehrenreich's claim that we hate our bodies?
2. Assuming you watch films that contain violence, why do they appeal to you?

Writing: Extended Response

1. Choose a popular movie that you enjoyed, and analyze why you enjoyed it. If you have a video or, better still, a DVD of the film, you'll be able to stop the action and replay key scenes, which will make it easier to gather evidence for your paper.
2. Leaf through a popular men's or women's magazine, looking for how the human body is portrayed. Look at the ads, the table of contents, the articles, and photographs. What conclusions do you draw? Write an essay defending your main point, using your examples as evidence.

COMPARING THE SELECTIONS

1. The idea of stereotyping runs through the selections by Lena Williams and Natalie Angier. Williams is assumed to like only "black" music, and, according to Angier, Hollywood casts women according to youthful sex appeal. While Williams' essay is subjective, focusing on her own experience, Angier's article is more objective, focusing on observations. Which of the two deals with stereotyping more effectively?

2. The purpose of an obituary is to sum up a person's life, but any obituary of George Harrison must also deal with his popularity and success. Popularity and success also form the basis for Joyce Millman's analysis of "Seinfeld." Of the two, which does the better job of analysis and why?

3. Societal attitudes lie behind the selections by Barbara Ehrenreich and Natalie Angier. According to Ehrenreich, violent films are popular because our culture hates the human body; according to Angier, films reflect Hollywood's gender bias. Both writers depend heavily upon example to back up their claims. Which is the more compelling and why?

4. Jane and Michael Stern go out of their way to discover good "road food," with Keaton's as an example. In somewhat the same manner, Lena Williams goes out of her way, culturally speaking, to discover music that speaks to her. Reread both selections, noting the attitudes of the writers toward their subjects. How would you characterize those attitudes—genuine or posed, appreciative or condescending, trustworthy or false, forthright or glib, what? Of the two selections, which do you find the more credible and why?

The Media

6

Introduction

Until a few years ago if someone referred to the media, the listener automatically thought of newspapers, magazines, radio and television—print and electronic means of conveying information and entertainment. Today, many of us get that information or entertainment from computers courtesy of the World Wide Web. Want to know the best-selling fiction or non-fiction books in 1950? The Web will give you a quicker answer than an almanac or encyclopedia, for using a search engine is a lot faster than finding a book and consulting an index.

Computers have become so much a part of our lives that virtually all major newspapers now have electronic editions, and the same is true of television stations. If you want to follow up on a news story you've just seen on CNN, you can find an expanded version on CNN.com, replete with sound and music. The Web has become a major source of information, so much so that many a student uses it instead of a library. How dependable that information may be is another question.

No matter how objective the news—in whatever form—may be, it still is written by one or more persons who must make decisions about what to include and what to exclude as well as what weight to give information and what words to convey facts. These human actions make the media informative and effective, but they also open up reporting to charges of bias. All you need to do is read your newspaper's letters to the editor to discover how a liberal or conservative slant can be found in almost any editorial or guest column.

Along with charges of bias come charges of sensationalism. Newspapers, magazines, television shows, even Web pages depend on advertising, which means that the greater the number of readers, watchers, or hits, the higher the cost of ads and the greater the revenue. Sensationalism is the main appeal of the tabloids you see as you wait in line at the supermarket checkout counter, but even seemingly sedate newspapers can go overboard when a juicy political scandal comes along, and talk shows on television or radio can rarely resist a satirical jab.

If you've worked for a student newspaper, you know the kinds of criticism leveled at the media, criticism that can serve as a good topic for an essay. But even without that experience, you are familiar enough with newspapers, magazines, and the electronic media to have opinions about them. For the next few days, try to analyze the information you come across, assessing it for its accuracy, appeal, and impact.

As you read the prose that follows, read each piece first for its basic meaning:

What aspect of the media is the author writing about?
What is the author's opinion about that subject?
How accurate is the writer's analysis of the subject?
What does the author want you to understand, think, believe?
How relevant is the piece to your own experience?

Then when you reread each selection, be aware of the techniques the writer uses:

What examples does the writer use?
What comparisons or contrasts does the writer use?
What descriptive language does the writer use?
How does the writer use cause and effect?
How does the writer try to keep your interest?

The selections that follow deal with a variety of media—newspapers, magazines, television, and radio. The selections themselves come from a newspaper and five very different publications—a professional journal, a weekly news magazine, a Web-based news site, an alumna publication, and a magazine focusing on community-service workers and documentary writers and photographers. Their subjects include the difficulty of being a reporter, the power of photographs, various critiques of the media, and a salute to an old-fashioned radio show.

My Sister's Dead Body Is No Longer News

Jim Heid

When Jim Heid's piece appeared in the "My Turn" spot in Newsweek *(September 17, 2001), the only identification given was that he "lives in Albion, California." But Heid's Web page tells you a great deal more. Were you to look at it (www.heidsite.com), you'd discover that Heid has a weekly column in the* Los Angeles Times, *writing about all matters related to Mac computers. His columns also appear on line at his Web site, along with some pages related to the selection below. There, he summarizes the* Newsweek *piece, lists various links "that you might find useful in learning more about the declining state of TV journalism," and provides some updates on articles dealing with the coverage of the September 11, 2001, disaster. As any Mac owner knows, the line of computers has a large and enthusiastic following. If you are among them, you'd enjoy Heid's reviews of Mac related products and programs, including a comparison of six DVD burners. His essay, however, deals with a far more serious subject.*

Before You Read   Think about local news programs. How large a part is played by violence?

1   In late august, Pittsburgh TV station WPXI ran a news report covering changes proposed for county parks in western Pennsylvania. The changes dealt largely with pedestrian-safety issues, and were inspired by a horrific accident that occurred in a park last March: an elderly driver suffered a fatal aneurysm and his car careered into three pedestrians on a jogging trail, killing them. One of those pedestrians was my sister.

2   As the news reporter spoke, a clip of the accident scene appeared. For several seconds, viewers saw a shot of the victims, their bodies draped with sheets, a crumpled Cadillac nearby. Unfortunately, my mother was watching.

3   Later in the week I called Mom to ask how she was doing. She hesitated, then admitted that she had recently had a "bad day." She explained how she had turned on the TV to get the morning news and saw an image that brought back the worst tragedy of her 82 years. She had not seen any pictures of the accident before, but now, she told me, the scene was burned into her brain.

4   When the accident first occurred, my mother and the rest of our family were too preoccupied to watch the news. When a local paper ran a photo of the incident on its front page, my brother and I intercepted it so Mom wouldn't see it. Then, when my mother was least prepared for it, a TV station managed to aggravate a wound that shows little sign of healing.

5   Video clips like the one my mother saw are called "B-roll"—they're intended to make a report more visually interesting than just a talking head. In the world of local TV news, where substance often takes a back seat to sensationalism, B-roll clips are often of graphic scenes: fires, crashes, sheet-draped bodies. Local TV newscasts have earned such a bad reputation for sensational reporting that an industry catchphrase describes their planning process: if it bleeds, it leads.

6   That creed appears to be in effect at WPXI. In the 1998 edition of an annual study conducted by Columbia University's Project for Excellence in Journalism, the station earned an F for newscast quality. The Pittsburgh market as a whole earned the dubious distinction of being the worst of the 20 markets studied.

7   Why is some local TV news failing? Because its priorities center on making money, not informing the public. It's simple: they believe blood sells. Viewers' morbid curiosity draws them in, and sensational reporting and graphic images keep them there. A 1998 study by Rocky Mountain Media Watch found that more than 40 percent of local TV newscasts was devoted to coverage of crimes, accidents and other violent events.

8   But what effect does a diet of bloody news have on a society? We become calloused and paranoid at the same time, hardened to violence but fearful that we might be next. And because TV news only glosses over issues of real importance, the more we watch, the less well informed we become.

9   It doesn't have to be this way. When I called WPXI to complain about the grisly footage it had shown, I was told that the station

had simply been trying to illustrate the safety issues the newscaster was talking about. I argued that if the station believed a visual was essential to the story, it could have done what another local station did: it could have used a long shot of the ambulances with their flashing lights, minus the victims' bodies.

10   Research indicates that stations that take the high road may be rewarded in the long run. Columbia University's annual studies consistently show that stations with high-quality newscasts build ratings more effectively than lower-scoring ones. It turns out that quality sells. We're smarter than news producers think we are—and the world is a better place than they portray.

11   What WPXI did is far from unusual, and TV news isn't the only guilty party. I've viewed—yes, with morbid curiosity—photos of plane crashes and accident scenes in newspapers and magazines. And while it might have occurred to me that the victims' loved ones would be pained by seeing these images, I'd have defended the news outlets' right to publish them.

12   And I still would. But I would also ask those news outlets to ask themselves two questions before publishing or broadcasting explicit images: is it news, and is it necessary?

13   You could argue that the scenes of my sister's death were news when they occurred in March. But they weren't news in late August. When WPXI broadcast those scenes in its most recent report, it was just scraping the bottom and feeding every negative stereotype about local TV news. My sister's sheet-draped body is no longer news, and by showing an image of it, WPXI didn't serve its viewers or its bottom line. It simply made a grieving mother cry.

Reading: Discussing the Text

1. Heid uses the example of his mother to open and close the essay. To what extent is he basing his argument on an emotional appeal?
2. Although the essay is grounded in personal experience, Heid is careful to back up his own views with evidence. How credible is that evidence?
3. The essay is structured around causal relationships. Trace their use in the essay. How effectively does Heid present them?
4. In his second to last paragraph, Heid proposes two questions that he believes would prevent the sensationalistic use of video footage. How successfully would they prevent what he perceives as the problem?

Writing: Brief Response

1. Watch a local news program and then use your notebook to record the extent to which Heid's objections seem justified.
2. After a serious accident or personal tragedy, the scene is usually visited by TV news reporters. What questions should they ask and why?

Writing: Extended Response

1. According to Heid, "substance often takes a back seat to sensationalism" (paragraph 5) on local news programs. Record the news segments of two or three local TV news programs so that you can test out his assertion. You can use examples from your videos to support your thesis.
2. Heid maintains that "bloody news" makes us "calloused and paranoid at the same time, hardened to violence but fearful that we might be next" (paragraph 8). Use your own experience, research, and interviews to evaluate the extent to which his claim is justified.

The School Shootings:
Why Context Counts

LynNell Hancock

With a BA from the University of Iowa and an MA in East Asian Languages and Literature from Columbia University, LynNell Hancock entered Columbia's Journalism School, where she earned her MS and where, a number of years later, she now teaches. In that interim, she investigated issues in education and wrote a column for New York City's Village Voice *before joining the* Daily News, *where she covered the many flaming issues that smolder and burn in a school system as huge as New York City's. She then became general editor at* Newsweek, *responsible for stories covering all levels of edu-*

*cation—public and private, national and international. She has re-
ceived a number of awards, among them the Association for Black
Journalists Prize, the New York Newswomen's Front Page Award, and
the National Press Club Consumer Journalism Award. Her articles
have been published in the* New York Times, Newsweek, U.S. News
and World Report, *and the* Columbia Journalism Review, *where the
article that follows appeared in the May/June, 2001, issue. Hancock
has contributed a chapter to* Public Assault on America's Children:
Poverty, Violence and Juvenile Injustice *(2000), and her own book,*
Hands to Work: The Stories of Three Families Racing the Welfare
Clock, *was published in 2002.*

Before You Read   On a scale of 1 to 10 (with 10 as the highest),
rank the present degree of violence in schools. Upon what do you
base your opinion?

1   The images are horrifying. Children are wheeled out of school
on stretchers, while medical workers chase them down pathways
with oxygen masks, bandages, intravenous drips. A security officer
is slumped in the hallway, his face bloodied by bullet spray. A gan-
gly fifteen-year-old is marched past TV cameras into custody.

2   This numbing scene was replayed on March 5 from Santana High
School in Santee, California. After a young student there allegedly
killed two classmates and injured thirteen others, Dan Rather led
the CBS broadcast with a sweeping introduction: "School shootings
in this country have become an epidemic." Within hours of the
California tragedy, MSNBC.com posted a package of stories, including a map of the U.S. that allowed readers to click onto each state's
previous violent school incidents. The cover of *Time* trumpeted,
"The Columbine Effect," illustrated by a bright blue schoolbag
packed with pencils, notebooks, and a revolver.

3   A national sense of dread took hold, again. Within days, more
than thirty children, from New Jersey to Georgia, were either ar-
rested or suspended for making threats that targeted kids or teachers. And beyond threats, a fourteen-year-old Pennsylvania girl shot
another student on March 7 in her school cafeteria. At the end of
the month, a sixteen-year-old in Gary, Indiana, was shot and killed
by a former classmate in their high school parking lot.

4   It seemed as if no school, no child, was safe from an enraged classmate with a gun and an urge to kill. Every American teen ambling down the sidewalk with a book bag became a suspect; every student a potential victim. An NBC/*Wall Street Journal* survey post-Columbine found that 71 percent of the people who were polled believed that school killings could occur in their communities.

5   Is the public's heightened fear based in reality? Or is it exaggerated, fed by saturation media coverage that is painting a distorted picture?

6   Despite the frightening shootings, from Paducah, Kentucky, to Littleton, Colorado, the numbers support the latter view. From 1992, when the National School Safety Center began keeping records, to 2001, the number of people shot and killed annually in elementary or secondary schools declined from forty-three to fourteen. The drop is not a straight line. During the tragic 1998–99 school year, for example, twenty-four were killed—more than half at Columbine. But the trend clearly shows that death by gunfire in schools is on the decline.

7   The downward trend also holds true for other school violence statistics kept by the center. When the numbers for total school deaths since 1992 are broken down, the categories for deaths by suicide and deaths for "reasons unknown" hold fairly steady. But "gang-related" and "interpersonal disputes"—the largest categories of causes of death outside "unknown"—show striking declines. Gang-related deaths drop from thirteen to one over the measured years, while deaths from "disputes" drop from eighteen to one. Bullying, an apparent factor in some of the recent shootings, was a factor in only twelve of the total 295 violent deaths recorded by the center since 1992.

8   It should be noted, meanwhile, that these 295 deaths occurred in a national school population of 52.7 million. Each American child, then, has only one chance in two million of getting killed on school grounds. With those odds, a student has a greater chance of being exterminated by a stray comet that wipes out the earth.

9   Other research groups support the argument that schools are safe and getting safer. The federal National Center for Education Statistics found that 25 percent fewer children brought weapons to school in 1997 compared to four years earlier. The study reported that "serious crimes" such as rape and sexual and aggravated assault declined 34 percent during the same period. Federal agencies from the Secret Service to the U.S. Department of Justice have re-

leased reports saying schools are one of the safest places for children to be.

10   "Stories about school shootings should mention these trends," argues Vincent Schiraldi, president of the Justice Policy Institute, a research and public policy group based in Washington, D.C. "You wouldn't write a story about Mark McGwire's home run streak without mentioning Roger Maris."

11   This is a simple matter of context. In its absence, "journalists are scaring the life out of parents and school officials about their violent kids," Schiraldi says. "The truth is, kids are no more violent today than they were twenty years ago. And schools are not the locus of homicide that the media portrays."

12   Certainly, media coverage of school shootings has significantly increased in column inches and broadcast minutes over the years.

13   • In 1974, a seventeen-year-old Regents scholar carted guns and homemade bombs to his upstate New York school, then killed three adults and wounded eleven others from his sniper post on the top floor. *Newsweek* carried only a 700-word story about the mayhem, well inside the magazine.

14   • In 1978, a smart, tormented fifteen-year-old in Lansing, Michigan, killed one bully and wounded a second. The story was front-page news in the local *State Journal*. But ninety miles away, the *Detroit Free Press* ran a much smaller story inside its pages.

15   • In 1988, a Virginia Beach sixteen-year-old armed himself with a semiautomatic weapon, 200 rounds of ammunition, and three firebombs before entering his Baptist school. He killed one teacher and wounded a second. The Associated Press sent a brief story about the murders over the wire that was picked up without much fanfare by a handful of papers around the nation. *The San Diego Union-Tribune,* for instance, ran a 360-word story on page three.

16   Neither MSNBC nor CNN existed when those teens opened fire. The national and international media did not descend on victimized towns and schools. Words like "rash of killings" and "epidemic" were not mentioned in the stories. " 'Epidemic' is exactly the wrong word to use when it comes to school crime in the nineties," says Lori Dorfman, director of Berkeley Media Studies Group, which urges reporters to add context and perspective to every violent-crime story.

17   Experts like Dorfman argue that real epidemics, which pose far more serious dangers to children than school shootings, go undercovered. Consider child abuse, for example. An average of five U.S. children are killed by their caregivers every day, according to the National Clearinghouse on Child Abuse and Neglect. Life is clearly more dangerous for children outside school walls than within. National education statistics show that, at most, thirty-five children were murdered in school during the 1997–98 academic year, while 2,752 were killed beyond the campus.

18   Yet the volume and intensity of coverage of modern school shootings focus public attention on children's safety inside school buildings. Many schools respond to this by adopting strict "zero tolerance" policies. New rules require kids to be expelled or suspended for everything from carrying a gun to carrying a nail file. In the wake of Columbine, a six-year-old from Harrisburg, Pennsylvania, was suspended for bringing a toenail clipper to school. A first-grader in Jonesboro, Arkansas, was suspended for aiming a chicken nugget at a teacher and saying, "pow, pow, pow." The Harvard Civil Rights project found that suspensions increased from 1.7 to 3.1 million from 1974 to 1997, and that black and Hispanic children were punished at far greater rates than their white peers.

19   Not all the coverage has had a punitive effect. Many of the stories led to constructive soul-searching on the part of schools, parents, and communities. Features following the Columbine massacre often tackled the root causes of violence. "More reporters asked why, not just what," says Dorfman, who studied juvenile violence stories for a year after Columbine. The community discussions went beyond improving law enforcement to such subjects as establishing open school environments, controlling guns, and increasing mental health services for adolescents. Schools developed emergency plans that included aerial maps and a network of counselors.

20   Santana High School was one of these. Yet after the two children died there, *The New York Times* reported on the following Sunday that Santee's citizens, and the public at large, had become strangely inured to the specter of teens mowing down their fellow students in a hail of gunfire. Reporters James Sterngold and Jodi Wilgoren wrote that public consciousness had shifted from disbelief to "a macabre sense of expectation and routine." In Santee, police and

school officials reportedly were already planning a training video, "to help them get ready for next time."

21   If the people of Santee believe that the statistically improbable horror that visited them in March is likely to occur there again, then the media have already wreaked significant collateral damage.

Reading: Discussing the Text

1. Hancock provides a great deal of evidence to support her claim. What evidence do you find the most compelling and why?
2. Reread the essay, looking for positive results of the news coverage of school shootings. To what extent does Hancock's article present a balanced view?
3. At times, an article can provide so many examples that they blur the overall point. If you find that true of Hancock's article, what would you cut and why?
4. If you would cut nothing, how do the examples differ?

Writing: Brief Response

1. Take another look at your rating in "Before You Read." How would you change it after reading the article?
2. Hancock compares earlier coverage of school shootings to the more recent ones, finding a significant increase over time. Use your notebook to speculate on the reasons for that increase.

Writing: Extended Response

1. The shootings at Columbine and elsewhere have given rise to the "zero tolerance" rule at many schools. Use your library or the Internet to explore how the rule has been implemented, its effect, and its fairness. Then use your evidence to support your evaluation of the rule.
2. Though Hancock focuses on students with guns shooting other students, violence against teachers has also become a problem, though that violence often takes lesser forms—threats, punches, knives. Use your library or the Internet to explore the nature and degree of the problem. Once you have accumulated enough evidence to find several examples, you will be in a position to select one and discuss it within its wider content.

Just a Little Honest

Maureen Dowd

> *Not many people can claim two Pulitzer Prizes, but that's what Maureen Dowd has won: in 1992, she was a finalist for national reporting, a warm-up to winning a Pulitzer in 1995 and again in 1999, both given for Commentary. As the category suggests, Dowd is a columnist, and her work appears regularly in the* New York Times *before being republished through syndication in many newspapers throughout the United States. Dowd's career is a fledgling journalist's dream. She started with the* Washington Star *as an editorial assistant, working her way up to become a reporter and feature writer as well sports columnist, then moving to* Time *magazine after the* Star *ceased publication in 1981. Two years later, she joined the* Times, *first as a metropolitan reporter, then as a correspondent for its Washington bureau before becoming one of the* Times' *most widely read columnists. Her "On Washington" appeared regularly in the* New York Times Magazine, *and now you can find her work on the newspaper's Op-Ed page. That's where the column that follows appeared on January 9, 2002. You'll find its wit typical of her writing.*

Before You Read   Take a minute to think about a news show you watch and then write down a description of the news anchor. What is the image that is projected?

1   "A gaffe," Michael Kinsley once observed, "occurs not when a politician lies, but when he tells the truth."

2   CNN made a terrible gaffe over the weekend and told a terrific truth.

3   It was refreshing to see somebody finally spit out what we all know but what the networks go to ludicrous lengths to deny: They hire and promote news stars based on looks and sex appeal.

4   About 10 times over the weekend, CNN ran an ad promoting Paula Zahn's new morning show, "American Morning," with a male announcer purring, "Where can you find a morning news anchor who's provocative, super-smart, oh yeah, and just a little sexy?" The

word sexy then flared onto the screen, accompanied by a noise that sounded like a zipper unzipping.

5   The ad's naked truth stunned television insiders. "If they're sexy, so be it," said Don Hewitt, executive producer of "60 Minutes." "It ain't necessary to say it. It's undignified.

6   "Whatever Paula brings to television," he said, "it's despite the fact that she's nicely put together. It diminishes a first-rate woman journalist to label her sexy. Why doesn't CNN say that Wolf Blitzer is sexy? He must be sexy to somebody."

7   On Monday the embarrassed CNN chief, Walter Isaacson, yanked the spot. "It was a bad mistake," he said. "I'm really sorry. The promotion department didn't get it cleared. You can say sexy about a man but not about a woman."

8   A CNN spokesman explained that the noise was not supposed to be a zipper sound, but more like a needle scratching across an LP record—a sound effect sometimes used on "Ally McBeal."

9   CNN's bitter rival, Fox News, which fired Ms. Zahn in September when it learned she was being wooed by CNN, immediately began crowing. In the absence of the usual Washington back-stabbing, Fox vs. CNN is the most entertaining contest going. The Fox anchor Brit Hume declared on air that the sexy ad was "a first in the history of television news."

10   Mr. Hume said off air he thought that in the old days CNN made news the star. But now, beset by lively cable competition and Ashleigh Banfield types, the network has to make stars the news.

11   "TV news is a peculiar hybrid medium with many imperatives," Mr. Hume said. "And attractive people, alas, is one of them."

12   As TV news has succumbed to glossy entertainment values, the executives in TV don't think so differently from executives in movies.

13   As Glenn Close recently told The Chicago Tribune, Hollywood always wants "the same old thing—young, sexy. I always have an image that there must be some room somewhere full of men saying," to paraphrase Ms. Close, "Would you date her?" "Yeah, I'd date her." "O.K., let's cast her."

14   The BBC's 56-year-old veteran news correspondent Kate Adie created a stir in October when she said TV bosses in England were more interested in the "shape of your leg" than professional credentials. Calling herself a "terribly old-fashioned old trout," she said the modern crop of BBC presenters had "cute faces and cute bottoms and nothing else in between."

15   American network executives have also been hiding their preference for the visual over the cerebral in plain sight over the years, as they paraded a bunch of glamorous cookie-cutter blondes, pretty conservative pundettes with gams longer than their résumés and dishy anchor studs across the screen, all the while pretending that it was more important for their journalists to be hard on the news than easy on the eyes.

16   The irrepressible Roger Ailes, head of Fox News, is chortling, declaring that in its "desperation" to add some Fox-like foxiness to its more staid network, CNN overreached.

17   He said he thought the ad was due to the influence of Jamie Kellner, the Turner Broadcasting boss who came over in March from running the WB network, where he used to oversee "Buffy the Vampire Slayer" and "Felicity." He does not buy Mr. Kellner's plea of ignorance.

18   "This has got Kellner's fingerprints, palm prints and face prints on it," Mr. Ailes said. "Nobody in the history of CNN in Atlanta would have used that zipper sound effect or the word 'sexy.' This is Hollywood. This is the way they promote a new sitcom. This is Kellner saying, 'I made "Buffy the Vampire Slayer." I can make Paula Zahn.'"

Reading: Discussing the Text

1. The first two paragraphs are intended to grab the reader so the person continues reading. How effectively do those two paragraphs do that?
2. Dowd implies that television news has crossed over to Hollywood. Examine the evidence she presents to support that claim. What is the most compelling and why?
3. To affect the reader, writers use appeals to reason, emotion, and their own sense of authority or credibility. Which appeal does Dowd depend upon the most? What evidence supports your view?
4. How would you characterize Dowd's attitude toward what she perceives as "what we all know but what the networks go to ludicrous lengths to deny" (paragraph 3)? Is she appalled? Disgusted? Amused? Bemused? Scornful? What?

Writing: Brief Response

1. Compare the notes you made in response to "Before You Read" to Dowd's claim in her essay. Use your notebook to record the degree to which she may be right.

2. Watch one or two shows of CNN's "Headline News." Is it Hollywoodized?

Writing: Extended Response

1. While the accuracy and depth of television network news is debatable, there isn't much question about the competition among networks. Select two network news programs, and compare their presentation of the news. Who wins and why?

2. The half-hour evening news show has a long history, but the amount of available information about the world has increased tremendously. To what extent is the half-hour national news show a dinosaur? What alternatives exist? What changes, if any, should take place? Narrow down to one question, and then research it so that you can back your opinion with evidence.

Staring Back

Francine Prose

If you were to pick up the New York Times Book Review *or the* Washington Post, *you might well find a book written or reviewed by Francine Prose. Novelist, essayist, short story writer, author of children's books, nonfiction writer, critic, writer of a screenplay about Janis Joplin, and teacher, she's hard to categorize, and her many interests make her an ideal book reviewer. As for her own work, it's an impressive list and a long one, some twelve in all. Her most recent book focuses on art—*Lives of the Muses: Nine Women and the Artists They Inspired *(2002)—and in 2000, a collection of her essays,* Scent of Women's Ink, *was published along with her novel* Blue Angel, *a satire of life in an English Department. That's a subject she is most familiar with, having taught at Harvard, Sarah Lawrence, the University of Iowa's Writer's Workshop, and Vermont's Breadloaf Writer's Conference. The essay that follows appeared in a special 2001 edition of* DoubleTake, *one focusing exclusively on the events of September 11, 2001.* DoubleTake *is published by the DoubleTake Community Service Corporation and, as its masthead proclaims, it is*

*"intended to further the ideas, the visions, and the ideals of commu-
nity-service workers and of documentary photographers and writers."
You'll see that Francine Prose's piece does just that.*

Before You Read   So that you can better appreciate the essay that
follows, use an unabridged dictionary to look up the meaning of
iconic, a word Prose uses twice.

1   Assuming that there is a future in which people can look at
photos of September 11 without such jolts of pain and grief that
they'd rather not look at all, the future will have plenty to look at.
The tragedy is fully documented—beginning with, however improbably, the initial moment of impact, which was recorded in the
course of shooting a fire department training video. Despite the
nightmarish velocity with which events seemed to be unfolding,
things transpired slowly enough that many people had time to duck
back into their apartments, grab their cameras, and turn their lenses
toward Lower Manhattan.

2   The astonishing number of witnesses moved to photograph the
catastrophe, and the immense range of images captured on film,
was made evident in a remarkable project, *This Is New York: A
Democracy of Photographs,* which turned a SoHo storefront into an
impromptu gallery displaying over a thousand photos of the disaster, taken by (and solicited from) working photojournalists and ordinary men and women. The snapshots that lined the walls included
many that had previously appeared in newspapers and magazines:
the cloud of dust and debris rolling through the city streets like
some threatening monster in a postwar Japanese horror film;
screaming pedestrians, firemen, and emergency workers helping the
injured or, in an two Jima–like tableau, hoisting the American flag;
survivors inhaling oxygen from masks; the interiors of downtown
apartments thickly coated with ash and debris; makeshift shrines displaying the innocent, heartbreaking faces of the dead and missing; a
cop, collapsed in tears; empty gurneys parked in front of a hospital
awaiting the wounded who never came.

3   Already the images of the disaster have ceded the front page to
scenes of conflict and destruction in Afghanistan and the Middle

East. But the pictures from September 11 continue to appear, it seems, everywhere we look—on T-shirts, in magazines, as punctuation for feature stories on network TV—prompting us to wonder which of these images will endure as the iconic representation of the event, which will function as the one recognizable image that, in the future, will provide a sort of visual shorthand, symbolizing and encapsulating all the horrors of that bright September morning.

4   In the past, our most renowned, most iconic—and, it might be argued, most powerful—images of disaster have tended to focus on the emotions of the living (shock, terror, grief) rather than the awkward, terrible, and somehow dehumanized disposition of the dead. The last few decades have provided a chillingly wide array of pictures that, like it or not, we cannot seem to get out of our minds: a naked, screaming Vietnamese child fleeing her napalmed village; a young woman grieving over the body of a Kent State student shot by the National Guard; an Oklahoma City firefighter cradling a tiny, bloodied one-year-old boy; W. Eugene Smith's photograph of a Japanese mother bathing her daughter, a victim of mercury poisoning at Minamata. We find ourselves searching the faces of these subjects and experiencing a sort of identification that's less voyeuristic than sympathetic: how do our fellow humans respond in such extreme and horrendous circumstances? How would we react if, by some appalling chance, we were in their places?

5   Perhaps one explanation for our continuing fascination with the doomed World Trade Center towers is that, despite the catastrophic loss of human life, there are almost no pictures of the dead. Never before have so many lives been lost in such a short time—and left so little physical evidence of their former presence. Images of the towers have become our only visible manifestation of the thousands of lives they housed. We stare at the buildings as if they can tell us something, as if they can unlock some riddle about the men and women who worked there every day or who just happened to be there at one profoundly unfortunate moment. What happened to all those people—how could they just vanish off the face of the earth—those men and women whose pictures and brief biographies now appear in some of our newspapers? From now on, when we look at the World Trade Center, we will in some sense be looking at the presence and absence of all those souls.

Reading: Discussing the Text

1. In paragraph 2, Prose gives examples of the photographic images in the SoHo exhibit. To what extent is the order of those examples effective?
2. Prose uses *iconic* in paragraphs 3 and 4. How is her use of the word appropriate?
3. According to Prose, the photographic images that have been the most powerful are those that "focus on the emotions of the living," not those that detail the "dehumanized disposition of the dead" (paragraph 4). To what extent is that statement true to your experience?
4. The last paragraph implies that "our continuing fascination with the doomed World Trade Center towers" exists because of what they symbolize. Explain the symbolism.

Writing: Brief Response

1. Use your notebook to answer whether the title of Francine Prose's essay is appropriate or not.
2. What one image of the September 11, 2001, tragedy do you most remember and why?

Writing: Extended Response

1. Photojournalists often risk their lives for the sake of a memorable shot. Use your library to find photographic records of memorable events so that you can write an essay on the power of photography. Mathew Brady's pictures of the Civil War, or any collection focusing on World War I or II, the Korean Conflict, or Vietnam, would be good sources, depending upon your interests.
2. In the last paragraph Prose states, "Never before have so many lives been lost in such a short time—and left so little physical evidence of their former presence." Test out that claim by researching some of the more disastrous natural disasters, such as floods, hurricanes, and earthquakes, and some caused by wars. If you find that the claim cannot hold up, you may wish to modify it and then use that new sentence as your thesis.

The Difficulty of Detachment

Mary Carmichael

At the time Mary Carmichael wrote the essay that follows, she was an intern at Newsweek, *having graduated from Duke University in 2001. She spent much of her time at Duke preparing for a career in journalism, using every opportunity to sharpen her reporting skills. In addition to writing for the* Chronicle, *the school newspaper, Carmichael contributed articles to the Duke University Medical Center newsletter* Inside DUMC *and* Duke Magazine, *the alumni publication, and she also edited the university's* TowerView *magazine insert. Meanwhile, she worked as a summer intern at the Charlotte, N.C.,* News & Observer *and contributed essays to the Student Success Web site put out by the publisher Prentice Hall. Her essays there focus on college life, as their titles attest; "Going to Class," "Rushing Back to School," and "Why Duke?" are some of them. The article that is included here, however, has a far more serious tone as befits the events that she witnessed. It was published in* Duke Magazine, *November–December, 2001.*

Before You Read   Burnout is possible on any job. How would you spot it in journalism?

1   I moved to New York five months ago, and when my boyfriend came to visit me, he wanted to see only one famous sight: the World Trade Center. We had dinner at Windows on the World on his last night in the city. We looked outside and saw the lights of Brooklyn, the Statue of Liberty. We danced on the wooden floor. Still, I grumbled that we were acting like tourists, that we should've gone to Nobu instead. I might have been right, Tim said as our cab pulled away: "It's not like the towers won't be here next time."

2   Every day since September 11, I've thought about that conversation, and about the little things I saw that night: the carpet at Windows on the World, with yellow WOWs emblazoned on the fabric; the Italian family on the elevator with us; how breathless and scared and delighted we all were on that elevator, zooming toward the top, our heads spinning, our ears popping as floor after floor

passed us by. I try not to think about the people who jumped, and whether their ears popped on the way down.

3   I try not to think, but it never works. It doesn't help that it's my job to think about these things, in accordance with the news cycle, twenty-four hours a day. I'm a reporter for *Newsweek*. When the towers crumbled, I went to the hospitals—not to give blood, not to find a loved one, but to pester grieving people. Later that night, I went to lower Manhattan. I climbed the rubble outside the World Financial Center, dodging a sharp scrap of metal that came screeching from the sky, trying to get facts, names, and numbers. I told my new sources I'd call them back "when things calmed down." Of course, things never did.

4   I suppose I should feel privileged that I got to cover this, the biggest story of my young lifetime. I suppose I should feel lucky that I was able to sneak past the barricades in the back of a squealing police car. I suppose I should treasure the dubious souvenirs— a hardhat, a gas mask, a stockbroker's notebook from the rubble.

5   Instead, I feel like one of those hundred people on the 106th floor, just one story under Windows on the World, whose final thoughts were recorded in a 911 operator's notes: "NEED DIRECTIONS ON HOW TO STAY ALIVE." Like most people, I try not to think about what's happened, but at the same time I can't stop thinking about it. The day of the attacks, I worked thirty-three hours straight. I didn't want to go home; I didn't want to be alone. The minute I sat down on my bed I bawled like a baby, then lay awake. It's happened every night since then. I don't go to bed until three a.m. now. Some nights I just stare out the windows.

6   At *Newsweek*, it's fashionable to say that we young reporters on "Team Terror"—most in their mid-twenties, a few in their early thirties, and me, the baby at twenty-three—have been turned into war correspondents. I don't think so. From what I've read, war correspondents are hardened and solitary. We still need each other. A week after the attack, we gathered at an Irish pub in midtown. Somebody played the piano. Somebody mentioned they'd seen body parts. Everybody smoked. Everybody threw back a shot of whiskey. Who needed the Employee Assistance Program? Like grizzled old newshounds, we were drinking our grief away.

7   But the next morning, our spiritual malaise lingered like a hangover, and it is with us still. Weeks after the attack, we are afraid to walk under bridges, afraid that the elevators in our building will come

crashing down, or worse, that the building will. We're not supposed to admit these fears. But I, at least, need to keep worrying, keep calling my parents every night, because as long as I keep talking about it, that's all it is: talk. To stop worrying would be to acknowledge the futility of worry in the face of certain attack. I can't do that.

8   For now, the plan is to stay in New York and keep doing my job, a job I was just learning when I was plunged into all of this. I've done cop reporting before, and I've seen a man executed; I thought I would be prepared. I wasn't. Three weeks after the attack, I received a reporting assignment more heinous than any trip to Ground Zero: Call the victims' families and ask them how much they've lost. How could I have prepared for that?

9   As I sat there on the phone, listening to stories of best friends and T-ball coaches and husbands of fifteen years gone, I felt it creeping in. Jaded, I was going to become jaded. And oh, the relief it would bring—if I didn't care, I wouldn't fear. Reporting would be so easy if I just didn't think.

10   But I kept going back to a column that Anna Quindlen wrote after the terrorists shattered our safety: We are not them, and we will never be like them unless we fail to value human life. So maybe our grief and terror is merely a reminder that we are still human, still alive. I read once that fear is an evolutionary gift to keep us out of danger. What better proof is there that we still value our lives than a nagging worry that we may lose them?

11   I'm glad I'm not an aged war correspondent, out on front lines that look to my eyes like any other. I'm glad that when I do sleep, I dream I'm dancing on the wooden floor again, looking out those windows on a world that is no longer there. In a way, I'm glad my daily life is still tinged with fear, because as long as I can feel fear, I can also feel hope.

Reading: Discussing the Text

1. The essay is structured chronologically, moving from past to present. Write out a timeline for the piece. How effective is its structure?
2. Carmichael examines various causal relationships. What are they? Which is the most effective and why?
3. The essay deals with a horrific event and its aftermath. How would you characterize Carmichael's attitude toward her experience? Is she pessimistic? Optimistic? Jaded? Vulnerable? What?
4. Explain whether the title is appropriate.

Writing: Brief Response

1. Carmichael uses a lot of details in her essay. Which one stands out and why?
2. In paragraph 6, Carmichael states that it was "fashionable to say that we . . . [had] been turned into war correspondents," but she disagrees. Explain whether her reasons are credible.

Writing: Extended Response

1. Look through a newspaper to find an article on a particularly horrible event and then read it carefully, noting the writer's choice of examples and words. Then use evidence from the article to explore the writer's degree of detachment.
2. Pick out one of the more sensationalistic weeklies—the *Star, National Enquirer,* and the like—and choose a story to analyze. What does the writer emphasize and why? What is underplayed or not mentioned? How credible is the story? Your essay will use examples from the story to support your evaluation of the article.

Mike's On: Radio's Obscure Comic Genius, Michael Feldman

Scott Shuger

One of the first and foremost Internet journalists (and surely the only one with a PhD in philosophy), Scott Shugar learned to write under pressure in the Navy. There he worked in intelligence, writing reports that had to be accurate, brief, and written quickly, experience that served him well in journalism. As a freelance writer, he first wrote book reviews for Amazon.com and went on to have his work published in the Washington Monthly, *the* Los Angeles Magazine, *the* New York Times, *and* Salon. *He is best known, however, for his association with* Slate, *the daily electronic newspaper published by*

Microsoft. At Slate, *he wrote "Today's Papers," a column that critiqued the lead stories from the* Los Angeles Times, *the* New York Times, *the* Wall Street Journal, *the* Washington Post, *and* USA Today. *Then in September, 2002, he became* Slate's *primary writer on the fight against terrorism. The piece that follows was posted in* Slate *on July 10, 1996, but its subjects—Michael Feldman and* Whad'Ya Know?—*are still going strong on public radio stations. Unfortunately, that's not so for Shuger. He died at the age of 50 in a scuba diving accident on June 18, 2002. For more about Shuger, look at* <www.slate.msn.com>; *for more about the show, go to its Web site, ironically named* <www.notmuch.com>.

Before You Read   Why do you listen or not listen to talk radio?

---

1   Talk radio is uniquely American, it's democratic, it's interactive, it's . . . OK, OK, it's mostly Rush talking to wack-jobs on Social Security about the budget and Howard jawing with lowlifes on weed about breasts. But not completely. Further up the yak food chain, past the local politics and sports gabbers, you can find Garrison Keillor and the *Car Talk* guys and, if you're lucky, the gentle wit of *Whad'Ya Know?* and its host, Michael Feldman.

2   This is talk radio for the rest of us—people who like information and words, have the conventional concerns of family and work, and enjoy a little innuendo now and then.

3   "Our listeners read," says Feldman, a 47-year-old former English teacher who looks and sounds fully capable of being beaten up by Woody Allen. "They play racquetball. They disproportionately own foreign cars. They carry dental insurance."

4   When asked if his marketing people are satisfied with this following (after 10 years of national broadcasts, the show, syndicated by Public Radio International, now reaches a total of 1 million people every week via more than 200 stations), Feldman responds, "What are marketing people?"

5   Although such comments reflect *Whad'Ya Know?'s* let's-go-in-the-barn-and-put-on-a-show feel, the show is a full-time gig for Feldman, who describes his salary as "about .4 Keillor units."

6   The two-hour Saturday morning show airs live, usually from a 175-seat classroom at the University of Wisconsin (in Madison,

where Feldman attended college and now lives with his wife and two young daughters). But sometimes Feldman takes it on the road to places like Northfield, Minn., and Springfield, Mo. The show always opens with a five-minute topical monologue ("One thing you gotta say about Congress: They can't run the government, but they've made it a federal offense to fire your travel agent.") and then segues to an interview with a guest or two (recent visitors included novelist Jane Smiley and a Democratic Party adviser who witnessed Bill Clinton and Helmut Kohl's glutton-off at a Milwaukee diner). Next comes the *Whad'Ya Know?* Quiz, which pairs a member of the studio audience with a caller. Quiz categories include "People," "Science," "Odds and Ends," and "Things You Should Have Learned in School (Had You Been Paying Attention)." (Sample question: Are more people injured by clothing or by razors? Answer: Clothing.) Kitschy prizes—like a book called *Songs for Dogs and the People Who Love Them* or a pair of underwear with the "Contract With America" printed on them—go to the winners.

7   There's also the phone call to an inhabitant of the "Town of the Week." The town is selected by a dart thrown at a map, and Feldman dials the town randomly until someone answers and chats with him (the feature ran eight years before he lighted upon an inhabitant who'd heard of the show). But most of the show is just Feldman pacing the audience and being funny. "It's sort of like *Donahue* without the issues," Feldman once told a Wisconsin magazine. "Or better yet, without Donahue."

8   WOMAN AUDIENCE MEMBER: *How can I wean myself from sleeping with a fan?*

9   FELDMAN: *I say marry him.*

10   In an age when even the most seemingly spontaneous public events are in fact preceded by stacks of memos and weeks of meetings, extemporaneous entertainment like this is no mean feat. And it's no *mean* feat either. Unlike Howard Stern and Dave Letterman, Feldman sees to it that his foils have as much fun as he does.

11   FELDMAN: *What's your name?*

12   AUDIENCE MEMBER: *Hankus Netsky.*

13   FELDMAN: *Is that the Pig Latin version? I'm being serious with you, now give me a serious answer. What's your name?*

14   HANKUS: *That's really it. . . .*

15   FELDMAN: *Hankus is your actual name?*

16   HANKUS: *It's true. I was actually named Hankus because my mother . . .*

17   FELDMAN: *Why?*

18   HANKUS' GIRLFRIEND: *Tell him the truth.*

19   FELDMAN: *There can't be a good reason for it.*

20   HANKUS: *Well, let's see. . . . There's a Jewish tradition of naming kids after . . .*

21   FELDMAN: *Of giving kids lousy names . . .*

22   HANKUS: *Actually, my mother had to name me after a relative whose name started with an "H" and she didn't like any of the American names like Howard or Harry or any of that sort of stuff, so she got this name from a cartoon show, as a matter of fact. . . .*

23   FELDMAN: *What cartoon had a character named "Hankus"?*

24   HANKUS: *There was a cartoon in Philadelphia called* Hankus the Horse.

25   At this point Feldman dials Hankus' mother in Philadelphia.

26   FELDMAN: *Hello, Mrs. Netsky, this is Mike Feldman calling from the radio show* Whad'Ya Know? *with Mike Feldman. If you can answer a simple question, we have a wonderful prize for you. Got a minute?*

27   HANKUS' MOM: *Just a minute, yes.*

28   FELDMAN: *OK—the question is, "What famous cartoon horse is your son named after?"*

29   HANKUS' MOM: Hankus the Horse. . . . *The nurses in the hospital when I had to fill in the certificate didn't like that. They said you've got to give him a proper name. . . .*

30   FELDMAN: *They didn't think* Hankus the Horse *was a proper name for a baby?*

31   Playing the man from Mars, agog at Earthling ways, Feldman listens skeptically to a guy in the studio audience who describes himself as a "community planner" busy "coordinating a community's relationships with the state and federal government." Bearing down, Feldman gets him to admit that his real duties are to "beg for money for sewers."

32   But the Madison Martian will gladly play the butt of a joke if it'll help him figure out the locals. Acclimating himself to the online world in one show, he required callers to tap their words into a keyboard as they spoke. Meanwhile, he did the same with his manual typewriter.

33   "It's-very-nice-to-meet-you-over-the-Internet-What-do-you-look-like?" spoke/typed a caller named Julia. "Parentheses-smiling-broadly-six-foot-four-and-a-half-blond-Lutheran-type-you?"Feldman spoke/typed back.

34   "To communicate using only your typing skills—to me, that's a special level in hell." Besides, he confesses, "I don't like to be accessed."

35   Which makes public radio the perfect medium for him—and explains why the TV pilots he made failed to sell.

36   "The concept was for me to be a white Arsenio Hall," he says of one pilot. "I had the hardest time figuring out what that would be—not hip, not black, not up that late. It came out as Art Linkletter.

37   "To tell you the truth," he sighs, summing up his life on public radio, "I don't see any way out of this."

Reading: Discussing the Text

1. The article mentions a number of talk show names. What, if anything, do these allusions add to the article?
2. How can you explain Feldman's popularity?
3. How well does Shuger communicate Feldman's sense of humor?
4. Why would readers of an electronic newspaper like *Slate* be interested in Shuger's essay?

Writing: Brief Response

1. Use your notebook to explore why you would or would not listen to Feldman's show.
2. What do you listen to on the radio and why?

Writing: Extended Response

1. Using Shuger's essay as a rough model, write your own review of a radio talk show. To make your analysis easier, you might tape several broadcasts so that you can later select examples and dialogue for your essay.
2. Radio is a relatively old medium far removed from the electronic world of MP3, CDs, and the Internet, yet it continues to be popular, offering talk shows, news, music, and variety shows. Write an essay in which you explore radio's popularity, comparing, for instance, what it offers that television or the Internet does not.

COMPARING THE SELECTIONS

1. Both Jim Heid and LynNell Hancock criticize the media, but the two selections differ in purpose and content. Heid emphasizes local television news, using an emotional appeal and addressing a mass media audience; Hancock emphasizes print coverage, using an appeal to reason and addressing a specialized audience. Which of the two makes the better argument and why?

2. Maureen Dowd and Jim Heid make similar points but based on different reasons. Dowd objects to appealing to viewers by using attractive female anchors and reporters, using sex to sell news. Heid objects to appealing to viewers by using graphic scenes, using blood and gore to sell news. At the same time, we live in a culture that emphasizes both sex and violence, so the line between Hollywood and news programs is a thin one. Where would you draw it and why? Use the two selections and your own experience as sources for your paper.

3. The events of September 11, 2001, provide the focus for the selections by Francine Prose and Mary Carmichael, but the two writers treat those events in different ways. Prose concentrates on photographs, providing many examples to make her main point; Carmichael concentrates on her first-hand experience, using her narrative to make her main point. Which is the more effective and why?

4. Log on to one of the many electronic news sources to find a story that you can also follow in print and on television or radio. You'll be doing a triple comparison to determine which is the fairer conveyer of news and why. As you do your research, test each medium against your own criterion for what a news story should be, looking for negative as well as positive qualities and the points made by at least three of the selections in this chapter. What is used to "sell" the news? How objective is the story? How thorough? How credible is the writer? What is the role of photography? The headline?

Education

Introduction

The figures involved in education are staggering. In the year 2000, 16- to 24-year-olds numbered 34.6 million, and over half of them were enrolled in our schools—8.7 million in high school and 9.6 million in higher education. Our colleges and universities have almost one million full- and part-time faculty members, and in 1996–97 public and private two- and four-year institutions spent over 196 billion dollars (figures from the US Department of Education). It's no wonder that education often heads the list of hot topics.

As a student, you have had a lot of first-hand experience with the more complex issues in education, those concerning the quality of teaching, the amount of homework, the courses that are required, the grades earned in those courses, and the kind of work those grades are based upon. And you have probably felt the double blows of the cost of tuition and textbooks. Too often, however, these issues and the minutiae of education get in the way of larger questions, questions such as "Why am I in school?" "What am I learning?" "What is education for?" Those are the kinds of questions worth pondering as groundwork if you were to write about any one of your day-to-day concerns.

You might also want to consider the educational choices you have had and why you made the decisions you did: four-year or two-year school; private or public institution; non-profit or for-profit entity; in-state or out-of-state; single-sex or coed; part- or full-time; residential or non-residential. Or perhaps you are among that growing part of a new student population, a student who is a "distance learner" or someone who takes courses on campus and a home computer. Once enrolled, another world of decisions awaits—what courses to take, what to major in, what to avoid. And, of course, there's the whole realm of extracurricular activities and the options they offer.

Thinking through those decisions calls upon cause and effect—why you chose what you did—and a process—the steps that led up to or followed your choice. Or if you are writing about an issue in education, you'd draw upon examples to explain your position, or perhaps you want to persuade your readers that your opinion is a correct one or to take a certain action. But first you need a subject, and the selections that follow should provide you with a number of ideas.

As you read the prose that follows, read each piece first for its basic meaning:

> What aspect of education is the author writing about?
> What is the author's opinion about that subject?
> How accurate is the writer's analysis of the subject?
> What do you think the author wants you to do, understand, think, believe?
> How relevant is the piece to your own experience?

Then when you reread each selection, be aware of the techniques the writer uses:

> What examples back up the claims?
> What comparisons or contrasts does the writer use?
> What descriptive language does the writer employ?
> How does the writer use cause and effect?
> How does the writer try to keep your interest?

The selections that follow begin with contested issues in higher education: the role of SAT scores, the fairness and meaning of grades, whether college is an entitlement, and the application of the business model of management to education. The last selection is from the Web pages for an editing service, and they have a dual purpose: providing information about the service and persuading prospective clients to use it.

Academia's Overheated Competition

Andrew Delbanco

In a sense Andrew Delbanco is a specialist in evil, having studied it in American literature from the Puritans to the present. One result of that study is The Death of Satan: How Americans Have Lost the Sense of Evil *(1995). While terrorist attacks have reminded Americans about evil, no one can challenge the depth and breadth of Delbanco's scholarship. In addition to various edited editions of Lincoln, Melville, and Emerson, he has published* William Ellery Channing: An Essay on the Liberal Spirit in America *(1981), The* Puritan Ordeal *(1989), Why Our American Classics Matter Now (1997), The Real American Dream (1999), and Writing New England: An Anthology from the Puritans to the Present (2001). Delbanco directs undergraduate studies in English at Columbia University, where he holds the title of the Julian Clarence Levi Professor in the Humanities. A trustee of various literary and educational organizations, Delbanco was recently elected to the American Academy of Arts and Sciences.* Time *magazine has honored Delbanco as "America's Best Social Critic," a label based on his work related to the humanities and published in various magazines and newspapers, including the* New York Times*, where his essay on the evils of the SAT and early admissions appeared on March 16, 2001.*

Before You Read   Based on your experience with the test you took, what is your opinion of the SAT or ACT?

1   **I** teach at Columbia, where I have wonderful students. Every year I read that our incoming students have better grades and better SAT scores than in the past. But in the classroom, I do not find a commensurate increase in the number of students who are intellectually curious, adventurous or imbued with fruitful doubt. Many students are chronically stressed, grade-obsessed and, for fear of jeopardizing their ambitions, reluctant to explore subjects in which they doubt their proficiency.

2   When President Richard C. Atkinson of the University of California recently proposed that the SAT I aptitude test no longer be required for college admission, he triggered an overdue national debate. Not only does excessive SAT preparation detract from real learning, but it has allowed affluent students, who are able to hire tutors to prepare them, to increase their competitive advantage. But the affliction in American education goes deeper. Our best universities are waging a take-no-prisoners war against each other—boasting to the world not only about the rising SAT scores of their students, but about the soaring numbers of applicants who want to come to their campuses. And they are doing everything they can to keep those numbers climbing.

3   At work, I lament these developments. But at home, I give in to them. I do not forbid my daughter, now a high school junior, from seeking help to raise her test scores. How can I when so many of her peers are doing just that? The rules of the game have become inequitable; but it is the rare parent with means who, out of moral compunction, requires his or her child to sit out the game.

4   America's colleges, though they express dismay at what is happening, are feeding the frenzy. Perhaps the most insidious and least understood development is the stampede in recent years toward early applications. At public schools in some wealthy communities the vast majority of seniors reportedly now apply early to college. At Groton, a prestigious prep school, the figure exceeds 90 percent. I also gave in to this phenomenon; I did not discourage my son, now a college junior, from applying early to the college of his choice.

5   Why? Filing an early application, for which many colleges require a promise to enroll if admitted, is a way to beat the odds. At highly selective colleges, the chances of getting in from the regular pool may be 1 in 10 or even lower, while chances in the early cycle may be 1 in 3 or 4 or better. At some universities, roughly 50 percent of incoming students are now admitted early; at Columbia, the figure for last year was 46 percent.

6   Certainly, the quality of early applicants is high, but the surge in their numbers may also raise the percentage of students who are able to pay their own way. Early applicants tend to come from families sophisticated about the college admissions process and less likely to need financial aid.

7   We need to slow down the spiral of irrational competition in which both students and colleges are caught. America's top univer-

sities should stop measuring the quality of their applicants by how much they outdraw the competition. The percentage of students admitted by early application should be capped. Most of all, a concerted effort should be made by presidents and deans to repudiate the idea that getting into college is about learning how to win in an unregulated marketplace. How can we foster critical thinking about inequities in our society if students turn cynical about the system before they arrive in college?

8   The frantic competition among top universities is distorting the admissions process and threatens to undermine the meritocratic ideal that these universities proclaim.

Reading: Discussing the Text

1. Delbanco finds that higher education's reliance on early-admission policies and SAT scores discriminates against low-income students. How valid is his claim?
2. Delbanco implies that the "good" students are those "who are intellectually curious, adventurous or imbued with fruitful doubt" (paragraph 1). How apt do you find that definition?
3. The emphasis on test scores and on grades, Delbanco implies, can produce students who are "chronically stressed, grade-obsessed and, for fear of jeopardizing their ambitions, reluctant to explore subjects in which they doubt their proficiency" (paragraph 2). How accurate is that statement?
4. Delbanco uses logical, emotional, and ethical appeals in his essay. Which do you find the strongest and why?

Writing: Brief Response

1. Write a brief entry explaining how you prepared for the SAT or ACT and evaluate the effectiveness of that preparation.
2. Delbanco criticizes how SAT scores are used but encourages his children to obtain a high score. To what extent is he a hypocrite?

Writing: Extended Response

1. The SAT and ACT tests have undergone a lot of recent scrutiny. Choose the one you took and research it. How accurately does it measure aptitude? How fair is it? Write an essay assessing one aspect of the test, using your own experience and your research as evidence.

2. Delbanco's essay and various letters to the editor that responded to it imply several different views of higher education. Delbanco sees it as a "meritocracy" that "foster[s] critical thinking"; one respondent believes it is a "ministry," not an "industry"; and another promotes it as a place where students should "compete" for "learning" rather than "prestige." Use your own examples and your own research to define what students should be obtaining from higher education.

California Makes College an Entitlement

Abigail Thernstrom

In 1997, President Clinton chose Abigail Thernstrom as one of the three authors to participate in what he called his first "town meeting" on the subject of race, and if you looked at her record of publications and service, you would see why. She is a member of the Massachusetts State Board of Education and a commissioner on the United States Commission on Civil Rights, as well as a Senior Fellow at the Manhattan Institute in New York. Her articles in publications such as the New York Times, Wall Street Journal, New Republic, *and* New York Post *cover issues such as race, testing, and violence in the schools. She has written* Whose Votes Count? Affirmative Action and Minority Voting Rights *(1987), which won several awards, including the American Bar Association's Certificate of Merit. Together with her husband Stephan Thernstrom, a historian at Harvard, she has published* School Choice in Massachusetts *(1991),* America in Black and White: One Nation, Indivisible *(1997), and* Beyond the Color Line: New Perspectives on Race and Ethnicity *(2002). Their new project,* Getting the Answers Right: The Racial Gap in Academic Achievement and How to Close It, *will be out by the time this book is published. The title of that book sets the larger context for her essay, which appeared in the* New York Times *on September 26, 2000, and provoked a number of responses, which follow the essay.*

Before You Read   Use an unabridged dictionary to look up *entitlement.* As a citizen of the United States, what are you entitled to?

1   California's legislature has created a new educational entitlement: lots of kids will be going to college free of charge. Sound good? It isn't. It's likely to harm the great public universities of the state, as well as undermine California's drive for standards in elementary and secondary education. And it won't address the real problem: the inadequate academic preparation of too many high school graduates, particularly those from low-income families.

2   Here's how the program works. Students who maintain a B average in high school are guaranteed a grant (called a Cal Grant) sufficient to cover the costs of attending a state college or university. Even those who plan to go to private institutions like Stanford University will receive impressive help in the form of vouchers worth up to $9,708 a year. Children of the rich won't qualify, but students don't have to be poor. The annual income ceiling for a family of four is $64,100; for a family of six, it's $74,100.

3   There's help as well for students whose high school grades average only a C, but who are from families earning less than $33,700 a year. If they go to a community college, the state will provide roughly $1,500 for books and living expenses. If that student later transfers to a four-year school, he or she will receive full tuition plus the same stipend for additional expenses.

4   It's the "most ambitious financial aid program in America," Gov. Gray Davis has noted. All of California seems to be in a swoon. Every legislator voted for it. Newspapers are lavishing praise. College administrators are ecstatic. "This reinstates the California dream," one state college chancellor said.

5   Promoting mediocrity on behalf of middle-class kids would be a more accurate description. The program is advertised as helping the "needy," but community colleges are free, California state colleges only charge student fees, and even the elite University of California schools are inexpensive compared with private schools. Low-income students are already served by federal, state, private and university programs, and California offered no evidence that financial need was a barrier to college attendance. More low-income students will attend college only when they have the skills to do the work demanded.

6   The main beneficiaries of the new policy are thus likely to be middle-class students who have traditionally had limited access to scholarships. This will especially be the case if colleges use funds typically reserved for low-income applicants to help the financially unchallenged. The academically accomplished kid from a family earning, say, $85,000 a year may now have a good shot at financial aid.

7   A high school diploma is already close to an entitlement in the view of the American public—an unacknowledged problem in states threatening to deny diplomas to students unable to demonstrate competency in core subjects. As Ward Connerly, a University of California regent, has noted, California is now "moving toward the notion that college, too, is an entitlement instead of something you earned." What school will have the courage to turn down applicants upon whom funds have been bestowed with a promise of "access"? Admissions standards to the selective public colleges will inevitably drop; course requirements will become less rigorous.

8   Already inflated grades at high schools are also likely to rise. In the last decade, while national SAT scores have dropped, the percentage of students taking the test who reported an average in the A range has risen from 28 to 40 percent. Governor Davis claims that the Cal Grants will encourage students to work harder. It is more likely to force high schools to inflate grades further. If a B grade is worth up to $9,000, what "caring" teacher will give anything less?

9   In any case, a B is hardly a bang-up grade, and its meaning differs from one school to the next. California could have tied grants to test scores, but the idea of merit has become an elitist notion. Instead of playing entitlement games of one sort or another and throwing money where it's not needed, why not just educate the kids?

Responses to Thernstrom

To the Editor:

Re "California Makes College an Entitlement," by Abigail Thernstrom (Op-Ed, Sept. 26): If every student in California goes to college, where will the masons, carpenters, electricians, auto mechanics and plumbers of tomorrow come from—the East Coast?

SALVATORE J. CATANIA
Garden City, N.Y., Sept. 26, 2000

To the Editor:

Re "California Makes College an Entitlement" (Op-Ed, Sept. 26): Perhaps Abigail Thernstrom is correct in asserting that the main beneficiaries of California's new education entitlement are likely to be middle-class students.

But the entitlement benefits all Californians by encouraging the best students to stay in the state for college. This makes it more likely that they will remain after graduation, enhancing California's work force with their skilled labor and improving the tax base.

ANTHONY Q. FLETCHER
New York, Sept. 26, 2000

The writer is an adjunct assistant professor of political science at City College, CUNY.

To the Editor:

Abigail Thernstrom's argument against California's expansion of scholarships for needy students who perform well in high school (Op-Ed, Sept. 26) demonstrates elitism and defeatism.

She acknowledges that the program is based on merit, with its requirement of a B average, and on need, with its limits on family income. So the only way left to discredit the idea is to say, without offering evidence, that the program will lead to grade inflation and lower standards. The logical conclusion of her argument is that some students are not cut out for college and would never get there unless high schools and colleges lowered standards.

We in California reject that gloomy assessment of our children and our schools. Gov. Gray Davis and the Legislature have demonstrated their belief that society is better served when our children are better educated.

JOHN MOCKLER
Sacramento, Sept. 26, 2000

The writer is California's interim secretary for education.

Reading: Discussing the Text

1. Reread John Mockler's response to Thernstrom's argument. To what extent, if any, is he correct?
2. Thernstrom maintains that a "high school diploma is already close to an entitlement in the view of the American public" (paragraph 7). How accurate is that statement?
3. Thernstrom's first paragraph identifies "the real problem: the inadequate academic preparation of too many high school graduates, particularly those from low-income families." The California proposal identifies access to higher education as the solution. What other solutions are there?
4. California's plan ties grants to grades, not test scores because, according to Thernstrom, the "idea of merit has become an elitist notion" (paragraph 9). What evidence can you find to support that view?

Writing: Brief Response

1. Salvatore Catania's letter implies that "masons, carpenters, electricians, auto mechanics and plumbers" have no need of college. Explain how that is or is not so.
2. Anthony Fletcher's letter asserts that if students "stay in the state for college . . . it [is] likely that they will remain after graduation, enhancing California's work force with their skilled labor and improving the tax base." How sound is that logic?

Writing: Extended Response

1. Thernstrom maintains that the program passed by the California legislature linking financial aid for higher education to a B average in high school will "force high schools to inflate grades further" (paragraph 8) by pressuring teachers to give higher grades. While much has been written about the pressure on college professors, not much has been written about high school teachers. Visit the high school you graduated from and interview some of your former teachers. To what extent are they pressured to give higher grades and why? Analyze those causes in an essay.
2. Thernstrom is correct in saying that "low-income students are already served [financially] by federal, state, private and university programs" (paragraph 5). Explore the subject of federal financial aid to students to determine just how much of a boon it is. What is the size of the average loan? How many years would it take to pay it off? At what cost? What is the default rate? The penalties for default? Your research will provide the evidence for your evaluation of the programs.

Grade Inflation Not Only About Harvard

Rosemary Roberts

As a columnist whose work appears twice a week in North Carolina's Greensboro News & Record, *Rosemary Roberts says she "lead[s] a low-tech life in a high-tech world," preferring a "creaky word processor of ancient vintage" to a modern PC and ignoring e-mail to the point of exceeding the size of the mailbox. But being low-tech doesn't keep Rosemary Roberts from covering a wide variety of subjects. Her recent columns take up issues ranging from the rightness of the United States' foreign policy in China and the Middle East to the reasons North Carolina should have a lottery. General subjects such as rudeness and the names of baseball teams fall somewhere in between. Many of her columns are written in response to what she has read in the news, and the one that follows comes after the issue of grade inflation at Harvard University hit the headlines. Education is a topic in which Roberts has a particular interest, as shown in her opinion pieces on the dearly departed practice of diagramming sentences and on the importance of teaching at the undergraduate level. The column reprinted here was published in the* Greensboro News & Record *on January 16, 2002.*

Before You Read   How would you define grade inflation?

1   Grade inflation is so rampant in America's public primary schools and secondary schools that some seniors can't read their diplomas. Whether that statement is true or false (and I suspect that it stretches the truth), grade inflation is a hot topic in public schools.

2   But now Harvard University, perhaps the nation's premier private institution of higher learning, has come under fire for inflating grades in wholesale numbers.

3   Last year nearly half the grades of Harvard students (48.5 percent) were A's and A−'s. Bad grades—D's and F's—accounted for fewer than 6 percent of Harvard grades. And last June a soaring 91 percent of Harvard seniors graduated with honors—an academic distinction based primarily on a student's grades. Rival universities

are chortling at Harvard because no other institution came close to Harvard's 91 percent honor roll.

4   So the question for Harvard comes down to this: Is it brains or grade inflation? Admission to Harvard is stringent, and its students are among the nation's brightest. But after they arrive at Harvard, are they all "A" students? Highly doubtful. One Harvard undergraduate told The New York Times: "I know I can do minimal work in some classes and get good grades."

5   Stung by criticism and derision from academe, Harvard is now encouraging professors to grade harder while a blue-ribbon panel studies grade inflation.

6   Harvard is not the only offender. Last summer I visited Stanford University for a class reunion of journalists who were Knight Fellows, a year-long intellectual enrichment program for professional journalists.

7   As I sentimentally ambled down the hall of my favorite building, I spotted a small stack of exam blue books on a table. Students had neglected to claim them before leaving campus for the summer. Stanford, like Harvard, attracts very bright undergraduates and is often called "the Ivy League university of the West."

8   Curious, I peeked at five or six of the exams. All students received A's or A–'s. But unlike Harvard's senior honor roll of 91 percent last year, Stanford's rate was only 20 percent (despite the A's in those exam books).

9   Though Harvard's deluge of A's and honors may be an extreme case, experts say grade inflation in higher education is a nationwide problem that started in the permissive 1960s and '70s and grew with ensuing decades.

10   Reasons for grade inflation, experts say, are varied. Some professors give high grades to encourage students. Some professors worry about student evaluations, fearful of administrative scrutiny if they grade hard and get negative student evaluations. Some professors give high grades to avoid the hassles of being challenged by students. Many college students nowadays regard a C as comparable to a D or F and some protest vehemently if their grade is lower than expected. (In my day, I was glad to get that C in college zoology and even a "D" in trigonometry, but that was decades ago.)

11   Another reason for grade inflation is a professor's difficulty in deciding what separates good work (B+) from superior work (A). In math, there is either a right or wrong answer, but in humanities classes—where most of the A's were dispensed at Harvard—the

defining line between good and superior is based on a professor's subjective opinion. In the interest of full disclosure, I should mention that I teach a journalism class at a local university and know there is a fine line between good papers and superior papers. But what if there are no "superior" papers? Should "good" papers become the "A" standard? I will confess to having erred, in some cases, on the side of generosity.

12   Harvard's much-publicized and embarrassing grade inflation problem has done higher education an enormous favor. Harvard is a bellwether, and scrutiny of Harvard's grade inflation compels all college and universities to scrutinize themselves. To do otherwise devalues a college diploma.

Reading: Discussing the Text

1. In what ways does the issue of grade inflation at Harvard contribute to Roberts' main point?
2. What does Roberts' personal experience add to the essay? To her main point?
3. In paragraphs 10 and 11, Roberts provides several reasons for inflated grades. Which strikes you as the most important and why?
4. Reread paragraph 8 in which Roberts presents some evidence from Stanford University. How solid is that evidence?

Writing: Brief Response

1. If you were the president of Harvard University, how would you explain the 91 percent honor roll?
2. At some point, more likely than not, you have received a higher grade than you deserved. Use your notebook to explain the situation and how you responded to it.

Writing: Extended Response

1. How real is the issue of grade inflation on your campus? To find out, track down several years of grade patterns so that you can compare them over a 10-year span or so. Also interview some members of the administration so that you can explore the possible reasons behind any changes you discover. Then write a report or an essay in which you explain whether grade inflation is a problem and, if so, its possible causes.
2. Roberts raises the question of subjective grading in humanities courses, stating that the "defining line between good and superior is based on a professor's subjective opinion" (paragraph 11). Explore the validity of that

opinion by interviewing several professors. The results of your interviews will provide you with the evidence you need to support or refute Roberts.

Angels on a Pin

Alexander Calandra

The essay that follows has a long history. In its present form, it appeared in Alexander Calandra's textbook The Teaching of Elementary Science and Mathematics *(1961) at a time when Calandra was teaching at Washington University. Though the title of the textbook suggests Calandra was teaching mathematics, in 1979 he received the Millikan Medal for "notable and creative contributions to the teaching of physics." The field of physics has changed a great deal since then, and Calandra is now Professor Emeritus at Washington University, but the problems in testing remain the same. How real Calandra's narrative may be is a matter of speculation, for it has passed into the eerie world of "urban legends," more specifically the realm of academic legends (for more about that subject, consult the Web site <www.urbanlegends.com>). The immediate context for the narrative, however, is factual. When "Angels on a Pin" was first published in the* Saturday Review *in 1968, the United States was in the middle of a push to surpass Russia's strides in scientific technology, strides that led to Sputnik, the first artificial earth satellite. Sputnik was launched in 1957. Now, close to 50 years later, we no longer have "Sputnik-panicked classrooms," but we are still trying to come to terms with our educational system.*

Before You Read   What part have rote learning and regurgitating information played in your education?

1   Some time ago, I received a call from a colleague who asked if I would be the referee on the grading of an examination question. He was about to give a student a zero for his answer to a physics

question, while the student claimed he should receive a perfect score and would if the system were not set up against the student. The instructor and the student agreed to submit this to an impartial arbiter, and I was selected.

2   I went to my colleague's office and read the examination question: "Show how it is possible to determine the height of a tall building with the aid of a barometer."

3   The student had answered: "Take the barometer to the top of the building, attach a long rope to it, lower the barometer to the street, and then bring it up, measuring the length of the rope. The length of the rope is the height of the building."

4   I pointed out that the student really had a strong case for full credit, since he had answered the question completely and correctly. On the other hand, if full credit were given, it could well contribute to a high grade for the student in his physics course. A high grade is supposed to certify competence in physics, but the answer did not confirm this. I suggested that the student have another try at answering the question. I was not surprised that my colleague agreed, but I was surprised that the student did.

5   I gave the student six minutes to answer the question, with the warning that his answer should show some knowledge of physics. At the end of five minutes, he had not written anything. I asked if he wished to give up, but he said no. He had many answers to this problem; he was just thinking of the best one. I excused myself for interrupting him, and asked him to please go on. In the next minute, he dashed off his answer which read:

6   "Take the barometer to the top of the building and lean over the edge of the roof. Drop the barometer, timing its fall with a stopwatch. Then, using the formula $S = 1/2at^2$, calculate the height of the building."

7   At this point, I asked my colleague if *he* would give up. He conceded, and I gave the student almost full credit.

8   In leaving my colleague's office, I recalled that the student had said he had other answers to the problem, so I asked him what they were. "Oh, yes," said the student. "There are many ways of getting the height of a tall building with the aid of a barometer. For example, you could take the barometer out on a sunny day and measure the height of the barometer, the length of its shadow, and the length of the shadow of the building, and by the use of a simple proportion, determine the height of the building."

9   "Fine," I said, "And the others?"

10   "Yes," said the student. "There is a very basic measurement method that you will like. In this method, you take the barometer and begin to walk up the stairs. As you climb the stairs, you mark off the length of the barometer along the wall. You then count the number of marks, and this will give you the height of the building in barometer units. A very direct method.

11   "Of course, if you want a more sophisticated method, you can tie the barometer to the end of a string, swing it as a pendulum, and determine the value of 'g' at the street level and at the top of the building. From the difference between the two values of 'g,' the height of the building can, in principle, be calculated."

12   Finally he concluded, there are many other ways of solving the problem. "Probably the best," he said, "is to take the barometer to the basement and knock on the superintendent's door. When the superintendent answers, you speak to him as follows: 'Mr. Superintendent, here I have a fine barometer. If you will tell me the height of this building. I will give you this barometer."

13   At this point, I asked the student if he really did not know the conventional answer to this question. He admitted that he did, but said that he was fed up with high school and college instructors trying to teach him how to think, to use the "scientific method," and to explore the deep inner logic of the subject in a pedantic way, as is often done in the new mathematics, rather than teaching him the structure of the subject. With this in mind, he decided to revive scholasticism as an academic lark to challenge the Sputnik-panicked classrooms of America.

Reading: Discussing the Text

1. Given that Calandra's essay is about grades, testing, and education in general, which do you find is his main subject? What sentences in the text support your claim?

2. What statement is the author making about education? What evidence supports your idea?

3. What do you interpret as the purpose of the essay? Does Calandra intend it to inform? To entertain? To persuade?

4. In every example the student gives, the barometer plays a role that belies its most important function. How do these roles subvert the instructor's questions?

1. Reread the essay, paying particular attention to the role of the narrator. Use your notebook to explain whose side he is on.
2. Look up the term *scholasticism*. How does Calandra's choice of title relate to his thesis?

1. Choose a test that you took recently and analyze it in terms of what it tests, whether that should be tested, and what it implies about learning. You can append a copy of the test, course and instructor omitted, as evidence, but use examples from it and from the syllabus to back up your points.
2. Multiple choice tests play a role in higher education, but that role varies from class to class and institution to institution. Research the subject and then use your findings, together with your own experience, to evaluate the effectiveness of this type of testing.

A Student Is Not an Input

Michele Tolela Myers

Michele Tolela Myers has the right job to implement what she believes in—the individuality of students—as she is now the president of Sarah Lawrence College. And she has the right background: a diplôme in political science and economics from the University of Paris, an MA and PhD in communication studies from the University of Denver, and an MA in clinical psychology from Trinity University (Texas). In addition to consulting with various business and educational groups, she has taught sociology and communication as they relate to management, negotiation, and behavior. Before her appointment at Sarah Lawrence, she was dean of undergraduate education at Bryn Mawr College and then president of Denison University. She is a past chair of the American Council on Education, a past director of the National Association of Independent Colleges and Universities and has served on the President's Commission of the National Collegiate Athletic

Association. Her work has been honored with the Knight Foundation Award for Presidential Leadership and by honorary degrees from the University of Denver, Denison University, and Wittenberg University. Together with Gail E. Myers, she has written Communication for the Urban Professional *(no date),* Communicating When We Speak *(1978),* Managing by Communication *(1982), and* The Dynamics of Human Communication *(1988). The argument she communicates here was published in the* New York Times *on March 26, 2001.*

Before You Read   To what extent does your college or university think of you as a number? As a consumer?

1   Attend a conference of higher education leaders these days, and you will hear a lot of talk about things like brand value, markets, image and pricing strategy. In the new lingua franca of higher education, students are "consumers of our product" in one conversation or presentation and "inputs"—a part of what we sell—in the next.

2   It's easy enough to see why academia has gotten caught up in this kind of talk. We borrow the language of business because we are forced to operate like businesses. Higher education has become more and more expensive at the same time it has become increasingly necessary. As we look for ways to operate efficiently and make the most of our assets, we begin learning about outsourcing, for-profit ventures, the buying and selling of intellectual property.

3   And as the public is well aware, colleges and universities are now in conscious and deliberate competition with one another. We "bid for student talent," as the new language would put it, because we know that "star value" in the student body affects the "brand value" of the university's name: its prestige, its rankings, its desirability, and ultimately its wealth and its ability to provide more "value per dollar" to its "customers."

4   But there is something troubling about the ease with which these new words roll off our tongues. I pay attention to words and how we speak about things because language tells us a good deal about how we think and feel, and ultimately, how we act.

5   What are the implications of thinking of a college or university as a brand? We know that some people will pay anything for prestige brand names. And as a result, some children are under unhealthy pressure from the time their parents begin panicking about which

nursery school they will go to. Yet, prestige sells, prestige provides value; we know it, parents and students know it. We at the colleges scramble to get up on that ladder.

6   A business professor told a group of us at one recent conference that to run a successful organization you had better make decisions on the basis of being "best in the world," and if you couldn't be best in the world in something, then you outsourced the function or got rid of the unit that didn't measure up. Have we really come to believe that we can only measure ourselves in relation to others, and that value and goodness are only measured against something outside the self? Do we really want to teach our children that life is all about beating the competition?

7   As we in the academy begin to use business-speak fluently, we become accustomed to thinking in commercialized terms about education. We talk no longer as public intellectuals, but as entrepreneurs. And we thus encourage instead of fight the disturbing trend that makes education a consumer good rather than a public good. If we think this way, our decisions will be driven, at least in part, by consumers' tastes. Are we ready to think that we should only teach what students want or be driven out of business?

8   Physics is hard, it is costly, it is undersubscribed. Should it be taught only in engineering schools? I don't think so. Should we not teach math because everyone can get a cheap calculator? Should we stop teaching foreign languages because English has become the international language? And what about the arts, literature, philosophy? Many might think them impractical.

9   I think we have a responsibility to insist that education is more than learning job skills, that it is also the bedrock of a democracy. I think we must be very careful that in the race to become wealthier, more prestigious, and to be ranked Number One, we don't lose sight of the real purpose of education, which is to make people free—to give them the grounding they need to think for themselves and participate as intelligent members of a free society. Obsolete or naive? I surely hope not.

Reading: Discussing the Text

1. To what extent is Myers opposed to "business-speak" and why?
2. Myers maintains "higher education has become more and more expensive at the same time it has become increasingly necessary" (paragraph

2). While there's no doubt about the increased cost, to what extent has a college degree become "necessary"?

3. Myers poses a rhetorical question: "Do we really want to teach our children that life is all about beating the competition?" She implies a "no" answer, but reread paragraph 6 to determine the extent to which Myers has stated the question fairly. Is the question the "correct" one?

4. In her last paragraph, Myers sets out what she believes to be the purpose of higher education. To what extent do you agree or disagree with her?

Writing: Brief Response

1. To what extent have you been treated as "input"? Explain.

2. Does "star value" (see paragraph 3) operate on your campus? If so, how? If not, why not?

Writing: Extended Response

1. Examine what your institution has as general degree requirements. Do some research and interview some administrators to determine their purpose. Based on your evidence, how effective are they?

2. To what extent does your institution market itself? To find out, examine all the promotional materials it puts out as well as any other possible marketing source, such as the catalogue and Web site. Based on what you discover, to what degree is your institution commercializing education? Analyze the situation and your response in an essay.

EssayEdge.com

EssayEdge.com was founded in 1997 as a Web-based editorial service designed to help students write successful letters of application for college admission or post-graduate programs in business, law, medicine, or for graduate school. According to the company's "Top 10 Reasons to Use EssayEdge Editors," and unlike some similar Web businesses, EssayEdge works with its clients' original prose, not only correcting errors but providing "a critique detailing new paragraphs to write and new ideas to pursue." Boasting "some of the finest editors in the world," EssayEdge claims its editors "have professional editing or admissions office experience, and hold graduate business, law, medical, and undergraduate degrees from Harvard University." You'll find out more from what follows—the site's home page and its "Top 10 Reasons to Use EssayEdge Editors."

Before You Read   What problems did you encounter with your college application, and how did you solve them?

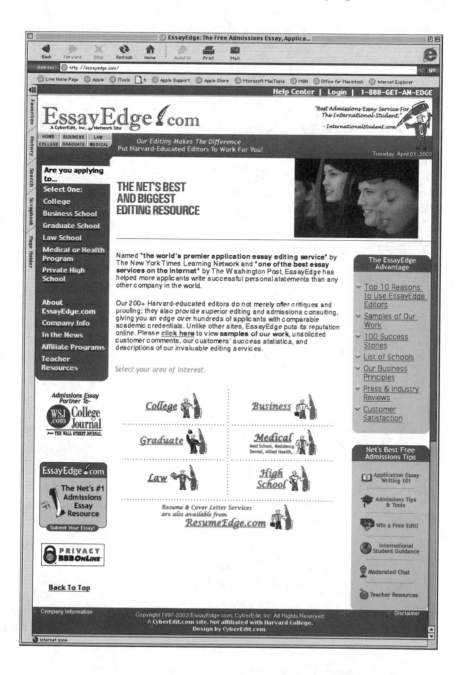

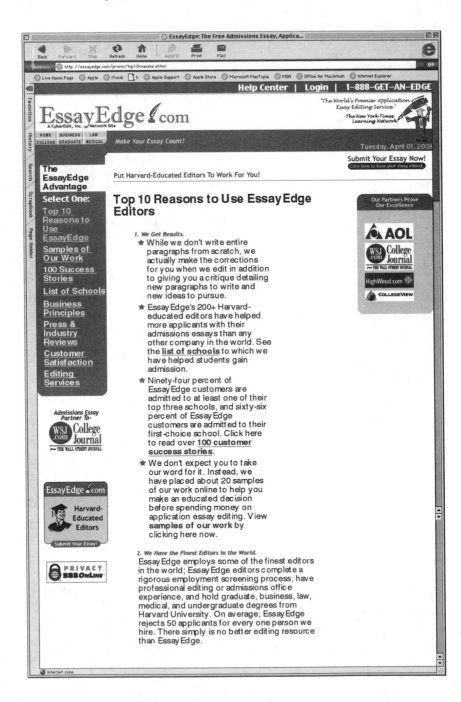

Help Center | Login | 1–888–GET–AN–EDGE

EssayEdge /com
A CyberEdit, Inc. o/ Network Site

"The World's Premier Application Essay Editing Service." -The New York Times Learning Network

HOME BUSINESS LAW
COLLEGE GRADUATE MEDICAL   *Make Your Essay Count!*

Tuesday, April 01, 2003

Submit Your Essay Now!
Click here to have your essay edited.

The EssayEdge Advantage

Put Harvard-Educated Editors To Work For You!

Select One:
Top 10 Reasons to Use EssayEdge
Samples of Our Work
100 Success Stories
List of Schools
Business Principles
Press & Industry Reviews
Customer Satisfaction
Editing Services

Admissions Essay Partner To-
WSJ.com College Journal
THE WALL STREET JOURNAL

EssayEdge /com
Harvard-Educated Editors
Submit Your Essay!

PRIVACY
BBBOnLine

Our Partners Prove Our Excellence
AOL
WSJ.com College Journal — THE WALL STREET JOURNAL
HighWired.com
COLLEGEVIEW

Top 10 Reasons to Use EssayEdge Editors

1. We Get Results.

★ While we don't write entire paragraphs from scratch, we actually make the corrections for you when we edit in addition to giving you a critique detailing new paragraphs to write and new ideas to pursue.

★ EssayEdge's 200+ Harvard-educated editors have helped more applicants with their admissions essays than any other company in the world. See the **list of schools** to which we have helped students gain admission.

★ Ninety-four percent of EssayEdge customers are admitted to at least one of their top three schools, and sixty-six percent of EssayEdge customers are admitted to their first-choice school. Click here to read over **100 customer success stories**.

★ We don't expect you to take our word for it. Instead, we have placed about 20 samples of our work online to help you make an educated decision before spending money on application essay editing. View **samples of our work** by clicking here now.

2. We Have the Finest Editors in the World.
EssayEdge employs some of the finest editors in the world; EssayEdge editors complete a rigorous employment screening process, have professional editing or admissions office experience, and hold graduate, business, law, medical, and undergraduate degrees from Harvard University. On average, EssayEdge rejects 50 applicants for every one person we hire. There simply is no better editing resource than EssayEdge.

Internet zone

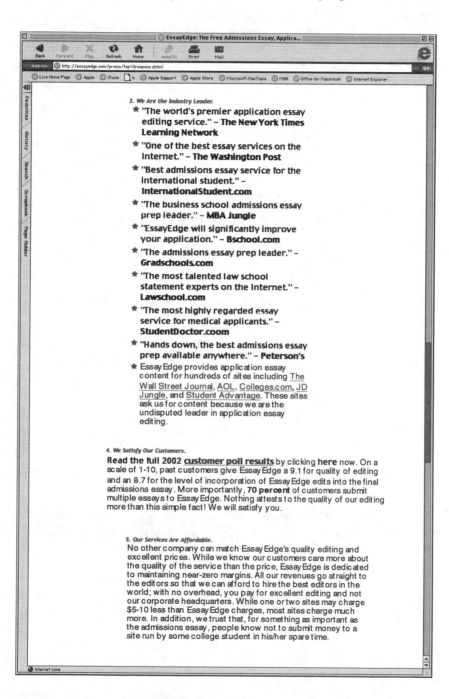

3. We Are the Industry Leader.

★ "The world's premier application essay editing service." – **The New York Times Learning Network**

★ "One of the best essay services on the Internet." – **The Washington Post**

★ "Best admissions essay service for the international student." – **InternationalStudent.com**

★ "The business school admissions essay prep leader." – **MBA Jungle**

★ "EssayEdge will significantly improve your application." – **Bschool.com**

★ "The admissions essay prep leader." – **Gradschools.com**

★ "The most talented law school statement experts on the Internet." – **Lawschool.com**

★ "The most highly regarded essay service for medical applicants." – **StudentDoctor.coom**

★ "Hands down, the best admissions essay prep available anywhere." – **Peterson's**

★ EssayEdge provides application essay content for hundreds of sites including The Wall Street Journal, AOL, Colleges.com, JD Jungle, and Student Advantage. These sites ask us for content because we are the undisputed leader in application essay editing.

4. We Satisfy Our Customers.

Read the full 2002 customer poll results by clicking **here** now. On a scale of 1-10, past customers give EssayEdge a 9.1 for quality of editing and an 8.7 for the level of incorporation of EssayEdge edits into the final admissions essay. More importantly, **70 percent** of customers submit multiple essays to EssayEdge. Nothing attests to the quality of our editing more than this simple fact! We will satisfy you.

5. Our Services Are Affordable.

No other company can match EssayEdge's quality editing and excellent prices. While we know our customers care more about the quality of the service than the price, EssayEdge is dedicated to maintaining near-zero margins. All our revenues go straight to the editors so that we can afford to hire the best editors in the world; with no overhead, you pay for excellent editing and not our corporate headquarters. While one or two sites may charge $5-10 less than EssayEdge charges, most sites charge much more. In addition, we trust that, for something as important as the admissions essay, people know not to submit money to a site run by some college student in his/her spare time.

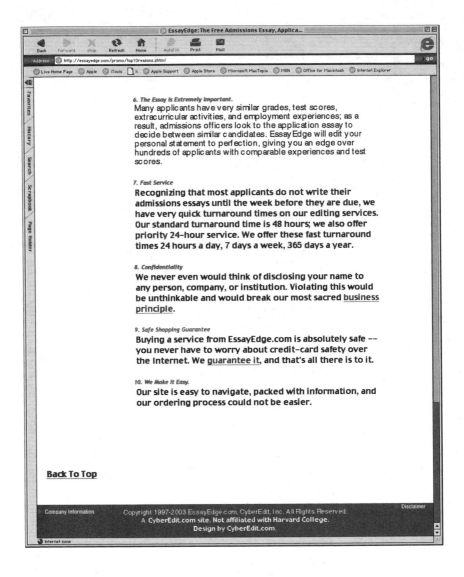

6. The Essay Is Extremely Important.

Many applicants have very similar grades, test scores, extracurricular activities, and employment experiences; as a result, admissions officers look to the application essay to decide between similar candidates. EssayEdge will edit your personal statement to perfection, giving you an edge over hundreds of applicants with comparable experiences and test scores.

7. Fast Service

Recognizing that most applicants do not write their admissions essays until the week before they are due, we have very quick turnaround times on our editing services. Our standard turnaround time is 48 hours; we also offer priority 24-hour service. We offer these fast turnaround times 24 hours a day, 7 days a week, 365 days a year.

8. Confidentiality

We never even would think of disclosing your name to any person, company, or institution. Violating this would be unthinkable and would break our most sacred business principle.

9. Safe Shopping Guarantee

Buying a service from EssayEdge.com is absolutely safe -- you never have to worry about credit-card safety over the Internet. We guarantee it, and that's all there is to it.

10. We Make It Easy.

Our site is easy to navigate, packed with information, and our ordering process could not be easier.

Back To Top

Company Information   Copyright 1997-2003 EssayEdge.com, CyberEdit, Inc. All Rights Reserved.   Disclaimer
A CyberEdit.com site. Not affiliated with Harvard College.
Design by CyberEdit.com.

Reading: Discussing the Text

1. The home page is designed to interest you and then direct you to various sources of information. How well does it succeed?
2. The "Top 10 Reasons to Use EssayEdge Editors" are intended to persuade the reader to become a client. How effective is it?
3. Based upon the Web pages you've read, explain why you would or would not use EssayEdge.
4. The whole idea of editing a person's admission application raises the question of ethics. How ethical is it?

Writing: Brief Response

1. Based on the information in the Web pages, explain why you would or would not use the service.
2. Does what's presented make you want to know more? If so, what? If not, why?

Writing: Extended Response

1. The lines between original, edited, and ghostwritten work can be fine ones. Write an essay in which you define each type, distinguishing among them in terms of what is ethical. Your purpose may be informative or argumentative, but if it's informative, make sure your thesis is an assertion and not a fact.
2. The Internet abounds with sites offering student papers for sale or free, though they usually have disclaimers about submitting those papers as your own work. Use a search engine to explore the number of sites available, and then choose two or three to investigate. What do they offer? How legitimate are they? How do they deal with the ethical issues? Your essay could explore one of these questions or one of your own.

COMPARING THE SELECTIONS

1. Both Alexander Calandra and Rosemary Roberts question the meaning of grades. Roberts explores the causes and effects of grade inflation, and Calandra investigates the legitimacy of an examination. What should grades measure, and what should they be based on? Use examples from the two essays and your own experience to support your view.

2. Michele Tolela Myers argues that applying the business model to higher education adversely affects learning, reducing students to "products" and education to a numbers game. Andrew Delbanco decries not only a different numbers game—competition based on SAT scores and early admissions—but also one that has a negative effect on education. Consider the situation at your institution. To what extent, if any, are you a number? To what extent, if any, does your institution play a numbers game? Back up your claims with references from the essays as well as your own experience.

3. Abigail Thernstrom maintains that the California legislature's proposal that links tuition and fees to grades will lead to grade inflation in the high schools, while Rosemary Roberts examines grade inflation on college campuses. How real is the problem of grade inflation at your institution? Use Thernstrom's and Roberts' claims and analyses to explore the question.

4. Reread the Delbanco and Myers essays paying particular attention to the kinds of qualities that their authors value, qualities that are difficult (if not impossible) to measure objectively. Then reexamine the information on EssayEdge's Web pages (consult more pages at that site if you wish). Use what you glean from the Delbanco and Myers essays to examine the legitimacy of what EssayEdge has to offer.

Language

Introduction

In a sense, all language is metaphor in that a word always stands for a thing and is not the thing itself. Sometimes a word comes close. The term used for words that approximate what they stand for is *onomatopoeia,* words such as *buzz* for the sound of a bumble bee or *hum* for the noise a person might make when puzzled. But switch languages, and the sounds change. Our English *bow-wow* is the French *ouah ouah* and the Russian *gav-gav* <http//www.georgetown.edu/cball/animals>. While such different sounds show that all languages are inextricably bound to their cultures, nowhere is that more evident than with words that stand for things, for such words are laden with multiple meanings.

To appreciate those meanings and the power of language, it's helpful to distinguish between the literal, connotative, and metaphorical senses of words. Think, for example, of *house, home,* and *sanctuary. House* is neutral, neither good nor bad unless another word is tacked on to it, as in *safe house* or *doghouse.* Look up *house* in a dictionary and you'll find its literal or denotative sense, nothing that has much appeal to the emotions. *Home,* however, carries with it notions of warmth and comfort, connotations that go beyond the literal meaning. *Sanctuary* takes you to the metaphorical level. You not only have all the meanings associated with safety and shelter but also those associated with religion—a holy place, a haven. All three words, however, can describe the same building.

Oral language can add another layer of confusion. A particular word can reveal a person's region, level of education, emotional state, and even age. Your *refrigerator* may be your grandmother's *icebox,* and if she says *frying pan* instead of *skillet,* she's probably from the South. Think, too, of *bad,* which may mean *good* or *bad* depending on the intonation. Given how slippery words can be, definitions are crucial, for much, as President Clinton once said, can "depend on what the definition of *is* is."

If you've analyzed a poem or short story in English classes, you're probably used to writing about language. You would have relied heavily on examples and explored the meanings and effects of certain words. Thinking about examples, definitions, and causal relationships will help you write about language, and the selections that follow should give you some ideas for topics.

As you read the prose that follows, read each piece first for its basic meaning:

> What aspect of language is the author writing about?
> What is the author's opinion about that subject?
> How accurate is the writer's analysis of the subject?
> What do you think the author wants you to do, understand, think, believe?
> How relevant is the piece to your own experience?

Then when you reread each selection, be aware of the techniques the writer uses:

> What examples does the writer use?
> What comparisons or contrasts does the writer use?
> What causal relationships does the writer analyze?
> What definitions does the writer use?
> How does the writer try to keep your interest?

Given the strong tie between language and culture, it's not surprising that the subject of language appeals to writers who are members of minority groups. In the selections in this chapter, for instance, four writers examine the link between language and culture—Maya Angelou, William Raspberry, Richard Estrada, and Louise Erdrich. Two additional selections address certain uses of language that can blunt, soften, or obscure meaning: Bryan A. Garner's entry on jargon for his *Dictionary of Modern American Usage* (1998) and Jonathan Yardley's column on euphemisms for plagiarism for the *Washington Post*.

In All Ways a Woman

Maya Angelou

If you happened to watch the inauguration of President William Jefferson Clinton on January 20, 1993, you heard Maya Angelou read her poem "On the Pulse of Morning." If not, you may know her from having read the first volume of her autobiography, I Know Why the Caged Bird Sings *(1969), when you were in high school. Maya Angelou has long been a celebrated writer and speaker. She is as apt to begin a speaking engagement with an a cappella blues song as with a narrative from her childhood. As an adult, she became San Francisco's first black streetcar conductor, studied dance in New York, sang in New York and San Francisco nightclubs, edited the* Arab Observer *in Cairo, taught music and dance in Ghana, and studied film in Sweden. Author of a large body of poetry, essays, children's books, and memoirs, Angelou is currently Reynolds Professor in the English Department at Wake Forest University. Her published poetry has been collected in* The Complete Collected Poems of Maya Angelou *(1994), and she has continued her autobiography in* Gather Together in My Name *(1974),* Singin' and Gettin' Merry Like Christmas *(1976),* The Heart of a Woman *(1981),* All God's Children Need Traveling Shoes *(1986), and* A Song Flung Up to Heaven *(2002). The essay that follows comes from* Wouldn't Take Nothing for My Journey Now *(1993), a collection dedicated to her good friend Oprah Winfrey.*

Before You Read   What images do you associate with the word *woman?*

1   In my young years I took pride in the fact that luck was called a lady. In fact, there were so few public acknowledgments of the female presence that I felt personally honored whenever nature and large ships were referred to as feminine. But as I matured, I began to resent being considered a sister to a changeling as fickle as luck, as aloof as an ocean, and as frivolous as nature.

2   The phrase "A woman always has the right to change her mind" played so aptly into the negative image of the female that I made myself a victim to an unwavering decision. Even if I made an inane and stupid choice, I stuck by it rather than "be like a woman and change my mind."

3   Being a woman is hard work. Not without joy and even ecstasy, but still relentless, unending work. Becoming an old female may require only being born with certain genitalia, inheriting long-living genes and the fortune not to be run over by an out-of-control truck, but to become and remain a woman command the existence and employment of genius.

4   The woman who survives intact and happy must be at once tender and tough. She must have convinced herself, or be in the unending process of convincing herself, that she, her values, and her choices are important. In a time and world where males hold sway and control, the pressure upon women to yield their rights-of-way is tremendous. And it is under those very circumstances that the woman's toughness must be in evidence.

5   She must resist considering herself a lesser version of her male counterpart. She is not a sculptress, poetess, authoress, Jewess, Negress, or even (now rare) in university parlance a rectoress. If she is the thing, then for her own sense of self and for the education of the ill-informed she must insist with rectitude in being the thing and in being called the thing.

6   A rose by any other name may smell as sweet, but a woman called by a devaluing name will only be weakened by the misnomer.

7   She will need to prize her tenderness and be able to display it at appropriate times in order to prevent toughness from gaining total authority and to avoid becoming a mirror image of those men who value power above life, and control over love.

8   It is imperative that a woman keep her sense of humor intact and at the ready. She must see, even if only in secret, that she is the funniest, looniest woman in her world, which she should also see as being the most absurd world of all times.

9   It has been said that laughter is therapeutic and amiability lengthens the life span.

10   Women should be tough, tender, laugh as much as possible, and live long lives. The struggle for equality continues unabated, and the woman warrior who is armed with wit and courage will be among the first to celebrate victory.

Reading: Discussing the Text

1. Explain the ways in which the title fits the essay's thesis and content.
2. What reasons can you find for Angelou's use of sayings and associations in paragraphs 1 and 2?

3. To what extent, if any, does Angelou make use of race in the essay? What purpose does it (or the lack of it) serve?
4. Although the essay is directed at readers of both genders, it focuses almost exclusively on women. To what extent does that focus limit the essay? What's in it for a man?

Writing: Brief Response

1. Use your notebook to explore what Angelou means by *tender*. What examples in your reading fit that definition?
2. If you prefer, explore what Angelou means by *tough*. Again, illustrate your points with examples from your reading.

Writing: Extended Response

1. Angelou points out the ways in which language can limit a person. Someone over 65, for instance, can be referred to as a senior citizen, golden ager, geezer, and the like. Choose an age group and consider the words, sayings, or metaphors associated with an individual in that group. Find all the examples you can and then use them as evidence to support your position as to whether the language limits the individual.
2. Look through a newspaper or magazine to find an article about a hard-fought game or hotly contested issue. Read it carefully, paying particular attention to the language used to describe the event or topic. What verbs are used? What comparisons? Write an essay in which you analyze how the language fits the topic.

The Handicap of Definition

William Raspberry

William Raspberry left the small and segregated town in Mississippi where he grew up to take a summer job with the Indianapolis Reporter, *moving on in 1962 to the* Washington Post. *Although he now teaches at Duke University, where he is the Knight Chair in Communications and Journalism, he is better known as a writer for the* Washington Post *and the author of a syndicated column that runs in more than 200 newspapers. His commentary on issues such as rap music, crime, and AIDS earned him a Pulitzer Prize in 1994. That same year, he received the Lifetime Achievement Award from the National Association of Black Journalists, and in 1997, Washington magazine named him "one of the top 50 most influential journalists in the national press corps." His book* Looking Backward at Us *was published in 1991. In the essay that follows, he writes about the terms* black *and* white, *words that have connotations we don't often think about. Raspberry shows us that if we stop to think about* black, *we'll see that it has so narrow a definition that it is "one of the heaviest burdens black Americans—and black children in particular—have to bear." Not much has changed since 1982, when this essay first appeared in Raspberry's syndicated column.*

Before You Read   What do you associate with the color *black*? With *white*?

1   I know all about bad schools, mean politicians, economic deprivation and racism. Still, it occurs to me that one of the heaviest burdens black Americans—and black children in particular—have to bear is the handicap of definition: the question of what it means to be black.

2   Let me explain quickly what I mean. If a basketball fan says that the Boston Celtics' Larry Bird plays "black," the fan intends it—and Bird probably accepts it—as a compliment. Tell pop singer Tom Jones he moves "black" and he might grin in appreciation. Say to Teena Marie or The Average White Band that they sound "black" and they'll thank you.

3   But name one pursuit, aside from athletics, entertainment or sexual performance in which a white practitioner will feel complimented to be told he does it "black." Tell a white broadcaster he talks "black," and he'll sign up for diction lessons. Tell a white reporter he writes "black" and he'll take a writing course. Tell a white lawyer he reasons "black" and he might sue you for slander.

4   What we have here is a tragically limited definition of blackness, and it isn't only white people who buy it.

5   Think of all the ways black children can put one another down with charges of "whiteness." For many of these children, hard study and hard work are "white." Trying to please a teacher might be criticized as acting "white." Speaking correct English is "white."

Scrimping today in the interest of tomorrow's goals is "white." Educational toys and games are "white."

6   An incredible array of habits and attitudes that are conducive to success in business, in academia, in the nonentertainment professions are likely to be thought of as somehow "white." Even economic success, unless it involves such "black" undertakings as numbers banking, is defined as "white."

7   And the results are devastating. I wouldn't deny that blacks often are better entertainers and athletes. My point is the harm that comes from too narrow a definition of what is black.

8   One reason black youngsters tend to do better at basketball, for instance, is that they assume they can learn to do it well, and so they practice constantly to prove themselves right.

9   Wouldn't it be wonderful if we could infect black children with the notion that excellence in math is "black" rather than white, or possibly Chinese? Wouldn't it be of enormous value if we could create the myth that morality, strong families, determination, courage and love of learning are traits brought by slaves from Mother Africa and therefore quintessentially black?

10   There is no doubt in my mind that most black youngsters could develop their mathematical reasoning, their elocution and their attitudes the way they develop their jump shots and their dance steps: by the combination of sustained, enthusiastic practice and the unquestioned belief that they can do it.

11   In one sense, what I am talking about is the importance of developing positive ethnic traditions. Maybe Jews have an innate talent for communication; maybe Chinese are born with a gift for mathematical reasoning; maybe blacks are naturally blessed with athletic grace. I doubt it. What is at work, I suspect, is assumption, inculcated early in their lives, that this is a thing our people do well.

12   Unfortunately, many of the things about which blacks make this assumption are things that do not contribute to their career success—except for that handful of the truly gifted who can make it as entertainers and athletes. And many of the things we concede to whites are the things that are essential to economic security.

13   So it is with a number of assumptions black youngsters make about what it is to be a "man": physical aggressiveness, sexual prowess, the refusal to submit to authority. The prisons are full of people who, by this perverted definition, are unmistakably men.

14   But the real problem is not so much that the things defined as "black" are negative. The problem is that the definition is much too narrow.

15   Somehow, we have to make our children understand that they are intelligent, competent people, capable of doing whatever they put their minds to and making it in the American mainstream, not just in a black subculture.

16   What we seem to be doing, instead, is raising up yet another generation of young blacks who will be failures—by definition.

Reading: Discussing the Text

1. The essay appeared in a large number of newspapers with equally large readerships, mostly white. What evidence can you find to show that Raspberry is trying to inform his white audience and persuade his black readers?
2. To what extent does Raspberry appear to be a credible person to write on this subject? What evidence supports your view?
3. A militant who read this essay would argue that Raspberry is trying to make blacks "better" by making them white. Is there any evidence to support this view? Explain.
4. A feminist who read the essay would argue that it is sexist. Is there any evidence to support that view? Explain.

Writing: Brief Response

1. To what extent do you agree with Raspberry's point? In what ways does your experience confirm or refute it?
2. Consider the associations with the term *college student*. To what extent are they accurate? Restrictive? Stereotypical?

Writing: Extended Response

1. Raspberry's essay was published in 1982. Use examples from your research to examine the extent to which his point still holds today.
2. Political correctness is an attempt to counter the negative effect that language can have on individuals. Choose one group of people and explore the language associated with it together with the more "politically correct" substitutes. Your research may lead you to any number of conclusions, so stick to one main point and use what you have discovered to back up your thesis.

Immigrants Need to Learn Language That Says Success

Richard Estrada

An eloquent spokesperson on issues related to immigration until his fatal heart attack at the age of 49, Richard Estrada was an associate editor of the Dallas Morning News's *editorial page. His column also appeared in that paper as well as in the* Washington Post *and was syndicated by the Washington Post Writers Group. Upon learning of Estrada's death, the publisher of the* Dallas Morning News, *Burl Osborne, commented that he was "an unusually gifted individual, combining his expertise in Mexican history and immigration with a sensitivity for all of the issues about which he wrote." That sensitivity is evident in the selection included here, one in which he reviews the controversy over second-language learning and argues for a balance between respecting different cultures and having a command of English. The column was published in the* Rocky Mountain News, *September 3, 1995. That was a number of years ago, but the controversy continues.*

Before You Read   To what extent was second-language acquisition an issue in your primary or secondary education?

1   Kid maids. It took a few seconds, but the meaning of this strange term finally dawned on me. I heard it a few years ago while having dinner in El Paso with an old friend, who, like myself, happens to be Mexican-American.

2   My friend casually recounted a story told to her by a male friend who isn't of Mexican descent. Apparently, her friend's young niece had just completed her first day at school. Asked if anything interesting had happened on that red letter day, the little girl nodded yes. "I saw kid maids," she said in wonderment.

3   The only thing I knew about this child was that she hailed from a fairly affluent non-Hispanic white family. But that information, together with her otherwise mystifying comment, made me suspect that the only persons of Mexican descent she had ever been around on a routine basis were domestic servants.

4   Intuitively, I grasped the youngster's reasoning: All people with brown skin and who speak Spanish are maids; therefore, she must have concluded, all children at school with brown skin and who may or may not speak Spanish are kid maids. Or, to put it in terms a child fortunately cannot understand, ethnicity and language are predictors of socioeconomic status.

5   This story came to mind after reading some controversial statements made recently in an Amarillo, Texas, child-custody case. State District Judge Samuel C. Kiser was upset because the mother of a 5-year-old Mexican-American child did not speak English to her child at home. He upbraided the mother in the following manner:

6   "If she starts first grade with the other children and cannot even speak the language that the teachers and the other children speak, and she's a full-blooded American citizen, you're abusing that child and you're relegating her to the position of a housemaid."

7   The judge notwithstanding, linguistics experts at Baylor University point out that children who have one parent speak to them exclusively in one language and the other parent in another, as the parents of the girl in Amarillo did, can become perfectly bilingual.

8   And as immediately pointed out by Texas attorney general Dan Morales, it's a gross distortion to call speaking Spanish to a child a form of child abuse. Besides in America, the cultural practices of people in their own homes is their business, not the courts'.

9   But Kiser had one thing right. Children face serious disadvantages for the rest of their lives if they don't learn English. At a time when job creation trends have placed a premium on communications skills, much more needs to be done to teach all students standard English rapidly, especially minority students.

10   The growing controversies over language are not about language, per se, but about language in the context of record levels of immigration and poverty. With nearly 23 million immigrants, legal and illegal, having entered the United States since 1970, the issue will continue to be with us for years to come. Fully 8.7% of the U.S. population today is foreign born, the highest percentage since World War II, and nearly twice what it was in 1970.

11   The American ethnic kaleidoscope, as Brandeis University professor Lawrence Fuchs calls it, is one of this nation's great features. But when it comes to the specific issue of teaching minority children how to fend for themselves in an increasingly competitive

world, policy-makers must find a balance between respecting diverse cultures and ensuring that students achieve a command of the English language.

12   Failing that, being a minority may increasingly be a predictor of low socioeconomic status. Everyone else will feel more inclined to use stereotypes against them. And innocent children of privilege on the Mexican border, both coasts and the nation's heartland will also come to speak of "kid maids."

Reading: Discussing the Text

1. Estrada begins his essay with a narrative. As an introduction, how effective is it?
2. In paragraph 4, Estrada tries to recreate the child's logic. How well does he do it?
3. Estrada's example of the child-custody case involves a judge, linguistics experts, and the attorney general. How essential are the three to his point?
4. Many essays are organized by first explaining a problem and then proposing a solution, but Estrada concentrates on the problem. To what extent is the essay strengthened or weakened by that focus?

Writing: Brief Response

1. The title was the newspaper's headline for the essay. Come up with two others. Which is better and why?
2. Explore the expression "American ethnic kaleidoscope" (paragraph 11). In what ways is the term *kaleidoscope* an apt metaphor?

Writing: Extended Response

1. In the 1990s, there was a surge of interest in making English the official language of the United States, and now and then the issue reemerges. Research the topic, using your library and electronic resources, to determine how you stand on the question.
2. Estrada states: "policy-makers must find a balance between respecting diverse cultures and ensuring that students achieve a command of the English language" (paragraph 11). What sort of balance has or has not been achieved in your community?

Jargon

Bryan A. Garner

In the minds of many, the words obfuscate *and* lawyer *are synonymous, but that's not Bryan A. Garner's fault. He has probably done more than any other single person, not to mention lawyer, to clarify the language of the legal profession. In addition to being the editor in chief of* Black's Law Dictionary, *7th ed. (1999), he has written* The Elements of Legal Style, *2nd ed. (2002) and* A Dictionary of Modern Legal Usage *(1995), among many other books. He also serves as a consultant, providing seminars for lawyers by way of* Law Prose, Inc., *a company he heads. Not content with cleaning up the prose of the legal profession, Garner has tackled everyone's writing in his* Dictionary of Modern American Usage *(1998), a surprisingly readable and not-so-surprisingly knowledgeable guide to American English usage. Ken Kister's review in the* Library Journal *sums up the book as "offer[ing] intelligent, sensible, readable advice concerning usage demons involving problems of grammar, spelling, homonyms, variants, clichés, skunked words, redundancies, phrasal adjectives and verbs, and more." Garner's entry on* jargon *follows.*

Before You Read   Look up *jargon, doublespeak, gobbledygook,* and *euphemism* in an unabridged dictionary and give an example of each.

1   **J**argon refers to the special, usually technical idiom of any social, occupational, or professional group. It arises from the urge to save time and space—and occasionally to conceal meaning from the uninitiated. The subject has magnified importance today because we live "[i]n an age when vague rhetoric and incomprehensible jargon predominate. . . ." Oliver Letwin, "Good Servant, Bad Master," *Times* (London), 25 May 1995, Books §, at 37.

2   Jargon covers a broad span of vocabulary. For the commonplace medical phrase *heart bypass surgery,* a range of jargon is available. There's the slightly more technical *angioplasty,* and then there's the technically precise (and more verbose) *coronary artery bypass graft.* From that phrase comes the acronym CABG, referred to in medical

slang as *cabbage* <we're going to have to give him a cabbage>. Some heart surgeons, who would have nothing to do with such slang, prefer the pompously arcane *myocardial revascularization.* But whatever the name, it's all bypass surgery.

3   Doctors also have several ways of saying that a patient is on a respirator (or ventilator). Some, of course, say that a patient is *on the respirator* or *on the ventilator.* Others, being fond of slang, say that the patient is *on the blower.* But then there are the stuffed-shirt doctors who say precisely the same thing in the most pretentious possible way: the patient is *being given positive-pressure ventilatory support.*

4   Similar levels of jargon exist in other fields. Consider AIRLINESE. In the late 1990s, a captain announced, in midflight: "We're about to *traverse an area of instability,* so I've *illuminated* the fasten-seatbelts sign." When a flight attendant was asked how she would say the same thing, she said: "We're going to *encounter some light chop,* so I've *turned on* the fasten-seatbelts sign." Another said, "We're about to *go through some choppy air,* so please fasten your seatbelts." Those quotations progress from the most to the least jargonistic—or, to put it judgmentally from the passenger's perspective, from the least to the most admirable.

5   True, jargon is sometimes useful shorthand for presenting ideas that would ordinarily need explaining in other, more roundabout ways for those outside the specialty. Jargon thus has a strong in-group property, which is acceptable when one specialist talks with another.

6   But jargon is unacceptable when its purpose is to demonstrate how much more the speaker or writer knows as a specialist than ordinary listeners or readers do. The intended audience, then, is the primary consideration in deciding which words will be intelligible.

7   In his book *On the Art of Writing* (2nd ed. 1943), Sir Arthur Quiller-Couch set out the two primary vices of jargon: "The first is that it uses circumlocution rather than short straight speech. It says: '*In the case of* John Jenkins deceased, the coffin' when it means 'John Jenkins's coffin'; and its yea is not yea, neither is its nay nay; but its answer is *in the affirmative* or *in the negative,* as the foolish and superfluous *case* may be. The second vice is that it habitually chooses vague wooly abstract nouns rather than concrete ones" (*id.* at 105). "To write jargon is to be perpetually shuffling around in a fog and cotton-wool of abstract terms" (*id.* at 117). See ABSTRACTITIS, DOUBLESPEAK & ABBREVIATIONS (C).

Reading: Discussing the Text

1. Garner chooses examples from medicine and airlinese to illustrate his point. What reasons can you think of for his choosing these fields?
2. How well do the examples support his point?
3. Garner is careful to point out the positive and negative qualities of jargon, using the notion of appropriateness as his standard (paragraph 6). How good a standard is it?
4. The entry on jargon, like others in the book, employs many citations. To what extent do they clarify or get in the way of understanding? Use examples to make your case.

Writing: Brief Response

1. Select a technical word from your major and define it. Then provide two substitutes for the word and their definitions. How essential are the technical terms?
2. Pick a particularly difficult passage from one of your textbooks, one that uses jargon. Is the intent to "save time and space" or "to conceal meaning from the uninitiated" as Garner states in paragraph 1, or something else? If it's something else, what is it?

Writing: Extended Response

1. Garner maintains "jargon is unacceptable when its purpose is to demonstrate how much more the speaker or writer knows as a specialist than ordinary listeners or readers do" (paragraph 6). Choose an article from a journal in your major and use it to test out whether the writer is guilty of using jargon to impress or obfuscate rather than to clarify.
2. According to Quiller-Couch, jargon has two vices: "it uses circumlocution rather than short straight speech" and "it habitually chooses vague wooly abstract nouns rather than concrete ones" (paragraph 7). Select an article from a specialized journal or newsletter and analyze it in terms of Quiller-Couch's criticisms. Government publications and policy statements on education are good places to look for texts.

In Search of the Appropriate Euphemism

Jonathan Yardley

Jonathan Yardley has a long and distinguished career in letters. Before joining the Washington Post *in 1981, Yardley had worked on the* Greensboro Daily News *(NC), the* Miami Herald, *and the* Washington Star. *But it is for his work at the* Post *that he is best known, both for his book reviews and his columns, some of which have been collected in books:* Out of Step: Notes from a Purple Decade *(1991) and* Monday Morning Quarterback *(1998). He has also written about his travels (*States of Mind: A Personal Journey through the Mid-Atlantic *[1993]) and his family (*Our Kind of People *[1989]) as well as biographies of sports writer Ring Lardner (1977) and novelist Frederick Exley (1997). In 1981, Yardley was awarded a Pulitzer Prize for Distinguished Criticism. As his works attest, Yardley has a keen ear for language and a perspective that some have called curmudgeonly. You can judge that perspective for yourself as you read his comments on euphemisms, particularly those weasel words that blur a writer's use of another's material. The column appeared in the March 4, 2002,* Washington Post, *in the midst of a controversy over "borrowed" words.*

Before You Read　　If you have not yet looked up *euphemism* in an unabridged dictionary or a dictionary of modern usage, do so. What examples can you think of based upon your own experience?

1　　In last week's homily it was noted that "one of the more appalling euphemisms of recent vintage" is "hospitality industry"—i.e., all those people who bring you hotel rooms and restaurant tables and bar stools—but in the splendid world where we are blessed to live, "recent vintage" must be brought up to date every five minutes or so. Now, thanks to that illustrious historian and distinguished television eminenta Doris Kearns Goodwin, we have a new euphemism that makes "hospitality industry" seem positively Shakespearean by comparison.

2   Goodwin, it will be recalled, has been locked into the pillory by journalistic moralists for what might be called questionable practices. Goodwin grinds out books the way Oscar Mayer grinds out wieners, though apparently with rather less attention to what manner of offal might end up inside. It was discovered last month, as a byproduct of the witch hunt that exposed Stephen E. Ambrose's penchant for using the words of other writers in his own texts without pausing to give the original authors due credit, that Goodwin has been guilty of what looks for all the world like exactly the same thing.

3   There are any number of good old-fashioned words for what this certainly seems to be, but the one that was most commonly used until recent vintage brought things up to date was "plagiarize." The ever-helpful and pithy Mr. Webster defines it as: "to steal and pass off as one's own (the ideas or words of another); use (a created production) without crediting the source . . . ; to commit literary theft: present as new and original an idea or product derived from an existing source." But Goodwin, in fessing up to her transgressions, said they were "absolutely not" plagiarism. Instead, she said, she had "borrowed" phrases and passages and facts from Lynne McTaggart (author of "Kathleen Kennedy: Her Life and Times") and others in her own book "The Fitzgeralds and the Kennedys."

4   Whether this is in truth "her own book" would seem to be a dubious proposition in light of the admission that Goodwin and her assembly line—three full-time researchers, according to the *New York Times,* and one part-timer—had "borrowed" the words and ideas of others, but one is forced to acknowledge that "borrowed" is about as ingenious a euphemism as one can imagine, right up there with "friendly fire" and "courtesy call" and "collateral damage." It simultaneously admits the offense and denies it: Yes, something was taken, but since it was merely "borrowed," it can be given back with no harm done. Why, it really didn't happen at all!

5   Not merely that, but the euphemism passed into the language in the blink of an eye, giving birth to baby euphemisms faster even than that. The same *New York Times* story that reported on her "team" of researchers contained these phrases for what she (and, one supposes, the "team") had done: "inappropriately copying," "borrowings," "failed to acknowledge," "unacknowledged repetitions," "sloppiness and inexperience," "repeated sentences," "borrowed phrases," "copied passages" and "derivative passages." No

doubt a heavy lawyerly hand had more than a little to do with this, but it remains that Goodwin, by introducing "borrowed" into the discussion, has managed to rewrite the language in which it is being conducted, and to muddy the waters most impressively in so doing.

6   Let it be said on Goodwin's behalf, though, that by contrast with Ambrose she is trying, after a fashion, to address the problem. She has gone back into the text of "The Fitzgeralds and the Kennedys" to give McTaggart proper acknowledgment both in footnotes and in a specific, highly laudatory reference to the latter's biography. She has even set aside work on her next book—a biography of Abraham Lincoln—to tidy up the mess she has, in all innocence, made.

7   Which leaves one to ask: Why, pray tell, do we need a biography of Abraham Lincoln by Doris Kearns Goodwin? What possibly can she bring to that task that has not already been brought by Benjamin Thomas or David Herbert Donald or Mark E. Neely Jr. or the zillions of others who have had their say on the Great Emancipator? The answer is all too simple: She will bring to it her byline and the vast sales it assures. Nothing more, nothing less. She is a celebrity—at least in the little world of books—and celebrity sells. The more that goes through the celebrity sausage grinder, the more money that is made. Never mind that too many researchers spoil the sausage—tossing in a little bit of this, a little bit of that and (oops!) forgetting to mention where it came from—what matters is that the apparently insatiable (if inexplicable) appetite in certain quarters for a product called Doris Kearns Goodwin be satisfied.

8   The pressure to produce product is intense, and the more product that's produced, the greater the pressure gets. So instead of doing your own work, you hire other people to do it for you. Don't think for a moment that pop historians and biographers are the only offenders. Novelists hire researchers to go out into the real world and tell them what it's like, and bigfoot journalists hire legmen to supply them with erudite quotations and other window dressing. When the ultimate goals are (a) to make as much money as humanly possible, and (b) to be on television as often as humanly possible, something's got to fall by the wayside. Integrity, scruples, dignity . . . take your pick. Or maybe you'd like to invent a euphemism for it.

Reading: Discussing the Text

1. Yardley refers to his last week's column as a *homily*. Look up the word in an unabridged dictionary. To what extent is the word appropriate for this column?
2. Reread paragraph 1. How would you characterize Yardley's attitude toward his subjects, his tone?
3. Yardley's support for his attack on plagiarism rests on two examples, Goodwin and Ambrose. Does he explain enough about those writers for his examples to be complete? How so?
4. You could make a case for Yardley's thesis focusing on euphemisms, plagiarism, celebrities, the public's taste, the worship of the dollar, or integrity. What do you find to be his thesis and why?

Writing: Brief Response

1. Choose one of the euphemisms Yardley mentions in paragraph 4. What is it covering up or softening? How well does it do it?
2. Write down all the words and phrases you can think of that can be substituted for *die*. Which is the most euphemistic and why?

Writing: Extended Response

1. Choose either Doris Kearns Goodwin or Stephen E. Ambrose as a subject and research the controversy surrounding their "borrowings" that hit the news in 2001 and 2002. Based on your research, write an essay in which you attack or defend Yardley's charge of plagiarism.
2. Yardley has been called a curmudgeon by more than one reviewer. Look up the word in an unabridged dictionary and then write an essay in which you explore the degree to which it describes the Yardley who wrote this essay.

Two Languages in Mind, but Just One in the Heart

Louise Erdrich

Two languages, if not three, come naturally to Louise Erdrich, for her mother is a Chippewa Indian and her father a German American. Erdrich grew up in Wahpeton, North Dakota, close to the Bureau of Indian Falls boarding school, where her parents worked, and the Turtle Mountain Reservation where her grandfather was the tribal chair. Her heritage figures largely in her work, whether she is writing poetry, short stories, essays, autobiography, children's books, or novels. Her first book of poetry was Jacklight *(1984), followed by* Baptism of Desire *(1989), but she is best known for her novels that treat many of the same characters and themes:* Love Medicine *(1984),* The Beet Queen *(1986),* Tracks *(1988),* The Crown of Columbus *(1991, with husband, Michael Dorris),* The Bingo Palace *(1994), and* Tales of Burning Love *(1996). In addition to exploring her ethnic heritage, Erdrich has always sought out practical experience of an unusual nature. While an undergraduate at Dartmouth, for instance, she found work as a lifeguard, construction flag waver, waitress, and teacher of poetry—the latter in a prison. She graduated from Dartmouth, where she later became a writer-in-residence, and then earned an MA from Johns Hopkins University. The essay reprinted here was part of the* New York Times *"Writers on Writing" series and was published on May 22, 2000.*

Before You Read   What has been your experience with learning a foreign language?

1   For years now I have been in love with a language other than the English in which I write, and it is a rough affair. Every day I try to learn a little more Ojibwe. I have taken to carrying verb conjugation charts in my purse, along with the tiny notebook I've always kept for jotting down book ideas, overheard conversations, language detritus, phrases that pop into my head. Now that little notebook includes an increasing volume of Ojibwe words. My English is jealous,

my Ojibwe elusive. Like a besieged unfaithful lover, I'm trying to appease them both.

2   Ojibwemowin, or Anishinabemowin, the Chippewa language, was last spoken in our family by Patrick Gourneau, my maternal grandfather, a Turtle Mountain Ojibwe who used it mainly in his prayers. Growing up off reservation, I thought Ojibwemowin mainly was a language for prayers, like Latin in the Catholic liturgy. I was unaware for many years that Ojibwemowin was spoken in Canada, Minnesota and Wisconsin, though by a dwindling number of people. By the time I began to study the language, I was living in New Hampshire, so for the first few years I used language tapes.

3   I never learned more than a few polite phrases that way, but the sound of the language in the author Basil Johnson's calm and dignified Anishinabe voice sustained me through bouts of homesickness. I spoke basic Ojibwe in the isolation of my car traveling here and there on twisting New England roads. Back then, as now, I carried my tapes everywhere.

4   The language bit deep into my heart, but it was an unfulfilled longing. I had nobody to speak it with, nobody who remembered my grandfather's standing with his sacred pipe in the woods next to a box elder tree, talking to the spirits. Not until I moved back to the Midwest and settled in Minneapolis did I find a fellow Ojibweg to learn with, and a teacher.

5   Mille Lac's Ojibwe elder Jim Clark—Naawi-giizis, or Center of the Day—is a magnetically pleasant, sunny, crew-cut World War II veteran with a mysterious kindliness that shows in his slightest gesture. When he laughs, everything about him laughs; and when he is serious, his eyes round like a boy's.

6   Naawi-giizis introduced me to the deep intelligence of the language and forever set me on a quest to speak it for one reason: I want to get the jokes. I also want to understand the prayers and the adisookaanug, the sacred stories, but the irresistible part of language for me is the explosion of hilarity that attends every other minute of an Ojibwe visit. As most speakers are now bilingual, the language is spiked with puns on both English and Ojibwe, most playing on the oddness of gichi-mookomaan, that is, big knife or American, habits and behavior.

7   This desire to deepen my alternate language puts me in an odd relationship to my first love, English, It is, after all, the language stuffed into my mother's ancestors' mouths. English is the reason

she didn't speak her native language and the reason I can barely limp along in mine. English is an all-devouring language that has moved across North America like the fabulous plagues of locusts that darkened the sky and devoured even the handles of rakes and hoes. Yet the omnivorous nature of a colonial language is a writer's gift. Raised in the English language, I partake of a mongrel feast.

8   A hundred years ago most Ojibwe people spoke Ojibwemowin, but the Bureau of Indian Affairs and religious boarding schools punished and humiliated children who spoke native languages. The program worked, and there are now almost no fluent speakers of Ojibwe in the United States under the age of 30. Speakers like Naawi-giizis value the language partly because it has been physically beaten out of so many people. Fluent speakers have had to fight for the language with their own flesh, have endured ridicule, have resisted shame and stubbornly pledged themselves to keep on talking the talk.

9   My relationship is of course very different. How do you go back to a language you never had? Why should a writer who loves her first language find it necessary and essential to complicate her life with another? Simple reasons, personal and impersonal. In the past few years I've found that I can talk to God only in this language, that somehow my grandfather's use of the language penetrated. The sound comforts me.

10   What the Ojibwe call the Gizhe Manidoo, the great and kind spirit residing in all that lives, what the Lakota call the Great Mystery, is associated for me with the flow of Ojibwemowin. My Catholic training touched me intellectually and symbolically but apparently never engaged my heart.

11   There is also this: Ojibwemowin is one of the few surviving languages that evolved to the present here in North America. The intelligence of this language is adapted as no other to the philosophy bound up in northern land, lakes, rivers, forests arid plains; to the animals and their particular habits; to the shades of meaning in the very placement of stones. As a North American writer it is essential to me that I try to understand our human relationship to place in the deepest way possible, using my favorite tool, language.

12   There are place names in Ojibwe and Dakota for every physical feature of Minnesota, including recent additions like city parks and dredged lakes. Ojibwemowin is not static, not confined to describing the world of some out-of-reach and sacred past. There are

words for e-mail, computers, Internet, fax. For exotic animals in zoos. Anaamibiig gookoosh, the underwater pig, is a hippopotamus. Nandookomeshiinh, the lice hunter, is the monkey.

13   There are words for the serenity prayer used in 12-step programs and translations of nursery rhymes. The varieties of people other than Ojibwe or Anishinabe are also named: Aiibiishaabookewininiwag, the tea people, are Asians. Agongosininiwag, the chipmunk people, are Scandinavians. I'm still trying to find out why.

14   For years I saw only the surface of Ojibwemowin. With any study at all one looks deep into a stunning complex of verbs. Ojibwemowin is a language of verbs. All action. Two-thirds of the words are verbs, and for each verb there are as many as 6,000 forms. The storm of verb forms makes it a wildly adaptive and powerfully precise language. Changite-ige describes the way a duck tips itself up in the water butt first. There is a word for what would happen if a man fell off a motorcycle with a pipe in his mouth and the stem of it went through the back of his head. There can be a verb for anything.

15   When it comes to nouns, there is some relief. There aren't many objects. With a modest if inadvertent political correctness, there are no designations of gender in Ojibwemowin. There are no feminine or masculine possessives or articles.

16   Nouns are mainly designated as alive or dead, animate or inanimate. The word for stone, asin, is animate. Stones are called grandfathers and grandmothers and are extremely important in Ojibwe philosophy. Once I began to think of stones as animate, I started to wonder whether I was picking up a stone or it was putting itself into my hand. Stones are not the same as they were to me in English. I can't write about a stone without considering it in Ojibwe and acknowledging that the Anishinabe universe began with a conversation between stones.

17   Ojibwemowin is also a language of emotions; shades of feeling can be mixed like paints. There is a word for what occurs when your heart is silently shedding tears. Ojibwe is especially good at describing intellectual states and the fine points of moral responsibility.

18   Ozozamenimaa pertains to a misuse of one's talents getting out of control. Ozozamichige implies you can still set things right. There are many more kinds of love than there are in English. There are myriad shades of emotional meaning to designate various fam-

ily and clan members. It is a language that also recognizes the humanity of a creaturely God, and the absurd and wondrous sexuality of even the most deeply religious beings.

19   Slowly the language has crept into my writing, replacing a word here, a concept there, beginning to carry weight. I've thought of course of writing stories in Ojibwe, like a reverse Nabokov. With my Ojibwe at the level of a dreamy 4-year-old child's, I probably won't.

20   Though it was not originally a written language, people simply adapted the English alphabet and wrote phonetically. During the Second World War, Naawi-giizis wrote Ojibwe letters to his uncle from Europe. He spoke freely about his movements, as no censor could understand his writing. Ojibwe orthography has recently been standardized. Even so, it is an all-day task for me to write even one paragraph using verbs in their correct arcane forms. And even then, there are so many dialects of Ojibwe that, for many speakers, I'll still have gotten it wrong.

21   As awful as my own Ojibwe must sound to a fluent speaker, I have never, ever, been greeted with a moment of impatience or laughter. Perhaps people wait until I've left the room. But more likely, I think, there is an urgency about attempting to speak the language. To Ojibwe speakers the language is a deeply loved entity. There is a spirit or an originating genius belonging to each word.

22   Before attempting to speak this language, a learner must acknowledge these spirits with gifts of tobacco and food. Anyone who attempts Ojibwemowin is engaged in something more than learning tongue twisters. However awkward my nouns, unstable my verbs, however stumbling my delivery, to engage in the language is to engage the spirit. Perhaps that is what my teachers know, and what my English will forgive.

Reading: Discussing the Text

1. Erdrich is safe in assuming that the great majority of her readers know little or nothing about the Ojibwe language. How well does Erdrich's introduction, paragraphs 1 through 4, address that problem?
2. Erdrich presents a number of reasons for her learning Ojibwe. Which do you find the most important and why?
3. Ojibwe differs from English in many ways. Choose one and explore its advantages and disadvantages.
4. Take another look at Erdrich's title. To what extent is it appropriate for the essay that follows?

Writing: Brief Response

1. What surprises you most about the Ojibwe language and why?
2. Erdrich speaks of the American English language as a "mongrel feast." In what ways might that expression be appropriate?

Writing: Extended Response

1. In paragraph 8, Erdrich briefly traces what has happened to the Ojibwe language, describing its suppression by the United States government. At that time, the government also suppressed the use of other Native American languages and, in Louisiana, Acadian French as well. Select one of those languages and research the ways in which its use was controlled and restricted. Your research can take you in a number of directions that can lead to an interesting essay: the government's motives, the manner in which the language was suppressed, the ways in which it is treated at present, and so on.
2. The number of students taking a course in a modern foreign language has almost doubled since 1960, even though many colleges and universities do not require the study of a foreign language for graduation. Do some research on the debate over requiring the study of a foreign language to determine where you stand on the issue. Then write an essay that explains and supports your stance.

COMPARING THE SELECTIONS

1. Maya Angelou and William Raspberry both emphasize how language can define a person or group. Which of the two makes a better case and why?

2. Richard Estrada, Louise Erdrich, Maya Angelou, and William Raspberry are all members of minority groups and therefore have a particular stake in the use of language. Choose two of the writers and analyze what language means to them. Which of the two makes the more compelling case about language?

3. In almost every English course, it's likely that your teachers praised the idea of clarity, an idea that crumbles into dust with the use of jargon and euphemism. Using examples from the selections by James A. Garner and Jonathan Yardley and other texts that you may find, write an essay in which you compare the two evils and argue for which is the worse.

4. The essays by Louise Erdrich and William Raspberry are structured according to causal relationships. Erdrich analyzes the reasons she studies Ojibwe and its effects on her; Raspberry analyzes how labels can limit performance and their effects. Which of the two essays analyzes causal relationships more effectively and why?

Ecology

Introduction

Because ecology examines how various organisms (including humans) relate to each other and their environment, it's no surprise that as scientific knowledge has expanded, the field of ecology has swelled. General interest in that field has grown as well. Colleges and universities in the United States now offer over 1,100 environmental studies programs. Groups concerned with preserving the environment have also expanded, representing views that range from those of the militant Earth First! to those of the much more moderate Audubon Society.

In fact, it's hard to pick up a newspaper today without running into an issue related to ecology. Scientists, special interest groups, politicians, and everyday citizens debate questions that affect our environment, questions that can be boiled down to three basic ones: What is the present state of our environment? What do we want our planet to be like in the future? And what can we or should we do to insure that future?

If you live in a city, you've probably been confronted with the population's need for more housing versus the preservation of green space, not to mention the problems related to automobiles—air quality, gasoline consumption, traffic, and parking space. Living in a rural area provides no relief, just different troubles—dwindling acquifers, erosion, chemical runoff from fertilizers, intrusions from wildlife. The problems are even greater in underdeveloped countries where deserts are spreading and forests are shrinking, while large numbers of people lack sufficient food and water.

The numbers keep increasing. As of 2002, the US census estimated earth's population at 6,234,277,496 and predicted that 22 years later it would be 8,034,487,427—an increase approaching two billion or 22%. According to the *New York Times*, as of 1998 one out of eight plant species in the world and one in three in the United States is "under threat of extinction." In 2000, the World Conservation Union <www.incn.org> put the rate for mammals at 25%. While those figures are based on any number of variables—war, disease, catastrophe on one end of the scale and advances in science and knowledge on the other—clearly our planet is in trouble. How deep that trouble may be is subject to debate.

Writing about ecological issues will lead you into a world of facts and arguments and opinions, many of which are at odds with each other. You might choose to examine one of those points of conflict, reviewing the arguments on both sides to decide which you find more compelling. Or if you already have a position, you will probably fight for it, marshalling the facts on your side and attacking the opposition. No matter what the purpose of your paper, you will be doing a lot of explaining and analyzing, examining causal relationships to support your point.

As you read the prose that follows, read each piece first for its basic meaning:

> What is the author writing about?
> What is the author's opinion about that subject?
> How accurate is the writer's analysis of the subject?
> What do you think the author wants you to do, understand, think, believe?
> How relevant is the piece to your own experience?

Then when you reread each selection, be aware of the techniques the writer uses:

> What examples does the writer use?
> What comparisons or contrasts does the writer use?
> What causal relationships does the writer analyze?
> What definitions does the writer use?
> How does the writer appeal to reason, emotion, credibility?
> How does the writer try to keep your interest?

The selections treat ecology in a broad sense. Here you'll find a critique of our use of natural spaces, a plea for environmental education, an argument about genetically engineered crops, together with a scientific look at the ocean's physical condition and two analyses of environmental issues.

The Road to Hell Is Paved

Chet Raymo

Known to the readers of the Boston Globe *for his weekly column, which he describes as thinking about the "human side of science," Raymo is better known to his students at Stonehill College in Massachusetts as a professor of physics and astronomy. Author of a number of books on science, three of which he illustrated, and two novels, Raymo describes himself as a "naturalist, exploring the relationships between science, nature, and the humanities." "The Road to Hell" was printed in* Orion's *slot "Curmudgeon in the Wild" on November 13, 2001.* Orion *is a magazine that seems tailor-made for Raymo, for as its Web site states, it tries "to reconnect human culture with the natural world, blending scientific thinking with the arts, engaging the heart and mind, and striving to make clear what we all have in common." Using paintings and photographs,* Orion *draws upon writers "who are shaping a new relationship with nature." That's what Raymo tries to do in the essay that follows.*

Before You Read   What role does the automobile play in your life?

1   "Stay away from anything that obscures the place it is in," writes poet Wendell Berry. The automobile is the perfect machine for obscuring places, especially an automobile with a cellular phone. "Honey, I'm just leaving the parking lot, I'll be home in an hour." "Honey, I'm on the expressway, home in twenty minutes." "Honey, I'm in the driveway." One place like every other. And if it's not, we'll make it so.

2   The natural contours of a landscape mean nothing to an 80-ton Caterpillar bulldozer. A stand of trees, an outcrop of granite, or a purling stream can be erased in a trice. Scrape it flat. Start from scratch. Most of all, make lots of room for cars. Pump asphalt up out of the ground and spread it on the surface. We are agreed that our ideal planet is as round and smooth as a bowling ball, asphalt black, painted with white lines.

3   Which is not to say that we can leave natural places alone. We no longer have that privilege. Maybe we never had that privilege.

When the first human crafted a chopping tool from stone, the wilderness was finished. When the first human struck a fire with flint, untrammeled nature was in retreat. The entire surface of the planet is inevitably going to be a human artifact. Wendell Berry, that champion of cherished places, is a farmer as well as a poet. He knows that a dairy cow and an ear of corn are artifacts. A farm is an artifact. The question is not whether we will live in artificial places, but whether we will know and love the place in which we live.

4   "If you know one landscape well, you will look at all other landscapes differently." says a character in Anne Michael's novel, *Fugitive Pieces;* "If you learn to love one place, sometimes you can also learn to love another." And that's what place is all about: learning to love. No one should love an automobile. No one should love an expressway. No one should love acres of asphalt marked with white lines. The automobile is the antithesis of love because it is the antithesis of place.

5   The place we learn to love can be a windowsill in a New York highrise, a patch of woods on Walden Pond, or a thousand acres of the high Sierras. Alaskan nature writer Richard Nelson says: "What makes a place special is the way it buries itself inside the heart, not whether it's flat or rugged, rich or austere, wet or arid, gentle or harsh, warm or cold, wild or tame. Every place, like every person, is elevated by the love and respect shown toward it, and by the way in which its bounty is received."

6   Civic planners have a responsibility to insure that our parks, greenways and open spaces remain bountiful. One thinks back to that grand era of public spaces designed and executed by the landscape architect Frederick Law Olmsted and his contemporaries. His was the generation who gave us our national parks, national forests, and great city parks. His was the generation who knew that we can't survive without roots in nature. His was the last generation who could imagine a landscape without an automobile.

7   New York's Central and Prospect Parks, Boston's Emerald Necklace, Chicago's Jackson Park and Montreal's Mount Royal Park are just a few of Olmsted's many splendid urban creations, feeding our need to connect to the natural world. He reshaped the landscape, to be sure, but in a way that lets organic nature shine through. Part of the requirement for the design competition for Central Park was provision for cross-town traffic; after all, the park was to extend fifty-one blocks up the center of Manhattan Island. Olmsted solved the problem by sinking transverse roads in deep-

walled trenches, thereby preserving the north-south visual integrity of the park, a strategy that minimizes the influence of vehicular traffic even to this day. Imagine what our cities and suburbs might be if those presently in charge of the planning and execution of public and private spaces where guided by Olmstedian principles.

8   Instead, we have created landscapes that cater to cars, not people, even to the point of sacrificing the esthetic integrity of some of our forbearers' most precious gifts, such as Charles Eliot's system of metropolitan parks and parkways around Boston, and Connecticut's Merritt Parkway. As early as the 1920s the writing was on the wall. On September 29, 1923, Charles Eliot's friend and coworker Sylvester Baxter wrote in the *Boston Evening Transcript:* "The parkways and boulevards . . . intended to be strictly subordinate . . . have become the primary factor in the scheme of the park system." The service of motor traffic had become the main consideration of the park administration, he complained.

9   If aliens from outer space visited this planet they would quickly decide that the ruling beings have four wheels; certainly, the two-legged creatures seem eager to sacrifice to the automobile their time, fortune, and quality of life. Add a lane, pave it over, build a strip mall. If there is a shred of natural beauty left, erase it. All hail to the automobile! The automobile rules.

10   The automobile is here to stay, of course, and properly so, but we are not required to love it, or sacrifice everything to it. Every acre of asphalt is one less natural place to love. A house with a three-car garage is unlikely to become a home. The number of miles on the odometer is a pretty good measure of how far we have gone from where we belong. If we had been wiser, we would have created a culture that emphasized place rather than mobility, nature rather than asphalt, public rather than personal transport. We chose not to and we are poorer for it.

Reading: Discussing the Text

1. Look up *artifact* in an unabridged dictionary. What does Raymo mean by saying: "A farm is an artifact. The question is not whether we will live in artificial places, but whether we will know and love the place in which we live" (paragraph 3)?
2. How well does Raymo define "natural places"?
3. To what extent does Raymo appear to be anti-automobile?
4. What, according to Raymo, have we lost by valuing the automobile over "natural places"? Is he right?

Writing: Brief Response

1. What "natural place" is important to you and why?
2. Consider your own campus from the perspective of planning and analyze if it values cars over people or vice versa. To what extent do you agree with that value?

Writing: Extended Response

1. The title refers to an old English proverb, "The road to hell is paved with good intentions." Think about the plan of your campus, and speculate about the intentions behind it. You will probably have to narrow your analysis to a particular building, open space, or pattern for pedestrian and vehicular traffic. What do you think were the planners' intentions? Write an essay in which you analyze the extent those intentions have been realized.
2. Raymo implies that in civic planning, we have lost the balance between "place" and "mobility," "nature" and "asphalt," "public" and "personal transport." Test out one or more of his three assertions, using a place you know well, perhaps a park or road system or a spot on your own campus. Write an essay exploring the extent to which Raymo's points hold.

Environmental Ed. 101

William H. Schlesinger

If you watch NOVA or CNN, you may have seen some of William Schlesinger's research, or you may have heard about it on National Public Radio or read about it in the New York Times, Discover, Scientific American, *or* National Geographic, *for his studies are timely. His work on how carbon dioxide affects the vegetation and soils of forests and on how global climate change affects deserts has won national recognition, and within his specialized area of research, he has written or co-authored over 130 scientific articles and a popular textbook,* Biogeochemistry: An Analysis of Global Change *(1997). A member of the American Academy of Arts and Sciences, the National Geographic Society's Committee on Research and Exploration, and the Committee on Global Change Research of the National Academy of Sciences, Schlesinger has testified frequently before the US House and Senate Committees. When he is not in the field examining deserts and forests, he is teaching at Duke University where he is the James B. Duke Professor of Biogeochemistry and Dean of the Nicolas School of Environment and Earth Sciences. The essay that follows appeared in the November-December, 2001, issue of* Duke Magazine, *a publication aimed at Duke alumni.*

Before You Read   What would you be willing to give up to improve the state of the environment?

1   When I was a young campus activist at Dartmouth College in the early 1970s, the issues of environmental degradation were clear. DDT was the nation's most popular pesticide, spread widely on farmlands to protect crops and in cities to control mosquitoes and Dutch elm disease. To ensure smooth engine performance, lead was added to gasoline and emitted as an air pollutant from the tailpipe of every car and truck in the United States. Phosphate was the basic active ingredient in nearly all detergents and in sewage effluents entering lakes and streams throughout the country. With all good intentions, we directly mined or manufactured these substances and added them to products designed to improve our daily lives—"better living through chemistry."

2   Subsequently, when environmental scientists found these substances were polluting the environment, appropriate regulatory procedures were obvious. The costs and risks of inaction were deemed unacceptable compared to using safer alternatives. And despite corporate objections, less harmful alternatives were found— many with significant profit potential for their inventors.

3   Today, bald eagles have returned to nest in most areas of the United States, where just a few decades ago, DDT residues had rendered their egg shells too thin for successful incubation. Urban children show lower levels of lead in their blood, and lower levels of lead are transported through the atmosphere and deposited in remote locations. Whitefish have returned to Lake Erie, which now seldom suffers the nuisance blooms of algae that choked its waters in the 1960s. Nearly all Americans enjoy clean air and water and,

despite corporate warnings to the contrary, our crops still grow, our cars still run, and our clothes are still clean.

4   Instead of being able to bask in these successes of the environmental movement, however, the American public now is faced with a baffling array of new environmental issues much more complicated than the problems we faced thirty years ago. Scientists recognize new threats to the biosphere—the fabric of natural ecosystems and the diversity of plants and animals that inhabit them. Unlike the obvious, toxic pollutants that spurred the environmental movement of the Sixties, we find that six billion humans on Earth, each in the pursuit of a higher standard of living, also cast subtle, diffuse, and long-term effects on nature.

5   Where we once focused only on the direct emissions of ozone as an air pollutant in cities, we now find that the forests of the eastern United States are often bathed in harmful levels of ozone, formed by the reaction of volatile organic compounds from the trees themselves with nitric-oxide gases emitted by fossil-fuel combustion and fertilized soils. Scientists have unraveled the complex photochemical reactions—that is, reactions mediated by sunlight—that form ozone in rural environments. We now know that the area affected by ozone pollution embraces more than just our cities. Rather than capping the obvious emissions from a smokestack, efforts to develop appropriate regulatory procedures to ensure safe ozone levels must involve broad participation of our citizenry.

6   Environmental scientists also tell us that rising carbon dioxide in Earth's atmosphere will lead to changes in climate that will disrupt much of our current social and economic system. But rising levels of this odorless, colorless, and unreactive gas are easy to overlook. No one wakes up in the morning and says, "Gee, the carbon dioxide level is awfully high today." Because it is well-mixed in Earth's atmosphere, each molecule of carbon dioxide (CO_2) contributes equally to the problem—whether it is emitted in Durham or Daulpur. Because each molecule added to the atmosphere is destined to remain there for decades, it will contribute to global warming well into the twenty-second century. Rising CO_2 in the atmosphere and climate change are long-term and global issues. Derived from the consumption of fossil fuels that drives nearly all of the world's economy, emissions of CO_2 will prove difficult to regulate.

7   When faced with complex and baffling issues of our own health, we trust the wisdom and treatment recommended by highly trained

doctors. Self-interest makes us listen to their advice. We may be curious about the levels of our blood chemistry, but few of us question how our doctor interprets the lab report. For centuries, we have held medicine among the most honored professions. The reputation of a good doctor travels fast, even in the world of managed care. Why don't environmental policy-makers—today's environmental health professionals—enjoy the same stature?

8   Strangely, despite increasing evidence that our own well-being is dependent on environmental health, self-interest often determines a different human behavior relative to environment—we act as if we are above nature, not part of it. For ourselves, doctors tell us the risk of smoking vastly exceeds the pleasure of doing so. But our love of large, low-mileage vehicles and our demand for low gas prices suggest that in issues of environment, we focus on today's pleasures rather than tomorrow's risks. Few voters link low gas prices to high gasoline consumption and to the urban sprawl that destroys natural land. Exploitation of nature is driven by short-term, personal economic reward, derived from a world that depends on the natural diversity of plants and animals to ensure the long-term stability of environmental conditions—clean air and water—that we take for granted with each new day.

9   In the face of an increasing onslaught and complexity of environmental issues, we will make only limited progress in protecting the environment until we have a cadre of highly trained environmental scientists who understand how the world works, policy-makers who can advise us on the best solution to environmental problems, and a citizenry that respects their judgments. But scientists and policy-makers have a poor track record of communication, because the training in one field has seldom included an appreciation of the other. Scientists must recognize and understand the complexity of environmental issues, engineers must develop solutions, and policy-makers must understand the magnitude of the threats so as to balance the risk of inaction against plausible alternatives. Most importantly, the public must have a basic appreciation of how nature works, so as to demand appropriate action.

10   As our population continues to grow, never before has there been a greater need for broad-based and interdisciplinary environmental education for our citizens. When I was a young environmentalist, the questions were obvious: How does nature operate and what impact do humans have on natural systems? Certainly, im-

portant scientific research remains to be done to improve our answers to increasingly complex environmental questions, but there is ample cause for immediate action on a large number of environmental threats that face us. When the scientific certainty approaches 95 percent, inaction leaves the world on a path that is increasingly difficult to change and frightening to those who know the prognosis for exponential population growth and resource use in a finite environment.

11   We must listen to environmental scientists and to their interpretation of our planet's lab report—recording changes in the chemistry of our atmosphere and oceans, and losses of the diversity of species that maintain the fabric of our natural ecosystems. Just as we respect the family physician, we must follow the regimen offered by professionals.

Reading: Discussing the Text

1. What evidence do you find that Schlesinger is writing for a non-technical audience?
2. To what extent does Schlesinger make resolving environmental issues the responsibility of a number of groups?
3. How effective is Schlesinger's comparison of physicians to environmental scientists?
4. How successfully does Schlesinger avoid blaming any one group for problems with the environment?

Writing: Brief Response

1. Explain why you would or would not take a course in environmental science.
2. Analyze why the state of the environment is or is not an important issue for you.

Writing: Extended Response

1. Schlesinger maintains, "Exploitation of nature is driven by short-term, personal economic reward" (paragraph 8). Analyze the validity of that assertion. You could choose examples from the corporate world—industries such as automobile, gas and oil, mining, timber, pesticide—or your personal world. For the latter, think about the ways in which you can be seen to exploit nature.

2. Consider Schlesinger's claim that "we act as if we are above nature, not part of it" (paragraph 8). How accurate is it? Think about our culture's relationship to the environment and select examples from one area to support your opinion. You might consider how we deal with waste, use plastics, recycle, or buy disposable items.

A Fight to Protect Home on the Range

Rene Sanchez

Rene Sanchez covers national news for the Washington Post *with articles that span a range of topics, from the general to the particular and rather odd, with breaking news stories somewhere in between. Of general interest are his stories dealing with first amendment issues, the homeless, hate crimes, "fixing" schools, and the like. For readers who might be more interested in the odd, there's his article on a proposed museum in Las Vegas that would feature mob figures or the story of a funeral for a teenager whose body was discovered some 80 years after he had fallen, been pushed, or jumped from a train. But Sanchez also covers breaking news, which, in 2002, meant the shooting at the Los Angeles International Airport on July 4 and the summer's forest fires in the west. Had you gone to the* Washington Post's *Web site in 2002 and clicked on* Archives, *typing in* Rene Sanchez, *you would have brought up 195 stories just within a span of two years. The article that follows appeared on March 24, 2002, with a dateline of Barstow, California.*

Before You Read   What do you think of when you hear the term "The American West"?

1   The cowboys on Dave Fisher's ranch have an unwelcome new chore: They are wrangling to save a reptile. In cattle roundups like none other in the West, they saddle up at daybreak and set out for

hours along rocky trails that wind through miles of grazing land here in the Mojave Desert, searching for cows that may be unwittingly wiping out small tortoises indigenous to the region.

2   The work is rough and slow, and Fisher, a grizzled rancher who prefers the old rules of the open range, would rather not bother with it. But for the first time, he has no choice.

3   "The environmental folks," he said, "are changing everything."

4   It all began this month. After years of lawsuits, studies and court hearings, he and every other cattle rancher in the Mojave are being forced to remove herds from nearly a half-million acres of federal grazing land during the six months the imperiled desert tortoises emerge from burrows to mate and forage for food.

5   The range may never be the same in this blazing and barren mountainous region 150 miles east of Los Angeles. It is the latest battleground in the West's chronic conflict over public land, which is escalating once more. Conservation groups are engaged in new fights over protections won for threatened species in recent years, and land interests that say their livelihoods are being ruined by such campaigns are hoping a sympathetic White House will defend their cause.

6   To keep cattle away from tortoises, federal land managers are erecting fences across long stretches of grazing areas. Once a week, they also are patrolling for cows now considered trespassers on turf they have long roamed. Ranchers, who face fines and other penalties if they fail to comply with the regulations, are shutting off water wells in some areas in the hope of moving herds.

7   Environmentalists say the steps are hardly too much to ask of ranchers to help save the desert tortoise, which the federal government declared a threatened species more than a decade ago. They say grazing cattle can crush tortoises or their burrows, eat vegetation they need to survive and trample ground plants they use to hide from desert predators.

8   The tortoises, about a foot long, are also vital to the health of desert wildlife, biologists say. Other species use their burrows as homes, too. By some estimates, hundreds of tortoises could once be found on every square mile here. Now the tally, at best, is dozens. The tortoises live underground when the desert climate is harsh but come out during the spring and fall, which is when ranchers now have to clear out their cattle.

9   "Livestock is certainly not the only threat these tortoises face. It's just the most unnecessary threat, and the one that we can most con-

trol," said Daniel Patterson, an ecologist with the Center for Biological Diversity, which has led the fight to limit grazing in the Mojave. "All ranchers have to do is move their herds off some of the land for some of the year. It's a real reasonable deal, and it's what's most in the public interest."

10   But ranchers say they are reeling from the restrictions. Rounding up and moving cattle from such large swaths of land is complicated and expensive, they say, because of the desert's difficult terrain and limited water supply.

11   Some ranchers contend the new rules could cost them several hundred thousand dollars and force them to reduce the size of their herds or drive them out of business altogether.

12   "This is giving us a real hard time," said Ron Kemper, whose cattle graze on 150,000 acres in the Mojave. "You just can't step outside and say, 'Come here, cows.' I really think some people hope this makes us all go bankrupt and leave the land."

13   Officials in San Bernardino County, in which most of the Mojave lies, are supporting the ranchers. Some say environmentalists are exaggerating the trouble that cattle cause and contend the tortoises face much more danger from ravens and the growing army of weekend warriors driving off-road vehicles through the desert. They also worry that the restrictions will harm the local economy.

14   Bill Postmus, a county supervisor, sees even bigger stakes. The clash over the tortoise, he said, is in many ways a struggle over what the priorities of the West should be. "It's not just about a few old ranchers out here," he said.

15   The plight of the desert tortoise has long been a subject of intense federal debate. Near the end of the Clinton administration, after years of scrutiny into what ails the species, the Bureau of Land Management negotiated a settlement with environmental groups that had sued to limit grazing in the Mojave.

16   Ranchers were supposed to be ordered off sensitive land last spring. But after dispatching investigators to the desert and spotting cows all over newly restricted areas, environmental groups charged that the federal land agency had decided to ignore the agreement after President Bush took office.

17   They returned to court and won another victory when U.S. District Judge William Alsup, a Clinton appointee who oversaw the settlement, accused the Bush administration of violating "the letter, the spirit and everything about" the limits on grazing. Alsup threat-

ened to hold federal officials in contempt and ordered the process to begin last fall. Furious, the ranchers appealed.

18   But an administrative judge appointed by the Interior Department to hear the case upheld the earlier ruling, although he said the BLM did not adequately consult with the ranchers about the change coming to the range.

19   Some ranchers appealed again and won temporary reprieves last fall just as they began removing cattle. Since then, ranchers have reached an uneasy truce over the issue and are cooperating with BLM officials. A few are still plotting legal strategies to try to overturn the grazing limits.

20   At times, local authorities have feared the tense dispute would erupt into violence, but none has been reported.

21   "So far, so good," said Larry Morgan, a conservationist with the BLM's Mojave office. "This is a big adjustment for everyone. The ranchers are pushing the cattle out, but in some places there's nothing to stop them from going right back. It's hard on them, and it's hard on us to get out there and monitor what's going on."

22   Environmentalists say they have doubts that federal officials are enforcing the grazing limits. They are sending their own investigators into the desert to make sure cattle are no longer in sensitive tortoise habitat.

23   "We realize things aren't going to change overnight," Patterson said. "But we're not going away on this issue."

24   Fisher, whose family has been ranching in the Mojave since the 1920s, sounds both defiant and defeated about the new policy. He is president of the local cattlemen's association and says that all the talk on the range these days is about whether to keep fighting or to give up and sell.

25   He owns about 400 cows and now has to keep them off 65,000 acres. Until BLM officials finish building a fence stretching 12 miles across the land he uses, he has cowboys working dawn to dusk to get cattle out and off the restricted area. Many of his cows are native, he said, and do not want to leave the only water spots and trails they know.

26   "We've never been kept out of our spring country before," Fisher said. "And when they want to start taking away my family's livelihood like this, I've got to say, 'Whoa.' But heck, I suppose what's happening is also probably just inevitable. It's all changing out here."

Reading: Discussing the Text

1. How does Sanchez humanize what could be reported as only a conflict of issues?
2. Outline the various levels of conflict in the article. Which is the most important and why?
3. What values are at stake in each of those conflicts? Which are the most important and why?
4. What evidence can you find that Sanchez supports one side over the other or that he is objective?

Writing: Brief Response

1. Given only the facts in the article, which side would you take and why?
2. Based on the article, explain whether Sanchez thinks of the rancher as a vanishing breed.

Writing: Extended Response

1. When first published the article was subtitled "Tortoise-Cattle Debate Illustrates Western Struggle." Think through the discussion surrounding questions 2 and 3 in Reading: Discussing the Text, and write an essay that defends what you believe to be the most important "struggle" and the values it represents. It's easy to get carried away with a topic such as this, so make sure you depend primarily on reason and example to support your view.
2. Few issues in the West have caused as much recent debate as grazing rights on federal land. Use your library or the Internet to explore that issue. The result may be a report that summarizes the arguments or an essay that takes a stand on the issue. If the latter, use what you discover through research to support your points.

Unknown Risks of Genetically Engineered Crops

Jeremy Rifkin

Jeremy Rifkin is a controversial figure. From his early days as a political activist to his most recent campaigns on ecological issues, he has gathered both critics and followers. Some of his book titles give you a good idea of the range of his interests: Who Should Play God? *(1977);* Declaration of a Heretic *(1981),* Green Lifestyle Guide *(1990);* Beyond Beef: The Rise and Fall of the Cattle Culture *(1992);* The Biotech Century: Harnessing the Gene and Remaking the World *(1998); and* The Hydrogen Economy: The Creation of the World-wide Energy Web and the Redistribution of Power on Earth *(2002). Some see Rifkin as a visionary, others as a crackpot. You can understand why from one of his statements: "It is possible to be in favor of progress, freedom of inquiry and the advancement of consciousness and still be opposed to essential elements of the prevailing scientific and technological world view" (quoted by* Newsmakers *1990). The essay included here was published in the* Boston Globe *on June 7, 1999. His concerns may not be too farfetched: genetically engineered corn has turned up in products we buy from supermarkets.*

Before You Read   What do you associate with the phrase *genetic engineering?*

1   On May 20, the term "genetic pollution" officially entered the public lexicon. Scientists at Cornell University reported in the Journal *Nature* that the pollen from genetically engineered corn containing a toxin gene called Bt killed 44 percent of the monarch butterfly caterpillars who fed on milkweed leaves dusted with it. By contrast, caterpillars fed with conventional pollen all survived. The results are all the more shocking given the fact that nearly 25 percent of the US corn crop now contains the Bt transgene and the Corn Belt states of the Midwest are where half of the monarch butterflies are produced each year.

2   In the wake of the monarch butterfly study, a growing number of scientists now say they wonder about the potential environmental effects of scores of other genetically engineered crops being introduced into the agricultural fields. Indeed, some critics are asking why these and other studies weren't done before introducing genetically engineered corn, soy, cotton and other crops over millions of acres of farm land.

3   The fact is, genetically engineered crops are radically different from conventional crops because they contain genes in their biological makeup from completely unrelated species. For example, scientists have introduced an antifreeze gene from flounder fish into the genetic code of a tomato plant to protect the plant from cold spells. While scientists have long been able to cross close relatives in the plant kingdom, the new genetic tools allow them to cross all of the biological boundaries, adding genes from viruses, bacteria, other animals and plants into the genetic code of traditional food crops.

4   Ecologists are unsure of the impacts of bypassing natural species boundaries. Consider, for example, the ambitious plans to engineer transgenic plants to serve as pharmaceutical factories for the production of chemicals and drugs. Foraging animals, seed-eating birds, and soil insects will be exposed to a range of genetically engineered drugs, vaccines, industrial enzymes, plastics, and hundreds of other foreign substances for the first time, with untold consequences.

5   Over the next 10 years, life science companies plan on introducing thousands of laboratory-conceived transgenic plants over millions of acres of farmland around the world. Ecologists tell us that the risks in releasing these novel crops into the biosphere are similar to those we've encountered in introducing exotic organisms into North America. While many of these nonnative creatures have adapted to the North American ecosystems without severe dislocations, a small percentage of them have wreaked havoc on the flora and fauna of the continent.

6   Whenever a genetically engineered organism is released, there is always a small chance that it too will run amok because, like nonindigenous species, it has been artificially introduced into a complex environment that has developed a web of highly integrated relationships over long periods of evolutionary history.

7   Much of the current effort in agricultural biotechnology is centered on the creation of herbicide-tolerant plants. To increase their

share of the growing global market for herbicides, life-science companies like Monsanto and Novartis have created transgenic crops that tolerate their own herbicides. Monsanto's new herbicide-resistant patented seeds, for example, are resistant to its best-selling chemical herbicide, Roundup.

8   The companies hope to convince farmers that the new herbicide-tolerant crops will allow for a more efficient eradication of weeds. Farmers will be able to spray at any time during the growing season, killing weeds without killing their crops. Critics warn that with new herbicide-tolerant crops planted in the fields, farmers are likely to use even greater quantities of herbicides to control weeds, as there will be less fear of damaging their crops in the process of spraying. The increased use of herbicides, in turn, raises the possibility of weeds developing resistance, forcing an even greater use of herbicides to control the more resistant strains.

9   New pest-resistant transgenic crops, such as Bt corn, are also being introduced for the first time. Monsanto and Novartis are marketing transgenic crops that produce insecticide in every cell of each plant. A growing body of scientific evidence points to the likelihood of creating "super bugs" resistant to the effects of the new pesticide-producing genetic crops.

10   Some ecologists warn of the danger of what they call "gene flow"—the transfer of transgenic genes from crops to weedy relatives by way of cross-pollination. New studies have shown that transgenic genes for herbicide tolerance and pest and viral resistance can spread by way of pollen and insert themselves into the genomes of relatives, creating weeds that are resistant to herbicides, pests, and viruses.

11   The insurance industry has quietly let it be known that while it will provide coverage for negligence and short-term damage resulting from the introduction of genetically engineered crops into the environment, it will not offer liability coverage for long-term catastrophic environmental damage because the industry lacks a risk assessment science—a predictive ecology—with which to judge the risks.

12   The industry understands the Kafkaesque implications of a government regime claiming to regulate the new field of biotechnology in the absence of clear scientific knowledge of how genetically modified organisms interact once introduced into the environment. Who, then, will be held liable for losses if a transgenic plant introduction were to trigger genetic pollution over an extended terrain

for an indefinite period of time? The life science companies? The government?

13   The introduction of novel genetically engineered organisms also raises a number of serious human health issues that have yet to be resolved. Most of these new crops contain genes from nonfood-source organisms. With 2 percent of adults and 8 percent of children having allergic responses to commonly eaten foods, consumer advocates argue that all novel gene-spliced foods need to be properly labeled so that consumers can avoid health risks.

14   The British Medical-Association has become so concerned about the potential health effects of consuming genetically modified foods that it has just called for an open-ended moratorium on the commercial planting of genetically engineered food crops until a scientific consensus emerges on their safety. And the European Commission recently announced a freeze on licenses for genetically engineered plants after learning about the monarch butterfly study.

15   A worldwide moratorium should be declared now on releasing genetically engineered food crops and other gene-spliced organisms into the environment pending further study of the potential environmental and health risks and liability issues at stake. It would be irresponsible and foolish to continue seeding farmland with genetically engineered food crops when we have yet to develop even a rudimentary risk assessment science by which to regulate these new agricultural products.

Reading: Discussing the Text

1. Rifkin's example in his first paragraph is intended to grab your attention and entice you to read on. How well does it succeed?
2. Genetic engineering is a complex concept. How well does Rifkin explain it?
3. Rifkin provides a number of possible negative effects of genetically engineered crops. Which do you find the most interesting and why?
4. The essay ends with a call for a moratorium. To what extent has Rifkin convinced you of that need?

Writing: Brief Response

1. What example in the essay do you find the most effective and why?
2. Rifkin points out that when some non-native creatures or plants have been introduced into the environment, they have "wreaked havoc" (paragraph 5). What examples can you think of?

1. Rifkin raises the question of increased herbicide runoff, a hazard that already exists. If you live near a large body of water or a river, more than likely your local newspaper has run stories on pollution caused by herbicides and other pollutants such as detergents and fertilizer. Track down one of those stories and investigate it. What was the problem? How bad was it? Has it been fixed? What were the issues involved? Depending upon what you discover, you can write an explanatory or argumentative paper.
2. The article was published in 1999 and much has happened in the field of biotechnology since then. Use your library or the Internet to update the risks and benefits of genetically engineered crops so that you can decide for yourself if Rifkin was right to call for a moratorium. You will find it best to limit your research to one type of crop, such as corn or soybeans.

2001: Year of the Ocean

Robert Kunzig

It's hard to read about oceans without running across Robert Kunzig's name. He is the European editor of Discover *magazine and author of* The Restless Sea: Exploring the World Beneath the Waves *(1999). His* Mapping the Deep: The Extraordinary Story of Ocean Science *(2000) won the Aventis Prize—England's most prestigious book award for the sciences. In an interview with BBC News Online, he remarked that we know little about oceans even though there has been a recent "revolution . . . in our understanding of marine science." What we know and don't know is the focus of his book, one described by Sir David Weatherall, chair of the panel that judged the Aventis Prize, as "open[ing] up a whole new world in a passionate, revelatory and scientifically rigorous way. It makes the mysteries of the deep sea really exciting." Those same qualities have earned Kunzig the AAAS-Westinghouse Science Journalism Award, presented by the American Association for the Advancement of Science, and the*

Walter Sullivan Award for Excellence in Science Journalism, presented by the American Geophysical Union. You can judge Kunzig's prose for yourself as you read the selection that follows. It comes from Discover's *Year in Science issue, January 2002.*

Before You Read   What benefits can you think of that you derive
from the ocean?

1   Late last summer the United Nations Environment Program published an unusual book: the first accurate atlas of the world's coral reefs. It showed that many reefs are in very bad shape, even the ones that aren't being dynamited as a fishing method. "Coral reefs are under assault," the program's executive director, Klaus Toepfer, said. "They are rapidly being degraded by human activities. They are overfished, bombed, and poisoned." The atlas was released on September 11. It did not get front-page coverage.

2   Not that it would have; it does not take terrorist mass murder or envelopes full of anthrax to make us forget the ocean. We have always paid it little heed—always treated it, a little paradoxically, as both an infinite food store and an infinite garbage can. But this past year we began to face up to its real limits. The coral atlas, for all its beautiful color, was not nearly so vivid as the European Union's decision last February to close a fifth of the North Sea to cod fishing during the spawning season; that hit the British right in their fish and chips. After the collapse of the Grand Banks fishery off Newfoundland in 1992 and the Georges Bank fishery in 1994, all the great stocks of Atlantic cod—the fish that fed the expansion of European civilization to America, the very fish people had in mind when they claimed the sea was inexhaustible—are close to exhausted.

3   And yet there is reason for optimism. Simply because we are beginning to understand the full extent of what we've been doing to the ocean, 2001 was a year full of hope—hope that we may finally be ready to slow the destruction.

4   "Every ecosystem I've studied is unrecognizably different from when I started," says Jeremy Jackson, a marine ecologist at the Scripps Institution of Oceanography, who has spent more than three decades among the reefs and turtle-grass meadows of the Caribbean. "I have a son who is 29, and I used to take him snorkel-

ing on the reefs in Jamaica to show him all the beautiful corals there. I have a daughter who is 15—I can't show her anything but big heaps of seaweed."

5 It was that personal sense of loss that prompted Jackson to bring together a group of 18 other scientists with similar stories from America and Australia. The idea was to arrive at some kind of overview, a big-picture understanding they could pass on to the rest of us. The results, published last July in the journal *Science,* are sobering. We have overfished coastal waters for centuries, Jackson and his colleagues found, and the effects of that overfishing have rippled through entire coastal ecosystems. In recent decades, just as we have acquired the submarines, cameras, and scuba gear that permit us to see the underwater world, the pace at which we are destroying it has accelerated frighteningly. Think of the sea around us as the Great Plains, teeming with buffalo, Jackson says; now think of the buffalo gone and the prairie turned into a monoculture of wheat—which in the case of the sea would be unpalatable plankton and jellyfish. That is the legacy we are preparing for our descendants.

6 Overfishing—by which Jackson and his colleagues mean excessive hunting of marine mammals and reptiles as well as fish—does not just destroy the animals we eat. Because what they used to eat no longer gets eaten, the whole ecosystem changes. The Caribbean, for instance, used to be swarming with green sea turtles. "The historical descriptions are incredible," says Jackson. "On Columbus's second voyage they feel as if they're running aground on the backs of the turtles, and they can't sail through them. And then there's this wonderful passage in a history of Jamaica in the 18th century—I can almost remember it verbatim: 'It is affirmed that vessels that have lost their way in hazy weather have navigated to the islands entirely by the sound of the beasts.'"

7 The cry of the green sea turtle was stilled long ago in the Caribbean; only a tiny fraction of the original population survives. When the British gained control of Jamaica in the 17th century, they began feeding turtles to slaves brought from West Africa to work the sugar plantations. Jackson unearthed historical records showing the British slaughtered as many as 13,000 turtles a year in the Cayman Islands alone. From those and other records, he estimates there were once 45 million turtles swimming around the Caribbean. "So you ask yourself the question," Jackson says, "what did all those turtles do?"

8   Among other things, they ate turtle grass. Turtle grass covers 10 to 20 percent of the shallow coastal seabed in the Caribbean; shrimp live in it, fish breed in it, and so it is an important resource to people too. According to a 17th-century natural history, turtle grass used to be four to six inches long—but that was when there were turtles around to crop it. "Now it's knee high, and it gently waves in the current," says Jackson. "And it grows from the bottom up, so the top part is the oldest, and it's rotten and foul and covered by all sorts of encrusting organisms and fungus." One of the things that grows on the rotting blades is a slime mold that in the 1980s laid waste to vast beds of turtle grass in Florida Bay and the Gulf of Mexico. Those outbreaks got fishermen very upset. The ultimate cause, Jackson believes, was a lack of turtles.

9   In the kelp forests off the Aleutian Islands, it is sea otters that are missing. Otters eat sea urchins, which eat kelp, and the three organisms achieve a stability—until people start eating otters and hunting them for their fur. Evidence from archaeological digs suggests that aboriginal Aleuts were wiping out local otter populations as much as 2,500 years ago, and European fur traders all but finished the job by the end of the 19th century. But in the 20th century, otter hunting was banned, and by the time Jackson's coauthor, marine biologist Jim Estes of the U.S. Geological Survey in Santa Cruz, went to the Aleutians in 1970, the otters had made a spotty comeback: Some islands had them and some didn't.

10   "It took about two seconds to see the difference," says Estes, recalling his first visit to one of the otterless islands. "We looked in the water and there were sea urchins everywhere—and no kelp." With no otters to eat them, the sea urchins had multiplied explosively and eaten all the kelp, converting the seabed to a pavement-like urchin barren. Both otters and kelp continued their comeback in the Aleutians until 1990, when killer whales started gobbling otters. Once upon a time, Estes believes, killer whales ate other whales, but human beings caught most of those in the North Pacific in the 1950s and 1960s. Though Estes can't prove it, he thinks the killer whales subsequently turned to other populations of marine mammals, first decimating seals and sea lions before doing the same to otters. He's not sure what they're eating now.

11   Elsewhere the story is similar—humans remove top consumers from the ecosystem; the ecosystem spins out of control—but the players are different. In the Chesapeake Bay, it was tall reefs of oysters rather than green turtles that once presented hazards to naviga-

tion, although there used to be lots of turtles there, too, and manatees and dolphins. Oysters feed by filtering plankton from the water, and they were so abundant in colonial times that they're estimated to have filtered all the water in the bay every three to six days. But mechanical dredging of oysters began in the late 19th century, and by the 1930s the oyster population had plummeted. The current problems of the bay, Jackson and his colleagues argue—above all, excessive plankton blooms that deplete the water of oxygen and kill fish—date from that decimation of plankton-eating oysters.

12 Some scientists disagree with the Jackson group's emphasis on "top-down" control of marine ecosystems. They place primary blame for the Chesapeake plankton blooms, for instance, on the huge amounts of nitrogen and phosphorus—plant nutrients—that now run into the bay from farm fields and subdivisions. But the argument is a bit academic: No one disputes that both top-down and bottom-up controls are important—or that the removal of top consumers through overfishing has had a huge effect on coastal waters. "Imagine a Serengeti," says Jackson, "where the wildebeests and the elephants and the buffalo and the hyenas and the lions are gone, and the top consumers are the termites and the locusts. That is what has happened."

13 So where's the hope in that?

14 The hope lies here: Overfishing is a catastrophe, but it's a uniquely tractable one. Nutrient runoff may well be creating dead zones in coastal waters, but we can't just stop fertilizing our fields; global warming is a serious threat to coral reefs, but we can't just stop emitting greenhouse gases, and at this point it would probably be too late. Those two assaults on the coastal ocean are backed by our whole economy. Overfishing is different. We can stop it, or at least contain it, if we really want to. And all over the world, on small scales, people are beginning to do that.

15 They're not doing it through the traditional techniques of fisheries management, in which scientists try to estimate how many fish there are and how many can safely be caught, and then try to enforce those estimates on recalcitrant fishermen. That's the system that gave us the collapse of the cod stocks. The technique that's working is much simpler, both to conceive and to enforce: It consists of establishing "no-take" reserves where no fishing is allowed, period. Where people have done that, they have discovered there is a free lunch. "It's been shown now from cases right across the

world, from the Caribbean and from the Pacific and Southeast Asia," says marine ecologist Mark Spalding, lead author of the UNEP coral atlas. "Closing off a small patch of reef has led to massive increases in the total fish yield. You've got a great improvement in the adult fish stock in this small area, and it actually exports fish to the surrounding reef."

16   "A reserve is win-win; the evidence is very strong," says fisheries biologist Jim Bohnsack of the National Marine Fisheries Service in Miami, who has recently shown the benefits of a no-take zone in the lagoons around the Kennedy Space Center. "It's kind of like we've discovered penicillin for the ocean."

17   The marine-reserve idea got a big boost in 2000, when President Clinton issued an executive order directing the federal government to set up a system of protected marine areas, analogous to the national parks on land. Last summer the Tortugas Ecological Reserve was established 80 miles west of Key West; it covers just 197 square miles of coral reefs and fish spawning grounds, but that makes it the largest reserve yet in American waters. The Bush administration has retained Clinton's order, but right now it is not a national priority. We all have other things on our minds these days.

18   But we have a chance now with the ocean that we shouldn't pass up. Not to bring back a paradise in which we run aground on oysters and catch fish with buckets, and green turtles guide us to shore—those days are gone, thanks to our forefathers. "We really couldn't see what we were doing under the ocean," says Bohnsack. "We could see it on land when the forests were clear-cut and the buffalo disappeared. It just wasn't obvious until we couldn't catch cod." Our forefathers could see what they were doing to the buffalo, but they did it anyway. We have a chance to be different—to be less ignorant. A hundred years from now, what will our descendants say about us? It depends on the ocean we leave them.

Reading: Discussing the Text

1. Kunzig maintains that the oceans are in terrible shape. How well chosen are the examples he uses to support that assertion?
2. *Discover* is a magazine aimed at an interested but non-technical audience. What evidence can you find that Kunzig is aware of that audience?
3. Kunzig points out that thanks to September 11, 2001, the plight of the oceans has had little publicity, for "we all have other things on our

minds these days" (paragraph 17). How well does he balance the concerns about terrorism with those about the state of the oceans?

4. Much of Kunzig's essay concentrates on the problems with the ocean and only the last five paragraphs deal with solutions. Explain why Kunzig might have chosen that emphasis.

Writing: Brief Response

1. What example in the essay do you find the most effective and why?
2. What comparison do you find the most effective and why?

Writing: Extended Response

1. About the ocean, Kunzig says "We have always paid it little heed—always treated it, a little paradoxically, as both an infinite food store and an infinite garbage can" (paragraph 2). Kunzig's essay includes examples to support the first part of his statement but not the second. Use the Internet or your local library to explore the degree to which pollution presents a threat to oceans. The result can take the form of a brief report on the state of things or an essay that takes a definite position.
2. Kunzig uses examples from the past in the paragraphs that focus on green sea turtles, sea otters, and oysters, implying that in the past the oceans were a kind of "paradise" (paragraph 18). Write a paper in which you analyze what those comparisons contribute to Kunzig's thesis and the overall effectiveness of his essay.

The Litany and the Heretic

The *Economist*

The tone of the British weekly the Economist *is indicated by the note on its table of contents: that it was first published in 1843, "to take part in 'a severe contest between intelligence, which presses forward, and an unworthy, timid ignorance obstructing our progress.'" That contest is evident in the magazine's coverage of world events, business, finance and economics, science and technology, and books and the arts—all regular features. The selection that appears here is from the February 2, 2002, Science and Technology section and is a review of Bjorn Lomborg's* The Skeptical Environmentalist, *published by Cambridge University Press in late 2001. In a way, the review is a follow-up of an essay Lomborg wrote called "The Truth about the Environment" that the* Economist *published August 2, 2001. An associate professor of statistics at the University of Aarhus in Denmark, Lomborg's critical analysis of the statistics used in ecological research and reporting has led to a heated debate in scientific journals and newspapers. Though once a self-proclaimed holder of "left-wing Greenpeace views," Lomborg's research has placed him firmly on the other side of the fence, as you will see.*

Before You Read   Using an unabridged dictionary, look up *litany* and *heretic.*

Why has Bjorn Lomborg created such a stir among environmentalists?

1   "I'm afraid there isn't much scientific controversy about Mr Lomborg. He occupies a very junior position in Denmark (an 'associate professor' does not exactly mean the same thing that it does in the United States), he has one possibly very flawed paper in an international journal on game theory, no publications on environmental issues, and yet manages to dismiss the science of dozens of the world's best scientists, including Nobel laureates, Japan and Crawford prize-winners and the like. As any sensible person would expect, his facts are usually fallacies and his analysis is largely nonexistent."

2   Those contemptuous words from Stuart Pimm, a professor of conservation biology at Columbia University, are fairly representative of the response from many environmental scientists and activists to Bjorn Lomborg's recent book, "The Skeptical Environmentalist". In the weeks since the book's release, virtually every large environmental group has weighed in with a denunciation. Numerous heavyweights of science have penned damning articles and reviews in leading journals: Dr Pimm, for one, railed against Dr Lomborg in *Nature,* while *Scientific American* recently devoted 11 pages to attacks from scientists known for their environmental activism.

3　　Dr Lomborg's critics protest too much. They are rattled not because, as they endlessly insist, Dr Lomborg lacks credentials as an environmental scientist and is of no account, but because his book is such a powerful and persuasive assault on the central tenets of the modern environmental movement.

Just the facts

4　Curious about the true state of the planet, the author—who makes no claims to expertise in environmental science, only to statistical expertise—has scrutinised reams of official data on everything from air pollution to energy availability to climate change. As an instinctive green and a former member of Greenpeace, he was surprised to find that the world's environment is not, in fact, getting ever worse. Rather, he shows, most environmental indicators are stable or improving.

5　　One by one, he goes through the "litany", as he calls it, of four big environmental fears:

- Natural resources are running out.
- The population is ever growing, leaving less and less to eat.
- Species are becoming rapidly extinct, forests are vanishing and fish stocks are collapsing.
- Air and water are becoming ever more polluted.

In each case, he demonstrated that the doom and gloom is wildly exaggerated. Known reserves of fossil fuels and most metals have risen. Agricultural production per head has risen; the numbers facing starvation have declined. The threat of biodiversity loss is real but exaggerated, as is the problem of tropical deforestation. And pollution diminishes as countries grow richer and tackle it energetically.

6　　In other words, the planet is not in peril. There are problems, and they deserve attention, but nothing remotely so dire as most of the green movement keeps saying.

7　　Nor is that all he shows. The book exposes—through hundreds of detailed, meticulously footnoted examples—a pattern of exaggeration and statistical manipulation, used by green groups to advance their pet causes, and obligingly echoed through the media. Bizarrely, one of Dr Lomborg's critics in *Scientific American* criticises as an affectation the book's insistence on documenting every statistic and every quotation with a reference to a published source.

But the complaint is not so bizarre when one works through the references, because they so frequently expose careless reporting and environmentalists' abuse of scientific research.

8   The replies to Dr Lomborg in *Scientific American* and elsewhere score remarkably few points of substance*. His large factual claims about the current state of the world do not appear to be under challenge—which is unsurprising since they draw on official data. What is under challenge, chiefly, is his outrageous presumption in starting a much-needed debate.

9   Some argue that scientists who favour stronger policies to improve the environment must use the same tactics as any other political lobby—from steel companies fighting for tariffs on imports to farmers demanding more subsidies. The aim, after all, is to win public favour and government support. Whether such a view is consistent with the obligation science owes to the truth is debatable, at best. If scientists want their views to be accorded the respect due to science, then they must speak as scientists, not as lobbyists.

10   Dr Lomborg's work has its flaws. He has made some errors in his statistical analysis, as he acknowledges on his website. And there are broader issues, especially to do with the aggregation of data and the handling of uncertainty, where his book is open to challenge. For instance, his approach of examining data at a global level, while statistically sound, tends to mask local environmental trends. Global marine productivity has indeed risen, as he says— but this disguises collapses in particular species in particular places. Dr Lomborg argues that such losses, seen in a long-term perspective, do not matter much. Many would disagree, not least the fishermen in the areas affected.

11   Allen Hammond of the World Resources Institute (WRI) makes a related point. He accepts Dr Lomborg's optimistic assessment of the environment, but says it holds only for the developed world. The aggregate figures offered in the book mask worsening pollution in the mega-cities of the poor world. Dr Lomborg agrees that there are local and regional environmental pressures, and that these matter a lot, but it is fair to point out that the book has little to say about them, except to argue that rising incomes will help.

---

*See the criticisms and Dr Lomborg's replies on his website, <http://www.lomborg.org/>. Last year, before "The Skeptical Environmentalist" came out, we ran a signed article by Dr Lomborg summarising his views. See <www.economist.com/science/lomborg/>

12   The book gives little credit to environmental policy as a cause of environmental improvement. That is a defensible position, in fact, but the book does not trouble to make the case. And another important question is somewhat skated over: the possibility that some environmental processes involve irreversible "triggers", which, once pulled, lead to sudden and disastrous deterioration. Climate scientists believe, and Dr Lomborg does not deny, that too much warming could lead to irreversible bad outcomes such as the collapse of the mid-Atlantic "conveyor belt" (an ocean current that warms Europe). The science here is thin: nobody knows what level of greenhouse gases in the atmosphere would trigger such a calamity. But the risk argues for caution.

13   Dr Lomborg's assessment of the science in this area leads him to venture that warming is more likely to be at the low end of the range expected by leading experts than at the high end. He argues that the most-cited climate models misjudge factors such as the effects of clouds, aerosols and the solar cycle. That is plausible, and there is science to support it, but the conclusion is far from certain. Again, it is reasonable to argue that such uncertainty makes it better to err on the side of caution.

14   Sensible people will disagree about the course that policy should take. Dr Lomborg—a courteous fellow—seems willing to talk calmly to his opponents. For the most part, while claiming in some cases to be men of science, his opponents do not return the compliment.

Homo ecologicus

15   Despite its limitations, "The Skeptical Environmentalist" delivers a salutary warning to conventional thinking. Dr Lomborg reminds militant greens, and the media that hang on their every exaggerated word about environmental calamity, that environmental policy should be judged against the same criteria as other kinds of policy. Is there a problem? How bad is it? What will it cost to fix? Is that the best way to spend those resources?

16   This is exactly what Tom Burke, a leading British environmentalist, denied in a debate he had with Dr Lomborg in *Prospect,* a British magazine. "What I find most egregious [in] your climate-change argument, however, is the proposition that the world faces a choice between spending money on mitigating climate change, and providing access to clean drinking water and sanitation in the

developing world. We must and can do both. Such artificial choices may be possible in an academic ivory tower where ideas can be arranged to suit the prejudices of the occupant, but they are not available in the real world and it is dishonest to suggest that they are."

17   On the contrary, Mr Burke. Only in an ivory tower could choices such as these be called "artificial." Democratic politics is about nothing but choices of that sort. Green politics needs to learn that resources are not unlimited.

Reading: Discussing the Text

1. The *Economist's* review is titled "The Litany and the Heretic." In what ways is the title appropriate?
2. What reasons can you find for the review beginning on a negative note?
3. To what extent is the review pro-Lomborg?
4. Explain whether the article is a review of the book or a summary of the controversy or an argument in its own right or some combination of types.

Writing: Brief Response

1. Does the review interest you to read Lomborg's book? Why or why not?
2. The reviewer raises the question of whether environmental scientists should "use the same tactics as any other political lobby" (paragraph 9). Explain your position on that question.

Writing: Extended Response

1. Reread the article noting Lomborg's argument, the counters to it, and the points where Lomborg's book, according to the reviewer, falls short. Write an essay in which you analyze the apparent validity of Lomborg's book.
2. The January 2002 issue of the *Scientific American* contains several articles on Lomborg's book. Look up the issue in your library or on the Internet and read the criticisms. To what extent is the *Economist's* reviewer's comment that the articles "score remarkably few points of substance" (paragraph 8) valid? Your answer is your thesis and the articles are your sources for evidence.

Comparing the Selections

1. Both of the authors of "The Unknown Risks" and "Environmental Ed. 101" use examples to emphasize existing and potential negative effects on our environment, and both authors call for action. Write an essay in which you draw your evidence from both essays to determine which does the better job of explaining the problems and presenting a solution.

2. Robert Kunzig, in "2001: Year of the Ocean," uses the past to highlight the present and argues for future action. Chet Raymo, in "The Road to Hell Is Paved," also uses the past to highlight the present, but he stops there. Which pattern of organization is the better of the two and why? Use examples from the essay to support your opinion.

3. Reread William H. Schlesinger's "Environmental Ed. 101" and the *Economist's* piece "The Litany and the Heretic." Using evidence from the two selections, analyze how Schlesinger's proposals might apply to the debate over Lomborg's book.

4. Conflict is at the heart of Rene Sanchez's "A Fight to Protect Home on the Range" and the *Economist's* account of Bjorn Lomborg's book. Analyze the various conflicts involved in both selections to decide which is the more important and why. You will have to do some research to find out if the debate over Lomborg's book has substance or is a clash of egos. To that end, you might examine Lomborg's Web site <www.lomborg.org>.

The Internet and Technology

Introduction

A hundred years ago, we lived in a world that knew nothing of much that we now take for granted: air conditioning, airplanes, cellophane, stainless steel, refrigerators, commercial radio, frozen food, television, jet engines, radar, atomic bombs, Velcro. And within the last 50 years, science and technology have given us plastic contact lenses, communication satellites, manned spacecraft, word processors, bar-code systems, video games, compact disk players, and cell phones. What's more, the Internet has enabled us to tell each other what is going on and find out what others are up to.

Our advances in technology have been so rapid that manuals and textbooks have to be updated every few years, and this year's new computer is apt to be outdated within another six months or less. DVDs are doing in VCRs in the same way that cassette decks replaced eight-track tape players. Add to the rate of change the degree to which the Internet has speeded up our lives. Turn on your computer, tap in <www.google.com>, type in your topic, and within seconds you'll have thousands of links. The rate of change is so rapid that what's new today may be old tomorrow.

As technology becomes increasingly complex, it also becomes increasingly hard for the untechnical person to understand or appreciate. It's also hard to foresee how some discoveries can or should be used, as debates over freedom of speech and privacy on the Internet illustrate. Should "hate sites" be censored or monitored? Should companies have the right to trace your buying patterns? As more and more questions arise, it becomes obvious that technology and the Internet may have developed faster than our ability to predict, examine, or control their uses.

You might see the topic "Technology and the Internet" and think that unless you're a computer geek or technology wonk you have nothing to write about, but that's not so. The ethical dimension of the Internet is something that concerns all of us, and we live in a world surrounded by technology—almost everyone has been defeated by a machine or been unable to reach a human being at an 800 number. On the other hand, if you do have a certain degree of knowledge about computers or technology, you might want to write a position paper that states your pro or con views of a particular type of software or explore the intricacies and attractions of "hacking." No matter what your topic, you'll be using causal analysis in much the same ways as the selections in this chapter.

As you read the selections that follow, read each piece first for its basic meaning:

> What is the author writing about?
> What is the author's opinion about that subject?
> How accurate is the writer's analysis of the subject?
> What do you think the author wants you to do, understand, think, believe?
> How relevant is the piece to your own experience?

Then when you reread each selection, be aware of the techniques the writer uses:

> What examples does the writer use?
> What comparisons or contrasts does the writer use?
> What causal relationships does the writer analyze?
> What definitions does the writer use?
> How does the writer appeal to reason, emotion, credibility?
> How does the writer try to keep your interest?

Three of the selections deal with the Internet—the joys the Internet offers for the hypochondriac, the effects of Internet gambling, and the "digital divide" between blacks and whites. The other three selections focus on technology—the difficulty of replacing the old with the new, the promise of mobile revolution, and the "coming fusion of biology and technology."

Internet Opens Up Whole New World of Illness for Local Hypochondriac

The *Onion*

Available weekly only on the web, the Onion *is a creature born of the Internet. Rated by* Entertainment Weekly *as one of the "Top Internet Sites of 2001," hailed by* PC Magazine *as "A Top 100 web Site," chosen in 2000 by the Academy of Interactive Arts and Sciences as the "Entertainment Site of the Year," praised by* Yahoo! Internet Life *as "Best Humor Magazine," and cited in 1999 by* Newsweek E-Life *as "The Funniest Site on the Internet," it comes as no surprise that as of May 2003 the* Onion *racks up 5 million hits a month. Its audience is young—over 50% between 18 and 34—and educated (88.30% of its readers have had some college, are college graduates, or have had postgraduate courses). The 'zine warns its first-time readers "it uses invented names in all its stories, except in cases when public figures are being satirized." Perhaps to protect the guilty, its stories list no authors. Given such freedom, you can understand why* Wired *claims "the* Onion *may be vulgar, insensitive, sexist, racist, against, antipapist, or even, on occasion, offensive, but unlike its web rivals, it's bankably funny." Judge for yourself.*

Before You Read   In an unabridged dictionary, look up *hypochondriac, satire,* and *irony.*

1   All her life, Janet Hartley has suffered from a host of ill-defined viruses and inexplicable aches and pains, diagnosing herself with everything from diabetes to cancer. But ever since discovering such online medical resources as WebMD, drkoop.com, and Yahoo! Health, the 41-year-old hypochondriac has had a whole new world of imaginary illnesses opened up to her.

2   "The Internet has really revolutionized my ability to keep on top of my medical problems," said Hartley, speaking from her bed. "For instance, I used to think my headaches were just really bad mi-

graines. But then last week, while searching Mt. Sinai Hospital's on-line medical database, I learned about something much more seri-ous called cranial AVM, or arteriovascular malformation, which, along with headache pain, may also result in dizziness, loss of con-centration, and impaired vision. I immediately thought to myself, 'Hey, that's exactly what happens to me.'"

3 In addition to regularly surfing various general medical-reference sites, Hartley makes frequent use of medical-school research sites, drug-company FAQs, and bulletin-board services for terminally ill patients in her ongoing quest to self-diagnose her hypothetical mal-adies.

4 "No more thumbing through the two-volume *Physician's Desk Reference,* a repetitive motion which led to my carpal tunnel syn-drome," said Hartley, her wrists wrapped in ointment-soaked Ace bandages. "It felt great when I could finally throw that old thing out. Except I think I slipped a disc in my back tossing it in the trash can."

5 Every day, provided she feels up to it, Hartley logs onto the Internet from her home. She also frequently logs on from work.

6 "Something in my office just isn't right," Hartley said. "I always feel fatigued there, and for a long time, I suspected that the fluores-cent lights were leaching the vitamins from my system. But accord-ing to a bunch of web sites I checked, that's unlikely. Then I thought maybe it was asbestos in the walls, but supposedly, there isn't any. So I spend some time on the Internet every day trying to figure out what exactly it might be."

7 With a vast array of medical resources available to her at the click of a mouse, Hartley has been able to investigate workplace maladies ranging from office-chair-induced lumbar-vertebrae dis-placement to the carcinogenic properties of coffeepot residue to the possibility of spinal-fluid poisoning resulting from carpet-fabric out-gassing. But perhaps Hartley's favorite thing about the Internet is its ability to connect her with other hypochondriacs.

8 "Just the other day, I was at the chronic-fatigue-syndrome mes-sage board, talking to other sufferers like myself," said Hartley be-tween coughing fits. "I can't tell you how reassuring it was to be in the company of people who are not only going through the same things I am, but who know I'm not just making this stuff up."

9 Despite her enthusiasm, Hartley cautioned that web-based med-ical diagnosis remains an inexact science.

10   "It's still far too common for a person who knows she's sick to enter her symptoms and get a response back from the web site that says nothing's wrong," Hartley said. "If that happens, you should get a second opinion from a different site. Or maybe take stock of your physical state again. You may have missed something that would alter your diagnosis. Or, if a web site is asking you 'yes or no' questions about the symptoms you're experiencing, just say yes to all of them. That way, you'll get a wider list of diseases, conditions, or syndromes you might have."

11   Hartley offered one final caution. "Computers are great, but if you spend too much time in front of them, you run the risk of developing chronic ocular strain," she said. "Not to mention the threat posed by monitor radiation, which I suspect played a part in my recent brain-cancer scare. Fortunately, though, if a computer makes you sick, you can then use it to help you get better."

Reading: Discussing the Text

1. Explain what in the article first tipped you off to the satiric tone.
2. The article claims Janet Hartley, thanks to the Internet, "has had a whole new world of imaginary illnesses opened up to her" (paragraph 1). What support can you find for that statement?
3. Make a case for what you find to be the focus of the satire. Is it Janet Hartley, hypochondriacs, medical Web sites, the Internet, or some combination?
4. Among many other functions, a conclusion can sum up, point to a new direction, emphasize overall tone, or call for action. What is the function of paragraph 11, and how successful is it as a conclusion?

Writing: Brief Response

1. Log on to one of the sites mentioned in the article. In what ways does it lend itself to satire?
2. Review the full definition of *irony* and analyze how it works in paragraph 9.

Writing: Extended Response

1. The Internet teems with opportunities for satire—chat rooms, pop-up ads, home pages, "blogs," even the layout and usability of Web designs. Choose a subject that appeals to you and write your own satire. Or, if you prefer, design a Web site that is a parody of an existing one.

2. Write an essay in which you analyze the tone of the article. Before you start, review the full definitions of *irony* and *satire* and look up *sarcasm* as well.

Upping the Ante

Jason Franchuk

Gambling on the Internet may be an odd subject for a sportswriter, but when gaming affects college students and college athletics, it's a natural for Jason Franchuk and the University Daily Kansan, *the University of Kansas' student newspaper. Franchuk did all the research for his story, which was edited by staff copyeditor Shawn Hutchinson and designed for the Web page by Palvih Bhana. The* Daily Kansan *is produced by the students enrolled in the William Allen White School of Journalism and Mass Communications, which is housed at KU's main campus in Lawrence. A member of the Big 12 Athletic Conference, the main campus has close to 20,000 undergraduates and over 6,000 graduate students, not counting the medical center. According to the* U.S. News and World Report's *"America's Best Colleges" issue for 2001, KU's academic reputation puts it among the top 50 public national universities. You will see some of the academic reputation shining through in Franchuk's article, which was published in the December 11, 2000, issue.*

Before You Read   Have you gambled? Why or why not?

1   Scott recalls numerous Saturdays he spent sitting at his computer with the sports section of his newspaper and a cold Corona within reach. But his fingers instead were clutching the mouse, poised to click in another $150 wager.

2   First bitten by the gambling bug when he visited Las Vegas with three buddies for a spring break trip, the 19-year-old no longer had to leave his own apartment to bet on college sports. Between

Internet betting and visits to Kansas City casinos, it didn't take him long to lose several thousand dollars that he had saved for college and run up $8,000 in credit card debt. He withdrew from the University and moved back to Colorado, too embarrassed about what had happened to want his name used in this story.

3   Scott, like many KU students, bet regularly on college sports. Just as it has been with pornography, the Internet has made gambling accessible to anyone anywhere who has a computer, Internet service, and a credit card. Such gambling remains illegal in Kansas—and every other U.S. state except Nevada. However, KU students like Scott can travel to the Bahamas, St. Kitts or other offshore Web sites to bet on college football, basketball and other sports.

4   According to the National Gambling Impact Study Commission Report, there were 800 gambling-related Internet sites in 1998, 60 of which offer real-time betting.

5   The ease with which students can now bet on games with the single click of a mouse threatens the integrity of college athletics, according to Kansas Athletics Director Bob Frederick, Kansas men's basketball coach Roy Williams and Kansas football coach Terry Allen.

6   This had been a concern at universities across the country, and a NCAA official, Bill Saum, has been appointed to work full-time as the organization's resident expert on college gambling.

Credit cards' contribution to the problem

7   When Scott lost a bundle on Saturday college games, he would try in vain to recoup the losses betting on Sunday NFL games. His credit card hole just got deeper.

8   "The computer and my credit card made it pretty easy to lose money quick," he said.

9   He's not the only one who could fall into the same problem—Saum estimated that 65 percent of undergraduates have credit cards.

10   Howard Shaffer, director of Harvard University Medical School's Division on Addiction, said research shows that more youth are introduced to gambling through sports betting than through any other type of gambling activity. Children are not likely to pick up a deck of cards or dice. Instead, they learn to gamble on sports by reading a newspaper's daily sports section or doing something as simple as participating in an office betting pool on the NCAA basketball tournament.

11   Not all gamblers take betting seriously.

12   Steven Kilby, Lawrence senior, saw his Internet sports betting as just another form of entertainment—like going to a bar or to a movie—even though he occasionally dropped $50 on a football game, as he did when the Kansas football team played their season opener against Southern Methodist in Dallas earlier this year.

13   He had an Internet connection that allowed him to place the bet and a satellite TV that allowed him to get constant updates of the game. The exhilaration of betting this season quickly disappeared with Kansas' chances of winning.

14   "I saw the first-quarter score, and I was just hoping they would cover the spread," Kilby said.

15   SMU was favored by five points, meaning Kansas could lose by four or less and Kilby would still win the bet. But the Jayhawks lost 31–17 and he lost $50 quicker than it took to sign on to his Internet account. To place the bet, he logged onto his favorite Internet site, punched in his ID name and credit card number and selected the bet. The money was posted to his credit card account as quickly as the game was finished.

16   Gambling is not like the Beach Boys tune, he learned. You don't have to be true to your school. Kilby bet on three Kansas football games this year. He won bets when he picked Kansas State and Nebraska to win big against the Jayhawks.

17   "I guess my friends could call me a jerk for not picking KU," he said. "But it's nothing personal. It's just about winning money."

18   Kilby now has two rules—don't bet with your heart, and don't bet more than you can afford to lose.

19   "You should never bet outside your means," he said. "Gambling is for entertainment. It gets a bad rap because of people who blow more money than they can afford to."

20   Kilby said he could see how others are suckered into placing big bets they cannot afford to lose.

21   "Look around campus," he said. "It's so easy to get a credit card here. And all you have to do is go onto the Internet and there are thousands of sites to choose from. And it looks like free money."

Betting with friends

22   The ease of placing a bet alone at the computer actually drove one KU gambler away from Internet betting. Eric Goodman, Omaha freshman, said he missed the social aspects involved in betting against friends.

23   He previously bet on games through the Internet. He had a few favorite Web sites where he could quickly make a bet, and the sites were reliable at paying when he won. But he gave up his computer betting and is now part of a group that regularly places bets with each other and then watches the games on TV together. He enjoys the thrill of having the game create friendly competition.

24   Goodman said he preferred to bet with friends because that way there's a face associated with the deal.

25   "It's better when you know the money isn't just going to some machine," he said. Even when Goodman loses and one of his pals has a big night, the friend is more likely to buy the beer or pizza to enjoy during the next game.

26   He said he sympathized with students who lose more money than they can afford to, but he thinks gambling should remain legal.

27   "As long as it doesn't make you lose all your money or your friends, I don't see anything wrong with it," Goodman said.

Gambling it all away

28   Scott, who left school last year after he spent his college savings on bad wagers, is trying to pay off his gambling debt. He now works two low-paying jobs in his native Colorado. He left behind a nice apartment, which he shared with three friends, and a girlfriend who finally grew tired of using her money to help cover his expensive habit. He is now a member of Gamblers Anonymous, a support group for addicted bettors.

29   Scott said he lied to friends about his reason for leaving the University. His mother was ill. He wanted to switch majors. As he packed his belongings, he sheepishly told his friends that he was not cut out for the rigors of college. In truth, his grade-point average when he left was 3.52.

30   "I'd do anything not to give the real reason," Scott said. "I still will not tell people."

31   He said it was slow-going trying to pay his credit card gambling debt.

32   "Working as a waiter and at a car wash is not going to make me nearly enough money to pay everything back," he said.

33   Scott considered himself an educated bettor. He used to call Kansas' sports information department to get inside information, so he could place a more knowledgeable bet.

Plaguing college programs

34   College coaches are familiar with the methods gamblers use to try to get information to gain an edge on the bookies, especially information regarding player's injuries.

35   "I've gotten plenty of phone calls from people who just want anything they can get on players," Allen said. "It's definitely not right, but I don't think it's a problem any other Division I program doesn't face."

36   Both Allen and Williams worry that college students who gamble will try to influence athletes on their campus who play the games.

37   "It's something a coach has to worry about every day now," Williams said.

38   Athletes at Arizona State and Northwestern have been convicted of sports betting crimes this decade. In each case, players were instrumental in fixing the game's scoring to help gamblers by not playing up to their full potential.

39   In the past 10 years, there have been 11 gambling scandals on college campuses, compared to the 10 that occurred during the 40 years prior to that.

40   NCAA officials have countered with a message that gambling on college athletics is wrong and dangerous.

41   Saum, the NCAA official who works as its college gambling expert, regularly visits college campuses to lecture teams about the dangers and pitfalls of gambling. Kansas' coaches have had Saum, other NCAA officials and even law enforcement officials talk to players about avoiding any connection to gambling.

42   "It's the single greatest threat to college sports and any university," Frederick said. "What a horrible thing it is to have happen to a university, because it completely destroys the institution's credibility."

43   Saum said part of the problem is how big college sports have become. College sports typically have either a football game or basketball game to bet on nearly every night, meaning there are plenty of options.

44   "There are two main factors to the success of gambling," Saum said. "One is a good economy. The other is having so many games to choose from on television."

45   Saum said even students without extra cash can gamble because 65 percent of undergraduate students have credit cards.

Legislative attempts to help

46   Saum has been part of a political effort to ban collegiate sports wagering.

47   He has worked with U.S. Sen. Sam Brownback, R-Kansas, who wants to ban all gambling on college sports. Brownback is a cosponsor of the Amateur Sports Integrity Act. ASIA, developed after a two-year study on the impact of legal gambling in the United States, is regarded by more than 1,000 U.S. universities, including Kansas, as a potential cure for the problem.

48   Brownback concedes that the plan is not a complete cure, but it is a start. However, NCAA's Saum and Frederick see the lobbying efforts of the American Gaming Association as a large obstacle because of the money it is willing to spend to save gambling on athletics.

49   "They're literally dumping millions of dollars in the laps of politicians to keep the bill from moving to the floor," Frederick said.

50   According to a story by Time magazine, the gaming industry gave Congress more than $16 million in the form of contributions in the past six years.

51   Saum said the Senate had adjourned without acting on the bill this fall, meaning it will probably have to start over.

52   "We have many high-ups telling us that if this bill gets to the floor it will pass," Saum said. "That's not bravado. We really believe that. But with all the money being poured into keeping it from getting there, it's a battle."

53   Frank J. Fahrenkopf, Jr., president and CEO of the American Gaming Association, said the bill, which underwent its latest revisions in September, won't end the problem of campus gambling.

54   "There's clearly a growing sense that this bill lacks the support its sponsors claimed," Fahrenkopf said. "As we have been saying all along, when people started focusing on the facts, they would recognize this bill for what it is: a cosmetic response to serious campus gambling problems. We're pleased that more members of Congress are now joining independent experts in disputing the NCAA's false assertions about sports wagering in Nevada."

55   Frederick chaired the NCAA men's basketball selection committee in 1994 and was responsible for selecting and seeding the 64 teams that played in the annual postseason tournament that decides the national champion. Next to the Super Bowl, it is the year's top

betting event, attracting more than $1 billion in wagers. When Frederick was chairman, the committee devised a plan to withhold credentials from any newspapers that ran betting lines for NCAA games showing favorites and point spreads.

56   The committee never implemented the plan.

57   Frederick said it would have been too much of a hassle because almost every major publication runs sporting odds, including the Lawrence Journal-World and Kansas City Star.

58   Saum said the plan also had legal problems. "I don't think we would have won that one in court," he said.

59   The betting lines on college games remain available in most newspapers, and Scott still said he checked them out. He even admitted that he placed an occasional bet with a friend for the sheer joy he experiences when he wins.

60   But he steers clear of the Internet because he said he is still tempted by the idea that he could quickly log on, place a bet and somehow win back the money he lost. Even when he conducts research for term papers he writes for the junior college classes he is taking, he goes to the library rather than uses a computer.

61   He can never forget that without traveling to Las Vegas and without leaving his own apartment, he sat in front of his computer, mouse in hand, and gambled away his college education.

Reading: Discussing the Text

1. What is the main purpose behind Franchuk's article—to explain, to persuade, some combination? What evidence supports your view?
2. Franchuk uses cause and effect throughout his article. Consider the ease with which students can obtain a credit card and place a bet as causes. What are the results?
3. What forces does Franchuk identify as contributing to gambling scandals on college campuses? Are they believable?
4. To what extent would banning gambling on college sports solve the problems that Franchuk points out?

Writing: Brief Response

1. Analyze the effectiveness of using Scott as an example of the hazards of gambling.
2. Explain the extent to which Franchuk's topic is or is not a real problem.

Writing: Extended Response

1. Gambling, in one form or another, is legal in many states. If your state has a lottery, explore whether its effects have been positive or negative. The state's official lottery office will be one source of information, as, of course, are newspaper articles and information from the Internet.

2. Franchuk emphasizes the ease of placing a bet over the Internet, but how true is that? Use the Internet to explore how gaming on the 'net gets around states' laws and whether such betting is indeed easy.

One Internet, Two Nations

Henry Louis Gates, Jr.

Henry Louis Gates, Jr.'s academic credentials and awards read like a scholar's dream: he was educated at Yale University and Clare College of the University of Cambridge; he has been a Mellon Fellow at Cambridge and the National Humanities Center, as well as being named a Ford Foundation National Fellow and a MacArthur Prize Fellow; he has been honored with the Zora Neale Hurston Society Award for Cultural Scholarship, in addition to receiving numerous other prizes. Gates chairs Afro-American Studies at Harvard University where he holds the positions of W. E. B. Du Bois Professor of the Humanities and director of the W. E. B. Du Bois Institute for Afro-American Research. Known for his scholarly books, he is that rare scholar who also addresses a general audience in books such as his autobiography, Colored People: A Memoir *(1993), and* Thirteen Ways of Looking at a Black Man *(1997), and in the PBS television series* Wonders of the African World *(1999). A regular contributor to the* New Yorker *magazine, he also serves on the Pulitzer Prize Board. The essay that follows appeared in the* New York Times *on October 31, 1999, and as its title suggests, Gates turns his attention to the electronic media and the Internet. It's an area he's familiar with, having co-edited Microsoft's* Encarta Africana.*

Before You Read   To what extent is the Internet an important source of information for you?

1   After the Stono Rebellion of 1739 in South Carolina—the largest uprising of slaves in the colonies before the American Revolution—legislators there responded by banishing two forms of communication among the slaves: the mastery of reading and writing, and the mastery of "talking drums," both of which had been crucial to the capacity to rebel.

2   For the next century and a half, access to literacy became for the slaves a hallmark of their humanity and an instrument of liberation, spiritual as well as physical. The relation between freedom and literacy became the compelling theme of the slave narratives, the great body of printed books that ex-slaves generated to assert their common humanity with white Americans and to indict the system that had oppressed them.

3   In the years since the abolition of slavery, the possession of literacy has been a cardinal value of the African-American tradition. It is no accident that the first great victory in the legal battle over segregation was fought on the grounds of education—of equal access to literacy.

4   Today, blacks are failing to gain access to the new tools of literacy: the digital "knowledge economy." And while the dilemma that our ancestors confronted was imposed by others, this cybersegregation is, to a large degree, self-imposed.

5   The Government's latest attempt to understand why low-income African-Americans and Hispanics are slower to embrace the Internet and the personal computer than whites—the Commerce Department study "Falling Through the Net"—suggests that income alone can't be blamed for the so-called digital divide. For example, among families earning $15,000 to $35,000 annually, more than 33 percent of whites own computers, compared with only 19 percent of African-Americans—a gap that has widened 64 percent over the past five years despite declining computer prices.

6   The implications go far beyond online trading and chat rooms. Net promoters are concerned that the digital divide threatens to become a 21st century poll tax that, in effect, disenfranchises a third of the nation. Our children, especially, need access not only to the vast resources that technology offers for education, but also to the rich cultural contexts that define their place in the world.

7   Today we stand at the brink of becoming two societies, one largely white and plugged in and the other black and unplugged.

8   One of the most tragic aspects of slavery was the way it destroyed social connections. In a process that the sociologist Orlando Patterson calls "social death," slavery sought to sever blacks from their history and culture, from family ties and a sense of community. And, of course, de jure segregation after the Civil War was intended to disconnect blacks from equal economic opportunity, from the network of social contacts that enable upward mobility and, indeed, from the broader world of ideas.

9   Despite the dramatic growth of the black middle class since affirmative action programs were started in the late 60's, new forms of disconnectedness have afflicted black America. Middle-class professionals often feel socially and culturally isolated from their white peers at work and in the neighborhood and from their black peers left behind in the underclass. The children of the black underclass, in turn, often lack middle-class role models to help them connect to a history of achievement and develop their analytical skills.

10   It would be a sad irony if the most diverse and decentralized electronic medium yet invented should fail to achieve ethnic diversity among its users. And yet the Commerce Department study suggests that the solution will require more than cheap PC's. It will involve content.

11   Until recently, the African-American presence on the Internet was minimal, reflecting the chicken-and-egg nature of Internet economics. Few investors have been willing to finance sites appealing to a PC-scarce community. Few African-Americans have been compelled to sign on to a medium that offers little to interest them. And educators interested in diversity have repeatedly raised concerns about the lack of minority-oriented educational software.

12   Consider the birth of the recording industry in the 1920's. Blacks began to respond to this new medium only when mainstream companies like Columbia Records introduced so-called race records, blues and jazz discs aimed at a nascent African-American market. Blacks who would never have dreamed of spending hard-earned funds for a record by Rudy Vallee or Kate Smith would stand in lines several blocks long to purchase the new Bessie Smith or Duke Ellington hit.

13   New content made the new medium attractive. And the growth of Web sites dedicated to the interests and needs of black Americans can play the same role for the Internet that race records did for the music industry.

14   But even making sites that will appeal to a black audience can only go so far. The causes of poverty are both structural and behavioral. And it is the behavioral aspect of this cybersegregation that blacks themselves are best able to address. Drawing on corporate and foundation support, we can transform the legion of churches, mosques and community centers in our inner cities into after-school centers that focus on redressing the digital divide and teaching black history. We can draw on the many examples of black achievement in structured classes to re-establish a sense of social connection.

15   The Internet is the 21st century's talking drum, the very kind of grass-roots communication tool that has been such a powerful source of education and culture for our people since slavery. But this talking drum we have not yet learned to play. Unless we master the new information technology to build and deepen the forms of social connection that a tragic history has eroded, African-Americans will face a form of cybersegregation in the next century as devastating to our aspirations as Jim Crow segregation was to those of our ancestors. But this time, the fault will be our own.

Reading: Discussing the Text

1. Gates begins his essay by referring to historical events and then does so again in paragraph 8. What do they add to his argument? To his credibility?
2. The first sentence of paragraph 4 makes a claim. What evidence does Gates supply for that claim?
3. Analyze the audience to which Gates' essay is directed. Is it African-American? White? Both?
4. In the essay, Gates uses appeals to reason, emotion, and his own credibility. Which appeal dominates?

Writing: Brief Response

1. Explore the implications of Gates' claim that the "Internet is the 21st century's talking drum" (paragraph 15).
2. Gates states, "Until recently, the African-American presence on the Internet was minimal" (paragraph 11), implying that it isn't much better today. Do a quick check using a search engine to assess the relative number of Web sites primarily aimed at an African-American audience. What do you find?

Writing: Extended Response

1. Gates' essay was published in 1999. Use your library or the Internet to investigate the "digital divide" and assess whether Gates' argument still holds true.

2. Write an essay in which you analyze Gates' use of appeals to reason, emotion, and his own credibility. Reach your own conclusions about which predominates and the effectiveness of the appeals, supporting your views with examples from the essay.

A Flat-Earther's Lament

Phil Leckman

One of the Arizona Daily Wildcat's *arts reporters, Phil Leckman regularly reviews CDs, videos, and films along with writing stories about topics such as Tucson's rodeo and the music on Mexican radio. With a circulation of 20,000, the* Daily Wildcat *is one of many services provided by the University's Arizona Student Media department, which also operates the* Wildcat Online, *KAMP Student Radio, and TV3. To staff those enterprises, the Media Department involves more than 300 students, both paid and volunteers, thus providing practical experience that augments what they learn in the classroom. According to the Department's Web site, its students "gain hands-on experience in writing, editing, design, broadcasting, film, marketing and promotions, advertising, computer graphics, website development, photography and accounting, among other areas of media management." If you were to check out* Wildcat Online *and do a search for* Phil Leckman, *you'd see that he often provides the photographs to accompany his stories. The article that follows was published on August 27, 2001.*

Before You Read   What machines do you feel emotionally attached to and why?

1   I've got a confession to make—I've committed a serious infidelity, a heartless betrayal of one of my truest companions. A few weeks ago, just before returning to Arizona, I bought a portable CD player, complete with adapters and headphones and a remote control, should I ever find myself at the gym (yeah, right). Most importantly, my shiny new toy connects right to my car stereo. And that's where the betrayal comes in.

2   I've never been exactly what you'd call "high-tech": I was the last person in my freshman dorm to own a CD player, and spent most of that year trying to complete my homework assignments on a 1988 Macintosh Classic, one of those boxy little old-school Macs best suited for use as a fishbowl. I'm doing slightly better these days, but my current computer is already hurtling toward obsolescence. And the telephone I use is a marvel of modern science purchased by my grandmother sometime back around 1986.

3   Some of this backwardness can probably be blamed on my upbringing. My parents didn't own an answering machine until I went to college, and didn't get a microwave until the mid-90s. Even today, my dad is still impressed by my ability to use advanced, complicated computer programs like Microsoft Word or Netscape, and insists that his 133-megahertz Pentium I is still as cutting-edge as it was when my brother and I talked him into replacing his IBM 386 in 1994.

4   But unlike my family, I'm no Luddite or Flat-Earther. I've got no problem with the newest and latest—I covet my friends' DSL connections and have wasted hours playing with the newest versions of Adobe Photoshop or Macromedia Flash in UA computer labs. I've even caught myself thinking favorably about cell phones lately. No, no technophobia here. No, my failure to "upgrade" is motivated not so much by fear of the new as it is by a nostalgic affection for the old. And there's no single object that motivates that nostalgia like the humble, much-maligned cassette tape.

5   Let me lead you on a guided tour of the battered blue tape box sitting in the back of my car. Right away, you'll notice the lack of organization, the cassettes scattered left and right. That faded one right on top? That's Fugazi's *13 Songs,* the album that opened my eyes to punk rock. Right next to it is U2's *The Joshua Tree,* my favorite album since 1987 and the soundtrack to first dates, first kisses and first break-ups. Then there's Faith No More's *Epic,* bought the

day after I saw them—my first rock concert ever. I haven't even mentioned mix tapes—this one with the torn label, for instance, was a gift from my first real girlfriend, a compilation of her favorite songs that would soon become our favorite songs.

6   And so it goes—each tape (OK, maybe not Europe's *The Final Countdown*—how did that get in here?) is a reminder, a soundtrack for some long-ago event that might otherwise be forgotten. Each battered cassette becomes a symbol, a signifier for the moments and memories that make me who I am.

7   Well, maybe that's a little too dramatic—there's actually quite a lot of crap in here too, so much that I've been feeling guilty lately for subjecting my friends to bad late-'80s metal and early-'90s punk. And tapes are bulky: my big cassette box can scarcely compete with the sleek efficiency of a CD travel case. The last straw was my vacation this summer—I almost drove off the interstate in northern Arizona while digging fruitlessly for something, anything, that wouldn't be embarrassing to share with my traveling companions.

8   So I bought the CD player, and have been quite happy with it. It sounds better, looks better, and there are no more tapes scattered everywhere. And it's nice to hear the music I actually like now, instead of feeling like every car trip is a time warp back to high school.

9   But I haven't forgotten my old friends. They still sit in my trunk, waiting patiently. They know that old favorites last forever, no matter how embarrassing they might be. One day soon, they'll get their chance to ride again. So if some day soon, you pull up next to a blue Subaru blaring Guns and Roses' *November Rain*, just look away. I promise I won't tell if you don't.

Reading: Discussing the Text

1. Use an unabridged dictionary to look up *Luddite* and *flat-earther*. To what extent is Leckman's title appropriate? Effective?
2. Leckman's essay can be said to touch on several topics—nostalgia for the old, the lure of the new, the importance of memories, objects as symbols, being "with it," among other possibilities. What do you find to be the main focus and what evidence supports your view?
3. Given the information in the essay, what can you deduce about Leckman's personality? His tastes?

4. How would you describe Leckman's tone? Is it formal, informal, conversational, colloquial, chatty, what? What examples support your point?

Writing: Brief Response

1. Explain the degree to which you can be labeled "high-tech."
2. Analyze your opinion of cassette tapes. If, unlike Leckman, they hold no meaning for you, explain why.

Writing: Extended Response

1. Assuming you have upgraded some kind of machine that has brought with it a different or new kind of technology, analyze the reasons behind your decision and how the result affected you.
2. Given the technological advances available today in electronics, and given no limit to what you could spend, what would you buy and why? What values are involved in your decisions?

Going Mobile

Jim Coates

If you have a question about your computer or its many programs, Jim Coates is the person who can probably answer it for he has a regular feature in the Chicago Tribune *that solves many of the problems that plague many a computer user. Want to know about "click-finger" pain? Windows ME lock-up? Vanishing icons? Jim Coates is your expert. Of course, he also writes a column for the* Tribune, *covering topics such as "Internet Demands Parental Guidance," "Copying Music Easy, Like Watching Paint Dry," and "3G Revolution is Fabulous, But Not for the Meek." If there's a new product on the market, Coates knows about it—its advantages and disadvantages. In the column that follows, he examines wireless technology and its future for the everyday Internet user. The piece was published by the* Los Angeles Times *(reprinted from the* Chicago Tribune*) on April 18, 2002. By the time you read it, you may be able to test his predictions and find out if they are true.*

Before You Read   Where do you fit in the wireless world? What devices do you use and why?

1   There's a strong whiff of the same old, same old wafting through the wireless world.

2   Billions of dollars are being spent to roll out networks and devices designed to foster a mobile revolution. They use high-speed radio technologies with names such as 3G, Wi-Fi, Bluetooth and ultrawide band.

3   Think of it as a marriage of the cell phone and the cable modem: a new generation of wireless hand-held devices such as the familiar Palms but capable of high-speed Internet features such as video e-mail, music and blazing file transfers from any place on Earth to any other place you happen to roam.

4   But what a bitter ring of familiarity it has, this talk about a third generation of mobile phones and allied devices that access the Internet without wires.

5   It hardly differs from the hype that fueled the first rush to get high-speed connections to home and office computers for e-commerce. That crusade to connect America to broadband lasted maybe four years before stumbling last year.

6   It's a bit premature to start passing out the party hats and confetti for the great revolution that wireless evangelists say awaits.

7   The question is: Can wireless somehow bring about the miracle that far-faster fiber-optic lines failed to produce?

8   Marketers have rushed to push anything that contains the "m" word, "mobile." But it's hard to forget that the last tech frenzy left us with an incredibly powerful global fiber-optic network that remains more than 90% unused.

9   All that dark fiber swallowed the hopes of companies such as Cisco Systems Inc., Nortel Networks Corp., Lucent Technologies Inc., AT&T Corp. and 3Com Corp. that now are gasping for air.

10   These companies stand to gain greatly—maybe even rebound to prior glory—if the world embraces all the new mobile devices that soon will pour onto the market.

11   It wasn't all disaster, of course.

12   Although the Internet meltdown blitzed the bulk of the dot-coms, e-commerce today is almost commonplace.

13   There is an important e-lesson here: Those selling the dream of using mobile phones or personal digital assistants to connect to the Net should remember and respect the lowly telephone modem.

14   Today, the majority of American Internet users remain content to dial up from their homes using roughly the same technology that existed when the information revolution began.

15   In fact, 88% of Americans accessing the Internet do so from conventional dial-up modems using connection speeds of 56 kilobits per second or slower. Only 12% of online Americans use cable modems, digital subscriber lines or other high-speed connections, according to the latest studies from the Progress & Freedom Foundation, a Washington-based technology policy think tank.

16   Internet service providers that use cable modems such as Princeton, N.J.–based RCN Corp. and AT&T Broadband are struggling to support existing customers and find new ones.

17   Those selling the dream of third-generation high-speed wireless access, or 3G, must convince the world that people who don't seem to want high speed in the comfort of their own homes will want it on their mobile phones.

18   But many of those who have experienced the excitement of the new wireless world are eager to embrace it. Consumers are buying mobile devices, such as the recently introduced Samsung SPH-1300 and the Handspring Treo, which combine a PDA with a cell phone. Businesses are adding wireless networks that can provide Internet access at airports, hotels and college campuses.

19   There is much to admire about the head-spinning array of clever wireless technologies. It is, after all, an engineering triumph to build systems that can slice and dice radio transmissions and create a 2-ounce telephone that carries moving pictures as effectively as a 40-pound television set.

20   Most likely, a 3G phone will always be on, just like a PC with a broadband connection. Link them with the new global positioning satellite radios, and employers suddenly know where each worker is at any given time.

21   Whether it's a cab service coordinating pickups, emergency operators dispatching police squad cars or a sales manager tracking order takers, 3G has huge new powers. Such gadgets will tell worried parents where their children are or how far a commuting spouse is from the front door.

22   Maybe Americans will learn to use a new palette of technology tools, such as sending a digital picture on 3G phones without making a full-fledged call.

23   Or maybe we'll just do what we did when the miracle of fiber-optic broadband was poised to change our world. Maybe we'll just stay at home, content to play with our trusty old 1G analog telephone modems.

Reading: Discussing the Text

1. Consider the audience to which Coates' article is addressed. How would you describe it, and what examples support your opinion?
2. Assuming cost is not a consideration, to what extent does the information in Coates' article persuade you to try the new generation of PDA-cell phones?
3. What issues are raised by Coates' speculation that the cell phone of the future will be always on and linked to global positioning satellite radios?
4. What answer does the information in the article imply in response to the alternatives Coates outlines in his last two paragraphs?

Writing: Brief Response

1. Write an abstract of Coates article, one that is no longer than 100 words.
2. Analyze why you do or do not use a cell phone.

Writing: Extended Response

1. While there's no doubt that cell phone use has expanded greatly, there's considerable concern that we have not developed a code of behavior to go with it. Write an essay in which you put forward such a code and analyze the reasons behind your proposals.
2. Coates' speculation that the cell phone of the future will be always on and linked to global positioning satellite radios suggests that some of our technological advances may be in conflict with our ethics or constitutional freedoms. Select one of those conflicts and explore the is-

sues involved. The result may be an informational report or an argumentative essay. Possible topics are cloning, euthanasia, vaccinations, and tracking devices.

Your Bionic Future

Glenn Zorpette and Carol Ezzell

Anyone who watches television or movies is used to seeing humanlike robots and magical substitutes for legs, arms, what-have-you. Popular culture has given us the likes of Robocop and the Bionic Woman, but all that is fantasy and science fiction. In real life, science fiction lives in the form of artificial limbs—hands constructed of various alloys that are connected to living nerves—or the relatively common artificial knee or hip replacement. From examples such as those, it's a relatively easy step to imagine new organs, even head transplants. That is the future outlined in the article included here. It is the introduction to Scientific American Presents, *a special issue devoted to "Your Bionic Future." Glenn Zorpette and Carol Ezzell wrote the introduction and edited the issue. Glen Zorpette is now at* IEEE Spectrum *magazine. Carol Ezzell continues to write and edit* Scientific American *where she specializes in biomedicine and biology, fields that mesh with a magazine that, according to its Web site, "identifies and delivers the latest developments in biotechnology and information science." You will see for yourself as you read Zorpette and Ezzell's article, dated September 20, 1999.*

Before You Read   What do you associate with the word *bionic*?

1   Television and slot machines notwithstanding, the point of technology is to extend what we can do with our bodies, our senses and, most of all, our minds. In the century now closing, we have gone from gaping at electric lightbulbs and telephones to channel-

surfing past images of a sunrise on Mars, to outbursts of pique if our e-mail takes more than a few minutes to get to the other side of the world.

2   And in the next decade or two, the revolution is finally going to get really interesting. Several of the most important but disparate scientific and engineering achievements of the 20th century—the blossoming of electronics, the discovery of DNA and the elucidation of human genetics—will be the basis for leaps in technology that will extend, enhance or augment human capabilities far more directly, personally and powerfully than ever before.

3   The heady assortment of biotechnologies, implants, wearables, artificial environments, synthetic sensations, and even demographic and societal shifts defies any attempt at concise categorization. But as our title boldly proclaims, we couldn't resist resurrecting the word "bionics," lately in a state of anachronistic limbo alongside the 1970s television adventures that made it a household word. Bionics often refers to the replacement of living parts with cybernetic ones, but more broadly it also means engineering better artificial systems through biological principles. That merger of the biological with the microelectronic is at the heart of most of the coming advances.

4   As scientists and engineers unleash fully the power of the gene and of the electron, they will transform bits and pieces of the most fundamental facets of our lives, including eating and reproducing, staying healthy, being entertained and recovering from serious illness. Big changes could even be in store for what we wear, how we attract mates and how we stave off the debilitating effects of getting older. Within a decade, we will see:

- A cloned human being. It is possible, in fact, that experiments are already under way in secret.
- An artificial womb for women who can't become—or don't want to be—pregnant.
- Replacement hearts and livers, custom-grown from the recipient's own versatile stem cells.
- Virtual reality that becomes far more vivid and compelling by adding the senses of smell and touch to those of sight and sound.
- Custom clothing, assembled automatically from highly detailed scans of the purchaser's body and sold at a cost not much higher than off-the-rack.

- Foods that counteract various ailments, such as noninsulin-dependent diabetes, cholera, high cholesterol or hepatitis B.
- A genetic vaccine that endows the user with bigger, harder muscles, without any need to break a sweat at the gym.

5   With only a few exceptions, the articles collected here extrapolate conservatively into the near future. Essentially all the predicted developments will follow directly from technologies or advances that have already been achieved in the laboratory. Take that genetic muscle vaccine: as this issue goes to press, a University of Pennsylvania researcher is exercising buff laboratory mice whose unnaturally muscular hind legs were created by injection. He has little doubt about the suitability of the treatment for humans.

6   The three exceptions to the mostly restrained tone of this issue are the articles by neurosurgeon Robert J. White, geneticist Dean Hamer and engineer-entrepreneur Ray Kurzweil, all of whom stake out positions that are controversial among their peers. White raises the possibility of making the Frankenstein myth a reality as he declares that medical science is now capable of transplanting a human head onto a different body. Hamer uses today's scientific fact and his best guesses about tomorrow's technology to sketch a fictional account of a couple in the year 2250 customizing the genes that will underlie their baby's behavior and personality. Kurzweil argues not only that machines will eventually have human thoughts, emotions and consciousness but that their ability to share knowledge instantaneously will inexorably push them far past us in every category of endeavor, mental and otherwise.

7   Regardless of whether we ever see Frankenstein's monster, much less conscious machines, we already have enough details of the more immediate bionic future to let us raise some of the deeper questions about what it means. Depending on your viewpoint, there are plenty of uncomfortable if not alarming possible outcomes. Athletic competition, for example, could devolve into baroque spectacles that decide, basically, whose genetic enhancements (and work ethic) are best. Of course, it would be difficult to argue that such games would be intrinsically less interesting than today's contests, which pretty much decide whose natural genes (and work ethic) are best.

8   Since the 1970s such possibilities have tended to inspire relatively dark cultural movements. Examples include an entire subgenre of

dystopian science fiction and one mad bomber. Historians and philosophers, too, are more likely now to analyze the negative ramifications of technology or even to attribute the endeavor to odd or unwholesome urges. Perhaps no one has written more entertainingly on the subject than the scholar William Irwin Thompson. In his 1991 book *The American Replacement of Nature,* he wrote:

> In truth, America is extremely uncomfortable with nature; hence its culturally sophisticated preference for the fake and nonnatural, from Cheez Whiz sprayed out of an aerosol can onto a Styrofoam potatoed chip, to Cool Whip smoothing out the absence of taste in those attractively red, genetically engineered monster strawberries. Any peasant with a dumb cow can make whipped cream, but it takes a chemical factory to make Cool Whip. It is the technological process and not the natural product that is important, and if it tastes bad, well, that's beside the point, for what that point is aimed at, is the escape from nature.

9   In the next decade or two the flight from nature will soar to new heights. The bright side of this transformation is potentially dazzling enough to drown out some of the dark visions. That is always the hope, of course. But the case now is unusually strong even if we base it on nothing more than the likelihood of powerful, sophisticated treatments for a host of dread genetic diseases and the frailties of old age. Those willing to grasp the implications of the coming fusion of biology and technology, with all its potential for beneficence and havoc, will find the exercise exhilarating.

Reading: Discussing the Text

1. The purpose of an introduction is to set up what follows and to entice the reader to continue. How well does the piece achieve the second goal?
2. The selection brings out both the dark and the dazzling aspects of what the future may hold. Which side predominates? What evidence can you find to support your point?
3. The readership of *Scientific American* is well educated, with some 64% having graduated from college and had postgraduate experience. What evidence do you find that the selection is pitched at that educational level?
4. What evidence can you find that the writers are concerned with more than purely scientific matters? Should they be?

Writing: Brief Response

1. What reasons can you find for the authors' inclusion of the excerpt from William Irwin Thompson's book (paragraph 8)?
2. To what extent does the authors' definition of *bionic* (paragraph 3) conform to what you know of the term?

Writing: Extended Response

1. William Irwin Thompson maintains that in America we have a "culturally sophisticated preference for the fake and unnatural . . ." (paragraph 3). Test out his assertion by thinking about your own tastes in food and the popularity of various food items. Write an essay in which you support or refute his statement.
2. Cloning is the most obvious form of genetic engineering, but, so far, genetically engineered humans have yet to become a reality. Even so, it is now possible to analyze a person's genetic code and identify the diseases that will probably develop at some time in the future. Choose either topic to explore, using your library or the Internet. The result may be a report aimed at the general reader or you may choose to take a position on the topic. If the latter, make sure you rely primarily on reason and evidence.

COMPARING THE SELECTIONS

1. The hazards of the Internet are brought out in the selections by Jason Franchuk and the *Onion*. Though the two articles differ in tone and intent, both use examples and quotations. Write an essay in which you compare the two to determine which one points out the Internet pitfalls more effectively.

2. Phil Leckman's "A Flat-Earther's Lament" and Jim Coates' "Going Mobile" focus on the value of the old while describing the advantages of the new. While one deals with a well-known technology, presenting a personal experience in familiar tone, the other focuses on a less common technology, exploring a subject in an informal tone. In short, one is a personal essay, the other an exploratory one. Which has the greater appeal, to whom and why?

3. The selections by Jason Franchuk and Henry Louis Gates, Jr. use causal analysis to explore the negative potential of the Internet. Consider the ways in which the two selections differ: the causes of the problems they address, the effects of those problems, and the solutions they propose. Which uses causal analysis more effectively?

4. In speculating and writing about what the future may hold, it's usually a good idea to bring out both the good and the bad, though one will probably get greater emphasis. Reread Coates' "Going Mobile" and Ezzell and Zorpette's "Your Bionic Future" noting the authors' treatment of examples and positive and negative views. Which presents the fairer picture?

CREDITS

Page 84: "Island" from ISLANDS, THE UNIVERSE, HOME by Gretel Ehrlich. Copyright © 1991 by Gretel Ehrlich. Used by permission of Viking Penguin, a division of Penguin Putnam Inc.

Page 91: "Legal Aide (First Job)" by Lorrie Moore, the *New Yorker,* April 23 & 30, 2001. Copyright © 2001 by Lorrie Moore. Reprinted by permission of Melanie Jackson Agency, L.L.C.

Page 94: "Ka-Ching! (First Job)" by Margaret Atwood. Copyright © 2001 by Margaret Atwood. Reprinted by permission of the author. First appeared in the *New Yorker* Magazine, April 23 & 30, 2001.

Page 98: "The Puritan Work Ethic" by Brian Dean, originally printed in *In Business.* Copyright © Brian Dean. Used by permission.

Page 102: "The Work Ethic, Redefined" by Virginia Postrel, *Wall Street Journal.* Copyright © Dow Jones Co., Inc. Used with permission.

Page 107: "Why Serve and Learn in Mexico?" © International Partnership for Service-Learning. Used with permission.

Page 112: "The Volunteers" by Peter Matthiessen, *Orion,* 2001. Copyright © 2001 Peter Matthiessen. Reprinted by permission.

Page 119: "A Black Fan of Country Music Tells All" by Lena Williams, *New York Times,* June 19, 1994. Copyright © 1994 New York Times Company, Inc. All rights reserved.

Page 123: "George Harrison" by Dave Laing and Penny Valentine, *The Guardian,* January 12, 2002. Copyright © 2002 David Laing. Reprinted by permission.

Page 129: "Chicken Riddle" by Jane and Michael Stern. Originally published in *Gourmet* Magazine, January 2002. Copyright © 2002 Jane and Michael Stern. Reprinted by permission of the authors.

Page 132: "Cheerio, Seinfeld" by Joyce Millman, *Salon.com,* May 4, 1998. Copyright © 1998 by Salon.com. Reprinted with permission.

Page 139: "Where Woman Was, There Gal Shall Be" by Natalie Angier, *New York Times,* November 19, 1995. Copyright © 1995 New York Times Company, Inc. All rights reserved.

Page 144: "Why Don't We Like the Human Body?" by Barbara Ehrenreich, *Time,* July 1, 1991. Copyright © 1991 Time Inc. Reprinted by permission.

Page 151: "My Sister's Dead Body Is No Longer News" by Jim Heid, *Newsweek,* September 17, 2001. Copyright © 2001 Newsweek, Inc. All rights reserved. Reprinted by permission.

Page 154: "The School Shootings: Why Context Counts" by LynNell Hancock. Reprinted from *Columbia Journalism Review,* May/June 2001. © 2001 by Columbia Journalism Review.

Page 160: "Just a Little Honest" by Maureen Dowd, *New York Times,* January 9, 2002. Copyright © 2002 The New York Times Company, Inc.

Page 163: "Staring Back" by Francine Prose. Copyright © 2001 Francine Prose. Used with permission from the Denise Shannon Literary Agency, Inc.

Page 167: "The Difficulty of Detachment" by Mary Carmichael, *Duke,* Nov/Dec 2001. Used with permission of Duke Magazine, Duke University. Copyright © 2001.

Page 170: "Mike's On" by Steve Shuger, *Slate,* 7/10/96. Copyright ©SLATE/Distributed by United Feature Syndicate, Inc. Used with permission.

INDEX